American Crusade

American Society of Missiology
Monograph Series

The ASM Monograph Series provides a forum for publishing quality dissertations and studies in the field of missiology. Collaborating with Pickwick Publications—a division of Wipf and Stock Publishers of Eugene, Oregon—the American Society of Missiology selects high quality dissertations and other monographic studies that offer research materials in mission studies for scholars, mission and church leaders, and the academic community at large. The ASM seeks scholarly work for publication in the Series that throws light on issues confronting Christian world mission in its cultural, social, historical, biblical, and theological dimensions.

Missiology is an academic field that brings together scholars whose professional training ranges from doctoral-level preparation in areas such as scripture, history and sociology of religions, anthropology, theology, international relations, interreligious interchange, mission history, inculturation, and church law. The American Society of Missiology, which sponsors this series, is an ecumenical body drawing members from Independent and Ecumenical Protestant, Catholic, Orthodox, and other traditions. Members of the ASM are united by their commitment to reflect on and do scholarly work relating to both mission history and the present-day mission of the church. The ASM Monograph Series aims to publish works of exceptional merit on specialized topics, with particular attention given to work by younger scholars, the dissemination and publication of which is difficult under the economic pressures of standard publishing models.

Persons seeking information about the ASM or the guidelines for having their dissertations considered for publication in the ASM Monograph Series should consult the Society's website—www.asmweb.org.

Members of the ASM Monograph Committee who approved this book are:

Paul V. Kollman, CSC
University of Notre Dame

Judith Lingenfelter
Biola University

Roger Schroeder, SVD
Catholic Theological Union

American Crusade

*Catholic Youth in the World Mission Movement
from World War I through Vatican II*

DAVID J. ENDRES

American Society of Missiology
Monograph Series

7

☙PICKWICK *Publications* • Eugene, Oregon

AMERICAN CRUSADE
Catholic Youth in the World Mission Movement from World War I through Vatican II

American Society of Missiology Monograph Series 7

Copyright © 2010 David J. Endres. All rights reserved. Except for brief quotations in critical publications or reviews, no part of this book may be reproduced in any manner without prior written permission from the publisher. Write: Permissions, Wipf and Stock Publishers, 199 W. 8th Ave., Suite 3, Eugene, OR 97401.

Pickwick Publications
An Imprint of Wipf and Stock Publishers
199 W. 8th Ave., Suite 3
Eugene, OR 97401

www.wipfandstock.com

ISBN 13: 978-1-60899-071-9

Cataloging-in-Publication data:

Endres, David J.

American crusade : Catholic youth in the world mission movement from World War I through Vatican II / David J. Endres.

xiv + 198 p. ; 23 cm. — Includes bibliographical references and index.

American Society of Missiology Monograph Series 7

ISBN 13: 978-1-60899-071-9

1. Catholic youth. 2. Youth movements. 3. Missions. I. Title. II. Series.

BV2300.C358 E53 2010

Manufactured in the U.S.A.

The author and publisher gratefully acknowledge permission to reprint, in revised form, previously published material from the *U.S. Catholic Historian*. "The Global Missionary Zeal of an American Apostle: The Early Works of Daniel A. Lord, S.J., 1922–1929," 24.3 (2006) 39–54, is partially reprinted in chapter three, and a portion of chapter four was published as "An International Dimension to American Anticommunism: Mission Awareness and Global Consciousness in the Catholic Students' Mission Crusade, 1935–1955," 24.2 (2006) 89–108.

Contents

Acknowledgments / vii

Introduction: Whatever Happened to the Crusade? / ix

ONE   Harvest of Souls: Christian Missions and American Expansion / 1

TWO   Coming Crusade: Catholic Missions and the Great War, 1914–1920 / 27

THREE   Knights and Ladies: The Call of the Crusade, 1920–1940 / 54

FOUR   Ramparts and Shields: Protecting American and Catholic Values, 1940–1960 / 91

FIVE   Age of Reform: Developments in Mission Theology, 1960–1971 / 123

SIX   The Final Generation / 153

Bibliography / 169

Index / 187

Acknowledgments

I OWE A DEBT of gratitude to many who have assisted with this work. I am grateful for the ongoing support of Dr. Christopher J. Kauffman, Emeritus Professor of American Catholic History at The Catholic University of America, who directed the dissertation from which this monograph has been based. I am appreciative to the American Society of Missiology for selecting this work as part of their ongoing scholarly monograph series.

I am grateful for the assistance of fellow historians of the American Catholic mission experience, especially Sister Angelyn Dries, O.S.F., of St. Louis University. During my research I was assisted by many kind archivists and librarians, especially the staff of the Historical Archives of the Chancery, Archdiocese of Cincinnati, and the librarians at the Athenaeum of Ohio/Mt. St. Mary's Seminary of the West.

I am thankful for the support offered by the Most Rev. Dennis M. Schnurr, Archbishop of Cincinnati, and the friendship of brother priests of the Archdiocese of Cincinnati and the seminarians at Mt. St. Mary's Seminary of the West. Lastly, I thank my family: my parents, James and Christina Endres, and sister, Elizabeth Oloffson for supporting me in all my pursuits. For each and for all, I echo the words of St. Paul to the Thessalonians: "I give thanks to God for all of you, remembering you in my prayers."

Introduction

Whatever Happened to the Crusade?

MISSION HISTORIAN ANGELYN DRIES in an article in *The Living Light*, poses the question, "Whatever happened to the Catholic Students' Mission Crusade?" Aware of the enduring memory of the movement by American Catholics who grew up in the 1920s through 1960s, Dries' article charted the rise and fall of what she called "one of the most extensive and successful movements to raise mission consciousness among Catholics in the United States."[1]

The Catholic Students' Mission Crusade (CSMC) was formed to educate American Catholic youth about the work of the missions, both foreign and domestic, and to bolster the support of the missions among Americans. The Crusade, envisioned from the start as a national youth organization, was formed through the efforts of two seminarians, Clifford J. King and Robert B. Clark, of the Society of the Divine Word. Impressed by the accomplishments of the Student Volunteer Movement for Foreign Missions, an American Protestant youth organization founded in the late nineteenth century, the founders of the CSMC endeavored to begin a similar organization for Catholic young people. With an initial involvement of only thirty students, the Crusade's program of "prayer, study, and sacrifice" spread to American Catholic seminaries, colleges and universities, high schools and elementary schools where local Crusade units were formed. Clergy and religious sisters and brothers moderated the units with the support of local bishops and religious superiors, while the youth themselves formed the core of the CSMC's action and zeal. Sponsoring oratorical, essay and play-writing contests, staging mission pageants, and organizing immense parades, rallies and open air Masses, student Crusaders from Boston to New Orleans and from Baltimore to Omaha

---

1. Dries, "Whatever Happened," 61.

joined the movement in large numbers, swelling its membership to 500,000 by the 1930s and to over one million by the 1950s. As the movement expanded, its outreach included the printing and distribution of a vast amount of educational material, including the movement's official periodical, *The Shield*, and its series of mission study guides utilized in countless classrooms.

The Crusade's civic and religious rituals, educational materials, and local activities evidenced a distinctive, public response by American Catholic youth to the needs of the global Church through involvement in the world mission movement. The CSMC propagated mission awareness through every modern means: the press, drama, radio, and public activities and rituals. The movement considered the broad reaches of the Church's potential influence, reacting to and incorporating national and supranational trends in politics, foreign policy, religious dialogue, education, and theological inquiry. Finding its source in multiple spheres of human experience, the CSMC was successful in navigating the world's complex and oftentimes-competing values, cultures, and beliefs. For many American students, involvement in the Crusade was a passkey to multiple worlds—sub-Saharan Africa, communist-dominated China, or war-torn Europe—each accessible through print, image, and occasionally first-hand experience as a missionary, in each case far beyond the confines of American Catholicism's ethnic neighborhoods or suburban *cul-de-sacs*.

Internationally conscious yet domestically shaped and sustained, the Crusade's relationship to America and the modern world was at times ambiguous. It could be simultaneously distrusting and critical even as it was romantically naïve and hopeful. From its origins, the movement experienced tension between the urge to yield to modern, American culture and a desire to forge a separate, Catholic subculture. For American Catholics in the twentieth century, this ambiguity was real. It was unclear whether the nation would play host to Catholicism as the core religious culture—as many Protestants feared—or whether these roles would be reversed and the Catholic Church would be subservient to national allegiances. The Crusade matured at a time when America was becoming convinced of its role as a world power, one that would call for the expansion of all things American: politics, culture, and Christianity. The expansionist rhetoric that was supported by many "mission-minded" Christians, however, could be in conflict with the American Catholic mentality to stand against materialism and individualism—supposedly secular and Protestant-inspired deviations that flourished within American culture.

Opposing this defensiveness, however, were those "Americanist" Catholics who wanted to fully integrate the faith into all areas of religious and civic life. This underlying tension resulted in the Crusade's frequent appeals to Americanism, a form of domestic nationalism, yet at times its bold opposition to the excesses of nationalism on the global stage. Its leaders could mirror the language of the late nineteenth century American imperialist and interventionist, while later articulating the isolationist "America first" position to avoid capitulation to communist Russia and entry into World War II. The Crusade could praise the "progress" of America yet denounce its wicked bedfellows: liberalism, materialism, and modernity. It could sympathize with conservative reactions to the war and communism abroad while embracing a liberal and progressive domestic social Catholicism that included interracial justice and voluntary poverty. The Crusade and its leadership operated within these ambiguities, often favoring a public engagement of culture, promoting a civic-minded, Americanist ideal that could be appreciated by non-Catholic America and a sectarian, theologically triumphant "gospel" that evidenced a sure commitment to the global Catholic Church.

Attentive to the Crusade's grounding in "local" American civic life and "universal" Catholic distinctiveness, this work explores the ways in which the movement continually reinvented itself according to perceived challenges to Church and nation. Employing a generational model, it charts four generations of the Crusade: the founding generation that matured at the time of World War I, those active in the movement during the interwar years, the generation influenced by World War II and the Cold War, and finally the last members of the Crusade who were impacted by the "sixties," especially social upheaval and the Second Vatican Council.

This history of an "American Crusade"—the Catholic Students' Mission Crusade—is part of the wider twentieth century American Catholic mission movement. The study of American Catholic mission history—a relatively new avenue for scholarly research—began largely with the publication of Angelyn Dries's *The Missionary Movement in American Catholic History*, helping focus attention on the breadth and depth of American Catholic participation in the foreign missionary enterprise. Dries's work along with historians such as Robert Carbonneau, C.P., Ernest Brandewie, and Jean-Paul Wiest are among the first scholars to be attentive to the distinctiveness of the American Catholic mission experience and its function within the global Christian mission movement.[2]

This study attempts to locate the missionary zeal of American Catholic youth within a broad framework that includes global Catholic history and the international Christian mission movement. The Catholic Church in America, which outgrew its own mission status in 1908, was, at least by early twentieth century standards, itself a "young church." In the early decades of the twentieth century, it quickly matured from the role of receiving missionaries to sending them to foreign lands while also cultivating a domestic "mission to America." During this process of national and religious maturation, Catholics in America founded a multitude of national organizations and networks to more effectively serve Church and society, including a strong thrust for Americans to serve the Church internationally and to assert their significance within a global body.

Divided into six chapters, this work's first chapter explores the context for the Crusade's founding by surveying the growth of the Catholic missionary impulse through the early twentieth century. The dynamics of Catholic and Protestant missionary efforts, youth involvement in the missions, and the relationship between mission and American expansionism are explored. Bolstered by rapid institutional growth and the perceived decay of American Protestantism, American Catholics during this time rejected a decades old "inferiority complex" and instead went on the offensive, convinced that they could fill voids both within American culture and the missionary enterprise.

Chapter two details the advent of the Catholic Students' Mission Crusade and the state of Catholic missions in the era of World War I. The founding generation, affected by the war and the United States' emerging national identity, exhibited the idealism and zeal characteristic of that era of American Catholicism. It was during this time that Catholics embraced a post-ethnic American identity, resulting in the close association of national and religious aims.

Chapter three explores the expansion of the Crusade during the interwar years, showing how the mission impulse was promoted through the medieval ideal. During these years the movement was influenced by neo-medievalism and the scholastic revival, accentuating the romantic

2. Notable contributions by these authors include Brandewie, *In the Light of the Word*; Carbonneau, "Life, Death, and Memory"; Dries, "'The Whole Way into the Wilderness'"; Dries, *The Missionary Movement*; Wiest, *Maryknoll in China*.

Whatever Happened to the Crusade?

allure and adventure found in a missionary vocation as well as the medieval "golden age" of Catholic society. Popularized by Father Daniel Lord's mission pageants, the movement successfully connected the idea of the hero-martyr crusader and the missionary. This generation of crusaders, the interwar generation, emphasized the need for a Catholic revival, exemplified in the program of Catholic Action. While asserting the triumph of Catholicism, they were attentive to America's shortcomings, especially in terms of racial justice. The chapter concludes with an analysis of the Crusade's turn to domestic concerns, chiefly the race issue, rural life, and the mission to America's non-Catholics.

In chapter four, the political-spiritual engagement of the Crusade in World War II and the ensuing Cold War is discussed, particularly how religious beliefs shaped attitudes regarding America's role in the world and how Catholicism in America was influenced by the international political situation. During the 1940s and 1950s, the movement focused on the intellectual and international threats of materialism and communism, working to protect American and Catholic values through the education of youth. The generation that matured during these years influenced the Crusade's fierce patriotism, animated by its anticommunist stance and hostility to the other chief "isms" of the age: materialism, individualism, and socialism.

The decade of the "sixties," the last decade of the Crusade, is analyzed in chapter five within the context of the CSMC's emerging focus on ecumenism, lay involvement in the missions, and the reassessment of mission theology and practice. During these years of reform and renewal, the members of the Crusade began to question their organization's methods, motives, and ultimately, the movement's very existence. This period of ferment within the Crusade culminated in the decision to dissolve the organization as a variety of local, decentralized initiatives of the Society for the Propagation of the Faith, were to continue its work.

The final chapter, chapter six, describes and analyzes the dissolution of the Crusade, taking into account the ecclesial, social, and cultural developments that contributed to the decision to disband the organization. The distinctiveness of the Crusade's final generation is explored. This generation was affected by the ecclesial reform initiated by the Second Vatican Council and the domestic tumult surrounding American involvement in the Vietnam conflict, the Civil Rights and youth movements. This generation advocated for ecumenism, humanitarianism, and peace, idealistically hoping to solve the evils of the age—war, poverty, and injustice—in a "single generation" much like their mission-minded predecessors. Ironically, perhaps, they did not envision the Crusade as a means to such progress. With heightened expectations and a broadening of the movement's scope, this last generation shifted the Crusade's emphasis from that of educating Catholic youth about the missions to an expansive humanitarian optimism linked to a hope in a new age of worldwide renewal and regeneration.

The four generations of the movement show the Crusade to be a vibrant model of cultural and religious engagement for the Church in America prior to Vatican II, challenging those conceptions of the preconciliar Church as only inward-looking, parochially centered, and uninventive. The history of the movement indicates the creative imagery and evolving methods necessary to sustaining a national movement within the global Church. It evidences that the Church in America was not static but constantly responding to cultural, political, and religious developments in ways perhaps not earlier perceived.

The story of the movement illustrates the powerful relationship between religion and culture and its impact on theological, political, and cultural perspectives. The participation of American youth in the CSMC shaped the wider worldview of its members. As an American movement with a global consciousness, the CSMC fostered a "mission mindedness" that cut across boundaries, enabling access to multiple "worlds" for the youth impacted by the Crusade. By enforcing a sense of Catholic idealism as an antidote to modernity and secularism and by broadening students' vision beyond the local and the national to embrace the global, the Catholic Students' Mission Crusade led youth to consider their role in an "American Crusade" to Christianize the world.

ONE

Harvest of Souls

Christian Missions and American Expansion

"MAKE DISCIPLES OF ALL NATIONS"

THE CATHOLIC FOREIGN MISSION impulse that developed in the United States in the early twentieth century had as its source the ethos of evangelization that emerged in the earliest ages of Christian history. Christ's charge, often called the "great commission," recorded at the conclusion of Matthew's Gospel: to "make disciples of all nations" baptizing them according to the Trinitarian formula of Father, Son, and Holy Spirit, took root in the Church in the first generations after the death of Jesus.[1]

Christians through the ages have sought to imitate those who preached the faith in distant lands, beginning with the missionary journeys of Paul and Barnabas recorded in the Scriptures and continuing with the political-religious expansion of Christianity into the Celtic and Frankish lands through the efforts of Patrick and Boniface of medieval fame. Christianity has attempted through the centuries to extend its influence to non-Christian peoples, first by way of neighboring regions along the Mediterranean and into Europe and later to the more distant continents of Africa and Asia.

The advent of the modern missionary movement was sparked by the geographic discoveries of the late fifteenth through sixteenth century and advances in technology and transportation, allowing for exploration of the "New World" and the Far East. The motivation for missions almost always involved a mixing of the sacred and the secular, "saving souls" and

1. Matt 28:19.

planting churches as well as establishing cultural and political dominance over indigenous peoples. Beginning in the fifteenth century, Rome granted permission for the kingdoms of Spain and Portugal to Christianize the "pagan" New World. The Treaty of Tordesillas of 1493 divided the globe in two with the Spanish and Portuguese each entitled to one-half of the "unclaimed" lands. This royal patronage colored the mission enterprise for centuries, assuring that political and religious aims would remain intertwined. The quest to conquer new lands and the challenge of the Protestant Reformation resulted in a flurry of missionary efforts in the sixteenth and seventeenth centuries, often led by members of the Society of Jesus and the Franciscans. Prior to this time, missionary efforts were local, sporadic, and tightly linked to the political extension of kingdoms.[2]

The pontificate of Gregory XV marked a turning point for the missions, the beginning of Catholic missionary efforts directed from Rome, not by the Catholic monarchs of Spain and Portugal. Flowing from the Reformation era Catholic counter-reforms of the Council of Trent, Pope Gregory instituted the Sacred Congregation for the Propagation of the Faith (usually known by its Latin title, *Propaganda Fide*, or simply the *Propaganda*) in 1622. Its initial work attempted to convert Protestants back to the old faith, however, its activities soon spread to lands outside Europe.[3] In the Far East, Catholic missionaries including the Jesuits Francis Xavier, Robert de' Nobili, and Matteo Ricci met their objectives with some success, as did missionaries sent to the Americas: "New France" and "New Spain."[4]

The missionary zeal that had been furthered in the seventeenth and eighteenth centuries by the *Propaganda Fide* flowered more dramatically in the nineteenth century through papal and local initiatives. This century, which has been called the "great century" for Protestant missions, was also an era of worldwide missionary expansion within Roman Catholicism.[5] The French Revolution's obvious attempt at de-Christianization had the

---

2. Jedin, *History of the Church*, 5:575–92 and 6:232–70; McManners, "The Expansion of Christianity," 301–37.

3. Metzler, *Sacrae Congregationis de Propaganda Fide*; Jedin, *History of the Church*, 5:610–14.

4. An accessible survey of mission history is Neill, *A History of Christian Missions*. See especially pp. 151–78 and 335–79 for Roman Catholic mission history beyond the year 1600.

5. Latourette, *A History of the Expansion of Christianity*, vol. 5.

inadvertent effect of awakening the people—both clergy and laity—to the need for evangelization and re-evangelization in European and "mission" lands. During this time the Church made great gains in Asia and Africa owing to new means of transportation, ease of travel and communication, an abundance of clergy, and the zeal of new missionary orders and lay associations. In the nineteenth century more religious orders came into existence than any time in the Church's history, a number of which were devoted to overseas missions: the Society of Mary (Marists), Holy Ghost Fathers (Spiritans), the Congregation of the Sacred Hearts of Jesus and Mary (Picpus Fathers), Missionaries of Our Lady of Africa (White Fathers), and the Missionary Oblates of Mary Immaculate. In addition to the missionary work of established orders such as the Franciscans, Dominicans, and Congregation of the Mission (Lazarists), mission manpower was increased with the 1814 restoration of the Society of Jesus, historically the Church's most important missionary order prior to its 1773 papal suppression.[6]

In imitation of Protestants, who often channeled their missionary efforts through particular societies, a number of Catholic mission societies were founded in France and Germany during the "great century." In France, a clerical society, *Missions Etrangères de Paris* (Society of the Foreign Missions of Paris), which had been founded in the seventeenth century and dedicated to the evangelization of Asia, grew considerably; the Society for the Propagation of the Faith, a lay movement founded by Pauline Jaricot in Lyons, France in 1822, was organized to enliven lay men and women to pray and support missionaries; and the Holy Childhood Association, founded in Paris in 1843 by Bishop Charles de Forbin-Janson, involved children in missionary support.

The papacy supported these local initiatives throughout the century, especially during the pontificate of Gregory XVI (1831–1846), a prefect of *Propaganda Fide* before his election as pope. Most noteworthy was Gregory's emphasis on evangelizing peoples outside of Europe, expanding the scope of mission beyond Protestants, Eastern Christians, and the Catholic diaspora in North America. The Church placed increased emphasis on mission in Africa, accompanying the European colonization of the "dark continent," and Asia, where the Church had made early gains

---

6. Verstraelen, *Missiology*, 230; Jedin, *History of the Church*, 8:175–78; J. Bruhls, "From Missions to 'Young Churches,'" in Aubert, Bruhls, and Hajjar, *The Church in a Secularised Society*, 385–93; Jedin, *History of the Church*, 7:193.

through the work of the Jesuits. During Gregory XVI's pontificate more than seventy mission dioceses and vicariates, often assigned to a single religious order, were created, and almost two hundred missionary bishops were appointed. Perhaps Gregory's crowning missionary accomplishment, the encyclical letter, *Neminem Profecto* (1845), provided a blueprint for missionary activity. The letter called for the division of missionary territories and the appointment of bishops to oversee these new dioceses, and advocated the recruitment and training of an indigenous clergy and episcopacy by establishing local missionary seminaries. The document asked that native clergy not be treated as second class auxiliaries to European priests and commanded missionaries to renounce the practice of permitting indigenous men to assist as catechists instead of encouraging them to pursue Holy Orders. The document additionally warned missionaries not to become entangled in politics and secular affairs.[7]

The missionary propagation begun under Pope Gregory XVI was continued by his successor, Pope Pius IX (1846–1878). While the first half of the century was marked by the emergence of French religious orders and mission societies, the second half saw many foundations in Italy and Germany. Religious orders dedicated to the missions continued to be formed: the Society of St. Francis de Sales (Salesians) was founded by Giovanni Don Bosco in 1859; Daniel Comboni formed the Society of the Sons of the Sacred Heart (Verona Fathers) for missions in Africa in 1866; the St. Joseph Society for Foreign Missions (Mill Hill Fathers) were founded in England for the African apostolate; and the German priest Arnold Janssen formed the Society of the Divine Word in 1875.[8] Within the German states, several mission-aid organizations for the laity were founded: the Leopoldine Society (*Leopoldinische Stiftung*), organized in Vienna in 1829 for the support of missions in North America, the Xavier Society of the Rhineland organized in 1834, and the Ludwig Society (*Ludwig Missionsverein*) formed in 1839 in Bavaria. By the century's end, more than one-hundred-fifty mission-aid organizations had been founded along with mission seminaries for secular priests in France at Paris and Lyons, in Italy at Milan and Verona, in Steyl, Holland and in Rome, assuring a steady stream of funds and missionaries from Europe.[9]

---

7. Jedin, *History of the Church*, 7:204–5.

8. Jedin, *History of the Church*, 8:175–78.

9. Kennedy, "Missions, Catholic"; Jedin, *History of the Church*, 7:193; Latourette, *A History of the Expansion of Christianity*, 4:59.

AMERICA AND THE CULTURE OF EXPANSION

American Catholics were largely absent from the stream of missionaries that swelled into Asia, Africa, and other mission regions in the nineteenth century. From the standpoint of Rome, the United States itself was officially mission territory and was consumed by the daunting task of building up the Church in its midst. Throughout most of the nineteenth century, the Church in America was continually expanding geographically as immigrants flooded westward and numerically with the steady flow of immigrants from Europe. The arrival of millions of German and Irish Catholics who had arrived *en masse* between 1830 and 1880 began to slow at century's end, enabling the church to evolve beyond its status as an "immigrant church" to instead foster a decidedly "national" understanding of church.[10]

The heralds of this theological, sociological, and historical concern for a national, "American Church" included several prominent Catholic leaders including Rev. Isaac Hecker, C.S.P., founder of the Paulist order, Archbishop John Ireland of St. Paul, Minnesota, Bishop John J. Keane, rector of Catholic University of America and later archbishop of Dubuque, Iowa, and Bishop Denis J. O'Connell, rector of the North American College in Rome and later rector of Catholic University of America and bishop of Richmond, Virginia. Known as the "Americanists," they envisioned a providential role for both America and for Catholicism within the world.[11] They believed that American influence could help save the faith in Europe and function as the torchbearer for Catholicism's universal mission to the unconverted. The Americanists recognized the unique role of the United States in the sweep of world history as well as the hand of "Providence" in the progress of the Catholic Church in America. They emphasized a developmental "theology of history" that subtly opposed the regnant scholastic viewpoint. In challenging scholasticism, the Americanist approach indirectly defied the philosophical basis for the dominant Catholic worldview. Such views, broadly grouped under the title "Americanism," however, fell under suspicion at home and in Europe, finally triggering

---

10. Church historians have ably documented this shift from the "immigrant" to a more national, post-ethnic Church. See, for instance, Carey, *The Roman Catholics in America*, 29–63.

11. This current of thought known loosely as "Americanism," has been the subject of many scholarly inquiries including McAvoy, *The Great Crisis in American Catholic History*; and O'Connell, *John Ireland*.

their condemnation in 1899 by the promulgation of Pope Leo XIII's letter, *Testem Benevolentiae*.[12]

Dubbed the Americanist heresy, the Americanist supporters believed that God was preparing the United States, through its political, cultural, and technological development for the reunion and expansion of Christianity. They maintained that if America were "won for Christ" the entire world could be converted to the Catholic faith. Those who supported the Catholic "mission to America" often viewed Protestantism as theologically bankrupt and hopelessly splintered. Only Roman Catholicism, they believed, could offer Christianity the order and unity it needed to expand across the globe.

Historian of mission Angelyn Dries has argued persuasively that Americanism was closely connected with the rise of a missionary impulse among Roman Catholics in the United States. Dries claimed that while Pope Leo XIII's letter, *Testem Benevolentiae*, served to stifle popular religious discourse on the subject, Americanism remained a latent theological reality, often converging into streams more acceptable to Church leaders in Rome. The missionary impulse among American Catholics emerged then as a form of "uncondemned Americanism,"[13] ideologically linked to the same streams of liberal and progressive American Catholic thought that had been partially condemned by the pontiff. The missionary movement proved to be an important outlet for Americanist thought and apostolic action, suitable to those who favored a developmental understanding of the Church and those sympathetic to a congenial relationship between Catholicism and American culture. Led by the first generation of Americanists like Archbishop John Ireland, the later "uncondemned" Americanists were often missionaries. Though their activity was transformed from theological speculation to

---

12. Though "Americanism" was not mentioned by name in *Testem Benevolentiae*, its approach was condemned as offering a challenge to *Aeterni Patris* (1879), Leo XIII's encyclical on the thought of St. Thomas Aquinas. For a brief account of the controversy, see Kauffman, "Americanism"; Fogarty, *The Vatican and the Americanist Crisis*; Fogarty, *The Vatican and the American Hierarchy*; Portier, "Two Generations of American Catholic Expansionism in Europe."

13. The author has borrowed this phrase from Dries, "'The Whole Way into the Wilderness.'" See Chapter 1, "Uncondemned Americanism: Walter Elliott and the Mission to Non-Catholics," 1–67.

practical action, they retained the thrust of the Americanist mission: to take Christ to America and the world.[14]

Owing to frequent outbreaks of hostility and obvious theological, social, and political disagreement, most viewed the relationship between Protestant and Catholic America to be one of inevitable conflict. Though their parallel, competing mission movements were often viewed as a "battle for souls" both in America and abroad, still the motivations and ideologies of liberal, Social Gospel, and mission-minded Protestants and Americanist Catholics were surprisingly similar.[15] Underlying the foreign mission impulse of the late nineteenth and early twentieth century for both Protestants and Catholics was the belief that Western culture was superior to that of "pagan" lands and that Western nations had been chosen by God to convert the rest of the world. Liberal Catholic clergy shared much in common with progressive Protestantism including an admiration for the aim of the Social Gospel movement: to Christianize and humanize society. Culturally and politically, both were influenced by America's "manifest destiny," the Spanish-American War, and the drive for Christian expansionism.[16]

The Paulist, Rev. Alexander Doyle (1857–1912), editor of *The Catholic World* and co-founder of the Apostolic Mission House—one of the first American Catholic missionary institutions—was an apologist of the progress of the Church and America. In his view, Church and nation enjoyed a special providential relationship. "We cannot be chided," he stated, "if we are forced to believe, then, that in these United States there is being prepared, in the providence of God, an arena where the Catholic Church will gain her most brilliant victories."[17] In 1904, Doyle wrote, "A Review of Catholic Growth and Progress: From the Planting of the Cross to the Dawn of the Twentieth Century," published in the Paulist-sponsored periodical, *The Missionary*. Doyle's view of Church history was distinctively

---

14. Dries, *The Missionary Movement*, 65–67, 78–80.

15. For Protestantism's influence on Americanism see Hitchcock, "Americanism," 107–8. For acknowledgment of shared Protestant and Catholic liberal "activism" during this era, see Hutchison, "A Moral Equivalent for Imperialism," 167.

16. Ricard, *An American Empire*; Gamble, *The War for Righteousness*; Valera, "The Social Gospel and Imperialism," 162–77; Wangler, "Myth, Worldviews, and Late Nineteenth Century American Catholic Expansionism"; Fishburn, "The Social Gospel as Missionary Ideology."

17. Doyle, "The Divine Guidance of Nations," *The Missionary* 3.10 (1898) 55.

American and Americanist; his article began with the landing of Christopher Columbus and ended with the establishment of the Apostolic Mission House, a center for training missionaries located in Washington, DC. Charting the history of the Church in America between these two events—the former being remembered significantly more by contemporary Americans—Doyle traced the remarkable numerical growth of the Church, but more importantly its intellectual and social contributions to America. The marks of American Catholicism he chose to remember are instructive: support for authority, obedience to law, respect for the rights of property holders, honoring the Sabbath, and speaking out against intemperance—traits important to the Americanists. Doyle cleverly, if not accurately, emphasized those virtues long association with Protestantism's social code, not those of the stereotypical Catholic, often a morally degenerate "foreigner" who was no stranger to intemperance, lawlessness, and poverty. Doyle ended his somewhat "selective history" with the assurance that "Catholicity and Republicanism are not radically opposed, but are twin sisters, born of the same mother at the same time."[18] Doyle envisioned a common mission between religion and nation and believed Catholicism to be a providential source of their mutual progress.

Americanist thought emphasized the active, natural virtues that were believed to be the proper hallmark of Americans. Following the thinking of Isaac Hecker and the Paulists, the Americanists accented the necessary inclusion of the natural virtues in any missionary undertaking. In the very first issue of *The Missionary*, Archbishop Ireland wrote that Americans had "as high an appreciation and as lively a realization of natural truth and goodness as [had] been seen in any people." Among the natural and social virtues particularly found in Americans was "truthfulness, honesty in business, loyalty to law and social order, temperance, respect for the rights of others." These virtues were completely consonant with mission of the Catholic Church in America, he believed. He wrote that the American Republic presupposed the Church's doctrine and that Americans were "naturally Catholic."[19]

---

18. Doyle, "A Review of Catholic Growth and Progress: From the Planting of the Cross to the Dawn of the Twentieth Century," *The Missionary*, special supplement 8.4 (1904) 1–15. For Catholic attempts to chart America's inherently Catholic character see Dohen, *Nationalism and American Catholicism*, 90–103.

19. Ireland, "Father Hecker and America," 5.

The Americanist emphasis on the nation's role in converting the world was due, in part, to the belief that "Old World" Europe had abandoned the faith, especially in France. One article in *The Missionary* compared the "virile state of Catholicity in the American Republic and the decadent state of religion among the French," concluding that the only hope for the Church in Europe was to put aside the "old methods" and adopt the "aggressive tactics of the Catholics in the United States."[20] Similarly, the decline of Protestant churches in America was seen as providential, opening the way for Catholicism's advances. "The generation that was reared in old-fashioned Protestantism will soon die out," one article claimed in 1901. "It is very evident to everyone that Protestantism is losing its hold on this generation."[21] The decay of European Catholicism and American Protestantism was simultaneously and providentially opening the door to a virile, practical American Catholicism destined to take root in the soil of every nation on earth. Doyle and others associated with the missionary movement in America believed that all the signs pointed to the conversion of the United States to Catholicism and the birth of America as a leader within the Church. They argued that if the Church could flourish in America—a free Church in a free land—then its success could be replicated around the globe. American Catholics could solve the problem of Christian unity and in doing so unite the world in its mission of Christian expansion.

Within Protestantism, the foreign missions also became linked to imperialism and the Social Gospel movement. As historian William R. Hutchison has argued, the mission to convert and civilize operated as the "moral equivalent for imperialism." Though liberal Social Gospel Christians most frequently propagated this approach to the foreign missions, both liberals and conservatives shared the belief that Christianity should be the basis for a thriving civilization.[22] One of the earliest and most ardent proponents of this form of imperialism was Josiah Strong, secretary of the Congregational Home Missionary Society. Written at the request of mission supporters, his book, *Our Country: Its Possible Future and Its Present Crisis* (1885), urged America to consider its international

---

20. "Converting the Old World," 27.
21. "We Cannot Escape It," 3.
22. Hutchison, "A Moral Equivalent for Imperialism," 167–77.

role especially in light of its duty to evangelize the world.[23] Called a "religious version of manifest destiny," Strong's work heralded an "evangelical imperialism" consistent with American political aims. In a vein similar to Strong's, the American Presbyterian James Dennis, in his three-volume, *Christian Missions and Social Progress* (1897–1906), extensively outlined the social deficiencies of other cultures, highlighting such depravities as polygamy, child sacrifice, and idolatry. These deficiencies could be erased and societal progress could be achieved, Dennis wrote, if the Christian Gospel were accepted. By exhibiting an ethnocentric melding of American ideals with Christianity, Dennis fostered a triumphalism that could be attached to both nation and Church, the ideal of a Christian Anglo-American empire.[24]

Though such works could appear as anti-Catholic, railing against the Church as backward and unenlightened and warning Americans of the seemingly endless immigration of ethnic Catholics to its shores, the Protestant ideology was shared in part by those Catholics who supported the foreign and domestic mission movements. Both shared a belief in America's providential role in history, foreseeing the potentially providential union of religion and societal progress. Echoing in part the aims of the Social Gospel movement, Americanists hailed their country's technological advancements and their potential in uplifting other cultures by aiding in the foreign missionary endeavor. For the Americanists, material goods were symbolic of the United States' growing influence. In addition to spiritual benefits, American missionaries could offer "something of this world as well: education, care of the sick, the poor, those especially on the 'edges' of their own civilization. Missionaries brought with them 'not a jungle, but a brotherhood of people cooperating in the development of the real, physical, intellectual, and moral good of the race.'"[25] Both Catholic foreign missionaries and Social Gospel Protestants could recognize the value of working for social progress along with the salvation of souls.

23. Reed, "American Foreign Policy," 230–45; Ricard, *An American Empire*, 35; Phillips, "Changing Attitudes"; Edwards, "Forging an Ideology for American Missions," 163. For Catholic reaction to Strong see Kauffman, "Edward McSweeney," 51–65.

24. Bosch, *Transforming Mission*, 293–94. See an analysis of Dennis's work in Hutchison, "A Moral Equivalent for Imperialism," 174–75. For another perspective see Forman, "Evangelization and Civilization," 54–56. Forman argues that Protestant missionaries were preeminently concerned with conquest of the faith, not political imperialism.

25. Quoted in Dries, "The Hero-Martyr Myth," 309. Original from *The Field Afar* 16.3 (1922) 3.

While Social Gospel Christians envisioned a divinely-inspired Protestant nation in America that would link the cause of Christ and human needs, activist Roman Catholics saw hope for the conversion of America to the "True Church of Christ," Catholicism.[26] Isaac Hecker, an early apostle of this ideal, believed that Americans would embrace the Catholic Church if the faith were presented in a way that emphasized its compatibility with culture. Consequently, he and those who followed his method attempted to erase any conceptions of Catholicism as "foreign" or as an enemy of liberty and democracy. They attempted to ease religious hostility by bridging the social and cultural divide between Protestants and Catholics, working for the day that America would be converted to one Church in Christ.[27]

AMERICAN CATHOLIC MISSION AWAKENING

America itself remained a mission territory through the early twentieth century, a longtime recipient of mission personnel from religious communities such as the Jesuits and Franciscans and mission alms from groups such as the Society for the Propagation of the Faith and the Leopoldine Society. When Pope Pius X issued the apostolic constitution *Sapienti Consilio* in 1908, he removed the U.S. as well as Great Britain, Luxembourg and southern Canada from the jurisdiction of *Propaganda Fide*. Within ten years time, America would progress from a mission-receiving to a mission-sending country. With an increasing number of priests and sisters, rising donations, and a growing international consciousness, the Church in America was poised to respond to the more distant needs of the Church. Called by some "America's hour" to participate in the foreign missionary movement, a variety of missionary groups were founded in America during the period, most notably the Maryknoll order, also known as the Catholic Foreign Mission Society of America, the first such missionary society of priests and brothers.[28] In the face of a perceived weakening of the Protestant missionary movement and a declining European contribution to the Catholic missionary enterprise,

---

26. Valera, "The Social Gospel and Imperialism," 165–66.

27. Jonas, *The Divided Mind*, 56–59, 172–73.

28. Dries, *The Missionary Movement*, 74–78, 86, 116–22. The Maryknoll order, also known as the Catholic Foreign Mission Society of America, was the first U.S. group to focus on the foreign missions.

American Catholics were eager to make an impact in the worldwide missionary campaign.

Increased interest on the part of American Catholics in the missions was evidenced by the work of the American branch of the Society for the Propagation of the Faith. While the existence of the propagation had been approved by the U.S. bishops at the Third Plenary Council of Baltimore in 1884, it was not incorporated until 1896 when a general director was named and a headquarters in Baltimore, Maryland was chosen.[29] The overseas mission movement paralleled rising interest in the domestic "mission to America." Beginning in 1904 and continuing through 1909, members of the Paulist order, chiefly Walter Elliott and Alexander Doyle, began sponsoring missionary conferences to discuss the mission to non-Catholics and rural peoples.[30] The same year that America was removed from mission status, 1908, the first American Catholic Mission Congress was convened in Chicago under the leadership of Rev. Francis Clement Kelley (1870–1948), the founder of the Catholic Church Extension Society and later bishop of Oklahoma City. Kelley had founded the Extension Society in 1905 to raise funds for priests in the home missions to better extend the reach of the Church into small-town and rural America.[31] A second mission congress convened in Boston in 1913, featuring addresses by American Catholics then serving in the mission field.[32]

The dramatic increase in mission interest among American Catholics was rooted in Americans' sense of having been divinely chosen for this task and the belief that it was America's opportunity to aid the missions—it was as if an unique alignment of location and time not before seen in history was shaping the movement. Early American Catholic mission periodicals focused on America's unique gifts to the mission movement, emphasizing the American missioner as industrious, practical and pragmatic. The missioner trusted God but also had confidence in his own

---

29. Ibid., 71–74.

30. Dries, "The Foreign Mission Impulse," 61–66.

31. Kelley, *The Story of Extension*; Gaffey, *Francis Clement Kelley*; Dries, *The Missionary Movement*, 69–71; Dries, "The Business of Missions," in "'The Whole Way into the Wilderness,'" 136–85.

32. For the proceedings of the mission congresses see Kelley, *The Two Great American Catholic Missionary Congresses*. For an interpretation of the congresses, see Dries, *The Missionary Movement*, 70–71.

human abilities.[33] The publications noted America's abundance of financial and material resources, further proof of its having been chosen by God to lead other nations.

In one particularly impassioned address, reprinted in the *Field Afar*, the publication of the Maryknoll order, Archbishop Ireland stated, "The Catholic Church must not allow the pall of death to spread over its missions in heathen lands. Those missions are its glory, the evidence of its divinely-given universality. . . . Catholics in large-hearted America will be the saviour of the Church in its missionary work." Ireland, continued, reminding all of America's great fortune:

> Our harvests are plentiful; our industries thrive. Wars in other lands bring us even greater prosperity than might otherwise have been ours. Let us show our gratitude to Almighty God by returning to Him, in service to charity and religion, a generous portion of the gifts with which His bounty has endowed us.[34]

Such early appeals frequently returned to the need for America to generously respond to the needs of the foreign missions. They argued that this was the only fitting response for a people so blessed materially and spiritually.

One of the most important American contributions to the missions was its overriding spirit of pragmatism. Archbishop Keane of Dubuque, on the occasion of the laying of the cornerstone of the Apostolic Mission House on April 24, 1903, lauded the practical actions of the missionary. The students of The Catholic University of America and those of the Apostolic Mission House were "not dreamers, lost in cloudlands of subjectivism, but practical men, thoroughly in touch with their generation, and eager to make their lives tell the utmost in manly endeavor." These men "in the very best sense of the word, are utilitarian" desiring "to do something good and noble for the glory of God and the advancement of humanity."[35] An article in *The Field Afar* echoed these sentiments: "As a people we are practical. Our wealthy men are engaged in business; our finishing academies for young ladies graduate business women who think it no disgrace to use their mental faculties . . . It is a pity, however, to waste on sport or business alone this God-given interest in the practical issues

---

33. Valera, "The Social Gospel and Imperialism," 164.
34. *Field Afar* 9.4 (1915) 50.
35. Keane, "The Apostolic Mission House," 9–11.

of life. Used for the greater good of pagan countries, this American characteristic would set things humming."[36]

In the minds of the missionary Americanists there was a definite relationship between financial success, practical knowledge, and religious truth. America had been divinely chosen and consequently its missionaries had the responsibility to spread their country's many blessings through its interaction with other cultures. Whether through exhibiting pragmatism or imparting its scientific and technical advances, Catholic missionaries attempted to uplift humanity and gain converts for the Church.

The Americanists, especially Archbishop Ireland, saw the cause of religion linked to that of democracy. In general they did not view such a "double loyalty" as dangerous, but saw that "altar and flag" could hardly be in conflict. This has led some to consider the Americanists as agents of imperialism. Such an indictment may be too harsh as the Americanists did not wish to spread the United States' influence for its own sake but as a means of spreading the Catholic religion throughout the world.[37]

Despite some use by Americanists of the vocabulary of "manifest destiny," there were many voices that criticized America's imperialist thrust. The mission-centered Americanists wanted to clearly distinguish between apostolic zeal and the conquering of peoples. In January 1898, only months before the United States declared war on Spain, a war that resulted in America gaining control of Cuba, Puerto Rico, and the Philippines, *The Missionary* stated that its aim was "not to conquer but to win." "Conversion is not conquest. Conversion is a work of grace done from within.... Every convert comes to the Catholic Church freely, conscientiously moved by himself and from within." The article concluded, "We do not expect to conquer America. We expect Americans to conquer themselves."[38]

While seeming to support America's nationalist thrust, a surprising number of articles were critical of nationalism. One articled decried nationalism's negative effect on religion: "'I have gone through Europe and

---

36. *Field Afar* 12. 7 (1918) 98.

37. Dohen, *Nationalism and American Catholicism*, 104–33. Dohen presents Archbishop Ireland as an example of a Church leader who wished to show "how American the Church is" at the risk of placing the nation above the criticism of religion. As a counter example, she introduces Bishop John Lancaster Spalding, a fierce opponent of American imperialism.

38. "We Come Not to Conquer but to Win," 50.

America,' writes a noted missioner: 'Here and there people said to me "we have enough works to patronize here at home without taking a part in those outside." That always pained me because, with St. Paul, I make no distinction between nation and nation.' One thing will lose all in a work like the propagation of the faith, and that is the spirit of *nationalism*."[39]

If there can be one term used to summarize the ideology of early twentieth century missionaries, the second generation of Americanists, it would be "supernatural patriotism."[40] While the religious mission of the Americanist drive to convert America and the world was preeminent in their thinking, their language was staunchly nationalistic. Their synthesis of national and religious rhetoric shows that they did not view these aims as distinctive as much as they were complementary. Their use of the word "supernatural" was meant to show the fundamental religious nature of patriotism or more specifically to hail the triumph of American Catholicism as God's will for the world and His Church. It this way, it can be seen that the Americanists viewed the Church as mediating the world rather than the Church acting against the world. This compatibility between the Church and nationhood they believed would lead to greater advances in Christian expansion.

"CRADLE OF FUTURE MISSIONARIES"

The Church throughout the late nineteenth and early twentieth century emphasized the important contributions that children and youth could make to the work of the Church.[41] A host of organizations were founded to engage the young in the foreign mission enterprise, properly calling such initiatives the "cradle of future missionaries."[42] In 1843 a French bishop, Charles de Forbin-Janson, founded the Holy Childhood Association

39. *Field Afar* 4.1 (1910) 8.

40. The term was used in *Field Afar* 11.11 (1917) 161.

41. The late nineteenth and early twentieth century gave rise to a variety of youth organizations emphasizing the spiritual development of its members and the work of the Church in the world. For instance, the French Catholic Youth Association (*Association Catholique de la Jeunesse Française*) was founded in 1886 by Albert de Mun to enable young people to help in rebuilding a thoroughly Christian social order. The movement was based on "piety, study, and action" not unlike the later Catholic Students' Mission Crusade model of "prayer, study, and sacrifice." See Aubert, *The Church in a Secularised Society*, 124–25, 137–38.

42. See "A Cradle of Future Missionaries," detailing one school's missionary support activities.

(*Association de la Sainte Enfance*) as an organization for youth to help aid children in mission lands. The movement quickly spread as a means for students to live out in a concrete way their devotion to the Christ Child. Inspired by the example of Pauline Jaricot who helped found the Society for the Propagation for the Faith in 1822, Forbin-Janson's aim was to interest children in the needs of young people in mission lands, particularly in China. Children could be admitted into the society from birth through the age of first communion, about age twelve. Members promised to remember in prayer children in mission countries and to make a sacrifice of at least one penny per month. They were required to pray the "Hail Mary" daily and conclude by saying: "Holy Virgin Mary, pray for us and for the poor pagan children."[43]

Almost from its inception, the link between Catholic youth and their foreign counterparts was established. Funds donated by children would be used to "ransom" children in "pagan" countries by guarding them from the possibility of physical slavery and the spiritual bondage of sin. To these ends, baptism was procured for them and their material needs were provided for in orphanages, schools, and hospitals staffed by religious sisters or priests. Noting the reciprocal relationship between the child offering his pocket change for the benefit of children in foreign lands, one publication related: "As the children of Europe would guarantee the rescue and salvation of the children of China, so would the little recipients of this charity be a means of salvation to their material and spiritual benefactors!"[44]

The forging of a bond between children who had never met—the one being in Europe or America, the other being in China or some other mission region—was accomplished through making the distant encounter real and immediate. Holy Childhood members or groups were encouraged to "adopt" or "ransom" an individual "pagan baby" with naming rights to the child—always choosing, of course, a proper Christian name. One publication claimed, "this plan was an inspired stroke of genius." "No work of charity has ever proven more appealing or exciting to Christian children," it claimed, "than this personalized drive to ransom and protect

---

43. "Save the Babies in Heathendom," 55.
44. Royer, *The Power of Little Children*, 70.

the countless babes who are each year born into suffering, ignorance, and poverty throughout the pagan nations of the world!"[45]

Expanding beyond France, the association was approved and recommended to the entire Church by Pope Pius IX in 1856 and the efforts of the association were extended to all mission territories. The association was established in America, still itself a mission territory in 1846, just three years after its founding, first in New Orleans, Louisiana, and later in Baltimore, Maryland. By 1851, the United States affiliates of the association were recognized along with those in Mexico and Canada. Its national office was established in New York City under the Jesuit Theodore Thiry from 1866–1889 and was later moved to Pittsburgh, Pennsylvania under the leadership of the Holy Ghost Fathers in 1892. Under Father Thiry's leadership the association grew to include a presence in thirty-seven American dioceses with a membership of 150,000 children and mission contributions of over $25,000 annually.[46]

At the first American Catholic Missionary Congress held in Chicago in 1908, Rev. John Willms, C.S.Sp., director of the Holy Childhood Association in the United States, commented on the aims of the association:

> First, to rally around the Infant Jesus our little Christian children from their tender years, so that with their increasing years and strength, and in imitation of Jesus their master, they may practice true Christian charity with a view to their own perfection; second, that by the practice of charity and enduring liberality those same little Christian children may co-operate in saving from death and sin, the thousands and thousands of children that in pagan countries like China are cast away and neglected by their parents and die unbaptized; to procure Holy Baptism for those abandoned little ones, and should they live, to make of them craftsmen, teachers, doctors, or priests, who all in turn will spread the blessings of the Christian religion amongst their countrymen.[47]

---

45. Ibid., 74–75.

46. Royer, *The Power of Little Children*, 66–75, 82–85, 99–100. See also Koren, *The Serpent and the Dove*, 148–50; Society for the Propagation of the Faith, *The Mission Apostolate*, 102–4.

47. Willms, "The Work of the Holy Childhood," in *First American Catholic Missionary Congress*, Kelley, ed., 73–74.

Willms clearly linked the participation of Christian children with the salvation of their non-Christian peers often living on the other side of the world.

By 1915 Catholics in America contributed more than $40,000 annually to the association's work of educating and saving children through the operation of orphanages, schools, and workshops. The leaders of the organization boasted that they had "sent directly to Heaven 20 million little ones" by procuring baptism for pagans and by "buying" children doomed to death or slavery. Paralleling the growth of enthusiasm and support for the foreign missions after World War I, Americans donated more than $140,000 annually by 1920, three times the total donations of five years prior.[48] The association received approval as a Pontifical Mission Society in 1922 by Pope Pius XI by which time nearly one in three American Catholic school children were enrolled.[49]

A laywoman, B. Ellen Burke of New York City, founded in 1905 another organization, similar in aim to the Holy Childhood Association. Burke, editor of two Catholic publications, the *Helper* and the *Sunday Companion*, organized a society for children to pray for the conversion of America. Called the "Child Knights of the Cross," and later as the "Knights of the Cross" when it began to incorporate adult members, the movement grew to 20,000 members within four years of its founding. The association required its members to say three Hail Marys each day for the nation's conversion, but did not collect monetary donations. Its goal was particularly to encourage spiritual practices among the young; according to Burke: "It was hoped that there would be a spiritual awakening, that a thirst for souls might be created, that habits of praying daily for the conversion of nations and people, as well as for individuals, might be fostered."[50] The movement was publicized in Burke's publications as well as the Paulist-sponsored publication, *The Missionary*.

By 1920, there were numerous publications and movements geared toward awakening missionary interest among the young. *The Field Afar* included a column, "Our Young Apostles," which later took the form of

---

48. *Field Afar* 9.9 (1915) 132; *Field Afar* 14.9 (1920) 196. For an analysis of *Field Afar*'s impact see Wiest, *Maryknoll in China*, 410–13.

49. Royer, *The Power of Little Children*, 90, 92.

50. B. Ellen Burke, "The Missionary Movement Among the Children," *The Missionary* 23.2 (November 1909) 56–59.

the "Maryknoll Junior" insert.[51] Beginning in 1915 the Society of the Divine Word published its own monthly missionary magazine for children titled *The Little Missionary*, aiming to cultivate the mission spirit among Catholic girls and boys. Founded by Rev. Bruno Hagspiel, S.V.D., the magazine cost just twenty-five cents a year and boasted 22,400 subscriptions by the end of its first year of publication. Within a few years the publication peaked at a readership of 150,000 per issue.[52]

Throughout the nineteenth and early twentieth century opportunities to support mission work expanded dramatically, especially for youth. Catholic children in America were invited to do their part by donating nickels and dimes to "save pagan babies," to remember the intentions of the missions in their prayers and to "offer up" small sacrifices for the success of the crusade to Christianize the world. A host of organizations sprouted from this desire for youthful involvement in the often-distant work of the missions. As participants in groups like the Holy Childhood Association and the Child Knights of the Cross, American boys and girls were invited to pray, study, and sacrifice for their non-Christian counterparts: youth in foreign lands.

COMPETITION FOR SOULS: MOTIVATION FOR CATHOLIC AND PROTESTANT MISSIONS

Though the rhetoric was usually neither fierce nor polemical, Catholics in America perceived the need to outdo or at least measure up to the work of their Protestant counterparts in the foreign missions.[53] As the foreign mission movement matured in the post-Reformation era, both Protestants and Catholics were cognizant of the double meaning of missions: to save "pagan" souls from unbelief and also from their Christian "competitor." For Catholics this meant claiming souls for the "True Church" and for

---

51. "Maryknoll Junior" insert in *Field Afar* 10.3 (1916) 1.

52. *Field Afar* 9.6 (1915) 85. See the advertisement for "The Little Missionary" on the back cover of Fischer, *For Christ's Kingdom*; see also Brandewie, *In the Light of the Word*, 113, 119.

53. For an analysis of the domestic "competition" for souls see Appleby, "Missions and the Making of Americans." Like their Catholic counter-parts, Protestants seemed to be aware of Catholic missionary efforts. See Dries, "The Foreign Mission Impulse," 61–66, who notes that former Protestant Student Volunteer Movement member and mission historian, Kenneth Latourette, was among the first to notice the rise of the American Catholic mission movement in his "The Missionary Awakening."

Protestants this was translated into saving unbelievers from the superstitions and un-biblical "inventions" of Romanism.[54]

Many Catholic mission publications of the early twentieth century highlighted the substantial Protestant mission enterprise as a motivating force in assembling a greater American Catholic influence in mission lands. At the same time that American Catholics only counted sixteen foreign missionaries, Protestant America could claim thousands of missionaries sent abroad and millions of dollars dedicated to the conversion of the world.[55] At the first American Catholic Missionary Congress held in 1908, Rev. Msgr. Joseph Freri, director of the Society for the Propagation of the Faith in the United States, spoke of the need for Catholic contributions to the foreign missions. He lamented American Catholics' meager influence and the substantial contributions of money and manpower by the Protestant churches. Protestants and Catholics were clearly in competition for souls in mission lands:

> Let us not delude ourselves that Protestant missions are a mere sham. With this enormous outlay they are obtaining remarkable results, and above all, they are raising powerful obstacles to the planting of the true Christian Faith. There are nations which, today, would be far in the road toward Catholicity were it not that when our missionaries arrived they found that Protestantism had already there, as everywhere, done its work of dividing the minds and leading toward incredulity and indifferentism.[56]

Another mission commentator attempted to shock his readers with the assertion that "so completely have American missions been Protestant that in many parts of the mission field the idea of an American Catholic missionary comes as a strange notion and is hard for the natives to believe at all."[57] The desire to overshadow the already immense American Protestant mission movement was a compelling motivation for further sacrifices and activity on the part of Catholics in the United States.

---

54. For Protestant efforts to emulate and surpass Catholic mission efforts see Beaver, "Mission Motivation Through Three Centuries."

55. See Carey, *The Roman Catholics in America*, 71; "Millions Let Us Pour Into the Missions."

56. Freri, "The Foreign Missions," in Kelley, *The First American Catholic Missionary Congress*, 70.

57. Keeler, "College Sodalities," 104.

The "competition for souls" between Protestants and Catholics impacted the youth mission movement, providing a powerful stimulus for involvement. Founded prior to the American Catholic mission awakening, the Protestant-sponsored Student Volunteer Movement for Foreign Missions (SVM) was the first large-scale student mission movement in the United States.[58] A survey of Catholic publications indicates that Catholics, especially those who envisioned a similar movement for their youth, followed the work of the SVM with muted admiration, lauding its organizational strength if not its evangelical content.[59]

The Student Volunteer Movement had a somewhat unlikely beginning in 1886, forming out of a summer Bible conference attended by some 250 evangelical Christians at Mount Hermon in rural Massachusetts. The meeting was presided over by Rev. Dwight L. Moody (1837–1899), a famous revivalist of the period. The missionary thrust of the meeting was due to the influence of Rev. Arthur T. Pierson (1837–1911), noted evangelist and biblical scholar, who spoke on the necessity for Christian evangelization—"all should go, and go to all," he preached to the students.[60] A portion of the meeting was set aside for a discussion of Christianity's role in the missions. Ten students, representing Asia, Europe, and indigenous America, were asked to speak on the progress of Christianity in their native lands. The speeches—each only three minutes in length—ended with the phrase "God is love" said in the native language of the presenter. These ten short pronouncements were so stirring that eventually one hundred of the conference attendees pledged to become foreign missionaries. Almost forty percent of the participants, called the "Mount Hermon One Hundred," committed themselves to mission service, an unexpected outcome of the meeting.[61] Many of those attending the conference called this "meeting of the ten nations" the highpoint of the gathering.

---

58. Parker, *The Kingdom of Character*; Showalter, *End of a Crusade*; Wallstrom, *The Creation of a Student Movement to Evangelize the World*; Phillips, "The Student Volunteer Movement"; Robert, "The Origin of the Student Volunteer Watchword," 146–149; Phillips, "Changing Attitudes," 131–45. The papers of the SVM are located at Yale University, Divinity Library Special Collections, New Haven, Connecticut.

59. As examples, see Schwager, "Mission Movement Among Protestant Students," and "Mission Movement Among Catholic Students."

60. Robert, *Occupy Until I Come*, 140–56 (148).

61. Wallstrom, *The Creation of a Student Movement to Evangelize the World*, 45.

One participant later wrote, "Seldom have I seen an audience under the sway of God's spirit as it was that night."[62]

The assembled students pledged to devote themselves to an intercollegiate missionary movement. The aim of the movement was fivefold:

> To lead students to a thorough consideration of the claims of foreign missions upon them personally as a lifework; to foster this purpose by guiding students who become volunteers ...; to unite all volunteers in a common, organized, aggressive movement; to secure a sufficient number of well-qualified volunteers ...; to create and maintain an intelligent, sympathetic, and active interest in foreign missions on the part of students who are to remain at home in order to ensure the strong backing of the missionary enterprise by their advocacy, their gifts, and their prayers.[63]

Attributed to Pierson in its final form, the students adopted as their motto, "the evangelization of the world in this generation," a testament to their optimism and the idealism of youth if not their naïveté. To make concrete the intentions of the movement, they drafted a pledge card to be signed by members, stating, "It is my purpose, if God permit, to become a foreign missionary."[64]

The SVM expanded swiftly with the support of a variety of established organizations such as the collegiate branch of the Young Men's Christian Association (YMCA), the Young Women's Christian Association (YWCA), the Inter-Seminary Missionary Alliance, and a number of college mission societies such as the Philadelphian Society then in existence at Princeton University. The leaders of the movement were prominent, educated laymen, attending universities such as Princeton, Yale, and Cornell.[65] They included the founder of the movement and general secretary, Robert P. Wilder,[66] longtime executive chairman, John R. Mott,[67] and committee

---

62. Parker, *The Kingdom of Character*, 1–3 (3).

63. Mott, *Five Decades and a Forward View*, 8; quoted in Howard, *Student Power in World Evangelism*, 86.

64. Howard, *Student Power in World Evangelism*, 86–87; See Wallstrom, *The Creation of a Student Movement to Evangelize the World*, 71–76, for the debate surrounding the pledge.

65. A brief introduction to the founders of the movement is found in Wallstrom, *The Creation of a Student Movement to Evangelize the World*, 4.

66. Patterson, "The Legacy of Robert P. Wilder," 26–32; Braisted, *In This Generation*.

67. Mott is perhaps best known for his service to the Young Men's Christian

member and prolific historian of the missions, Kenneth Scott Latourette. Others integral to the movement were Robert E. Speer, who later headed the Presbyterian Board of Foreign Missions,[68] and SVM missionary and evangelist G. Sherwood Eddy.[69] Within two years the founders had visited more than 160 educational institutions, pledging thousands as volunteers for the missions, including 500 women.[70]

Founded in an age of cultural and religious imperialism, anti-Catholicism, and romanticism, the movement drew strength from each. The appeal to the Student Volunteer Movement often utilized military terminology including references to "conquest," "crusade" and a "world-wide war" for Christ. Its members believed they possessed a special calling to spread "civilization" and aid "lower" nations and "backward civilizations" as citizens of the United States—a Western, largely Protestant country. The movement even appealed to a romanticized Christian past, adopting for its own uses the story of the "Knights of the Labarum," protectors of the symbol of the Emperor Constantine's dramatic victory in AD 312: Christ's monogram, the *Chi-Rho*.[71] Like American Catholic missionary efforts that gained strength from the myth of Protestant disintegration, Protestant missionaries often pointed to Catholic Europe and Latin America as evidencing a decline in faith, opening the door to proselytizing.[72]

Approaching the missionary calling with a uniquely Protestant sensibility, the missionaries of the SVM focused on the Victorian ideals of heroism, manliness, humanitarianism and self-sacrifice. The ideal Christian missionary was not the cleric but the businessman who approached his spiritual life in a worldly and practical way. According to one historian of the movement, the SVM members "saw themselves not only as evangelicals, but also practical, business-like, efficient, hard-working, virile Christians, who had the organizational skills, technical ability, and practical know-how to take the gospel of Jesus Christ around the world

---

Association (YMCA) in America, serving for nearly fifty years in the leadership of the organization. See Hopkins, "John R. Mott"; Hopkins, *John R. Mott, 1865-1955*.

68. Piper, "The Development of the Missionary Ideas of Robert E. Speer." Also, see his larger work, Piper, *Robert E. Speer*.

69. Nutt, "G. Sherwood Eddy," 502–21.

70. Howard, *Student Power in World Evangelism*, 84–85.

71. Phillips, "Changing Attitudes in the Student Volunteer Movement," 135–36; Showalter, *End of a Crusade*, 14; Parker, *The Kingdom of Character*, 78–79, 107 (79).

72. Parker, *The Kingdom of Character*, 68–69.

in a single generation."[73] The movement's ideals and its ethic were thoroughly American and Protestant.

In addition to recruiting missionaries for foreign service, the SVM engaged in educating youth who remained at home. The SVM publication, *The Student Volunteer*, which began in 1893, stressed the importance of mission education and often included outlines for mission studies. Additionally, the movement published dozens of studies detailing the progress of the missions in various countries and regions including China, Japan, the Philippines, South America, and Africa and comparative studies of Christianity's response to Islam, to relativism, and to various "social evils."[74]

The advent of the SVM in America spurred greater international cooperation in the mission field. Less than a decade after the volunteer movement's founding, John Mott helped organize the World's Student Christian Federation (WSCF), an international association of Protestant student mission movements.[75] In 1910 Mott chaired the first World Missionary Conference held in Edinburgh, Scotland. Though there had been similar conferences as far back at 1860, the Edinburgh conference was the first large scale, international gathering. Attended by some 1,200 participants, it is often cited as one of the first ecumenical meetings. Though no Roman Catholics were present, there is no doubt that the Catholic Church watched the Edinburgh conference closely.[76]

The SVM reached the height of its success in the early twentieth century, at which time it had been responsible for recruiting more than half of the foreign missionaries then representing mainline American Protestant denominations. The movement's strength flowed from its success in joining "theological liberals and conservatives, Social Gospelers, and premillenielists," representing a broad, yet diverse swath of Protestant America.[77] By 1920, the SVM had sent 1,800 volunteers to mission lands

---

73. Ibid., 19, 23, 24, 33 (33).

74. Ibid., 105, 111–20.

75. Showalter, *End of a Crusade*, 3–5; Rouse, *The World's Student Christian Federation*.

76. Neill, *A History of Christian Missions*, 331–32; Hogg, "Edinburgh 1910—Perspective 1980," 146–53; "World Missionary Conference," 2049–52; also Hutchison, *Errand to the World*. While no Catholic was present, Bishop Geremia Bonomelli sent a message to be read at the meeting. See Delaney, "From Cremona to Edinburgh," 418–31.

77. Parker, *The Kingdom of Character*, 103.

and had thousands of additional supporters praying and sacrificing for the missions from home.

The original zeal and unity of the movement, however, could not be retained among successive generations. As one historian recounted, by the 1930s the "well-outlined sense of purpose the watchword had originally served to focus so vividly now was projected as fuzzy and diffuse."[78] The number of students entering the missions plummeted as well as the numbers attending the organization's national conventions. While nearly 3,000 members enrolled in the SVM in 1920, only 25 did so in 1938 in the wake of the Depression and the rise of totalitarianism in Europe. Whereas almost 7,000 were present at the organization's convention in Des Moines, Iowa, in 1920, not even 500 delegates attended the meeting in 1940. By this time the organization had diminished to the point of being unrecognizable; the SVM had effectively ceased as an active promoter of the foreign missions among American Protestant youth.[79] After two decades of near inactivity, the SVM joined in 1959 with the United Student Christian Council and the inter-seminary committee to form the National Student Christian Federation (NSCF). In 1966 an alliance with the Catholic Newman Student Federation, among other associations, was forged, resulting in the formation of the University Christian Movement (UCM). The movement, however, was short-lived as its own members voted it out of existence in 1969, declaring itself no longer a national organization.[80] At one time among the most prominent and successful mission organizations in the world, the Student Volunteer Movement had gradually ceased to impact the work of the Protestant missions.

A century after the Catholic missionary awakening in Europe and the flowering of the Protestant mission movement in America, American Catholics became increasingly aware of the needs of the Church beyond their homeland. The parochial, ethnic-centered style of American Catholicism that was the hallmark of the immigrant Church was slowly

---

78. Wallstrom, *The Creation of a Student Movement to Evangelize the World*, 11–12, 86–87 (86–87).

79. For a description and analysis of the movement's decline see Howard, *Student Power in World Evangelism*, 90–95; Showalter, *End of a Crusade*, 161, 179–89. An unrelated organization, the Student Foreign Missions Fellowship, organized in 1936, helped fill the void left by the waning SVM.

80. Few studies analyze the decline of the movement, but the facts of its demise are related in Howard, *Student Power in World Evangelism*, 95–96.

giving way to a new vision. Disappointed by the Roman reaction, yet still active, the "uncondemned" Americanists emphasized a new role for Church and nation: to win the United States and indeed the world for Christ. This outward-looking thrust indicated the Church's newly realized institutional strength, its eagerness to espouse the ideals of the nation, and its assimilation of a political-religious ideal of expansion. Influenced by the ideology of liberal activism seen in the Social Gospel movement and the imperialist thrust of "manifest destiny," the drive for Catholic expansion reached new heights. The missionary awakening among American Catholics clearly has its roots in this political, cultural, and theological ferment of the late nineteenth and early twentieth century. Competition between Protestants and Catholics in the missionary quest, a strengthening national identity, and an increasing international awareness needed only the outbreak of war to fully ignite Catholic America's quest to Christianize the world.

TWO

Coming Crusade

Catholic Missions and the Great War, 1914–1920

THE FIRST WORLD WAR stands as a key moment for the Catholic missionary effort. For the European mission force, the war resulted in a disastrous loss of manpower as missionaries, mostly French and German, were recalled to their homelands to join in the armed conflict. Alternatively, for American Catholics, the "war to end all wars" signaled their arrival on the international mission stage. Viewing the war as an opportunity to advance domestically as well as internationally, American Catholics championed the United States' war aim to make the world safe for democracy, while remaining less enthusiastic about domestic reforms that included women's suffrage, prohibition, and immigrant restriction.[1] Though Catholics had not often promoted these causes, in a time of worldwide conflict, the qualities of unity, equality, and sobriety were emphasized over particular ethnic, sectarian, or local concerns.

In wartime, outward shows of patriotism remained significant, especially among immigrant groups. German Americans, in particular, descended from one of the "enemy" powers, jumped at the chance to prove their allegiance by purchasing "liberty bonds" and displaying the American flag, indicating they were "100% American" in their support of the war effort. Patriotism, though perhaps at times falsely emphasized, did serve to diminish ethnic separatism, eliminating the hyphenated status of such minority groups as Irish-Americans, German-Americans, and Italian-Americans.[2]

---

1. Kennedy, *Over Here*; Zieger, *America's Great War*; Keene, *The United States and the First World War*, esp. ch. 6, "The Meaning of the First World War for the United States," 85–87.

2. McKeown, *War and Welfare*; Meigs, *Optimism at Armageddon*, 17; Breen, *Uncle*

Equipped with increased financial and organizational resources and a resolve for at least surface-level cultural and moral unanimity, American Catholics harnessed the zeal that had spurred America's late nineteenth-century expansionism, transferring their idealism and confidence into wartime action. The most significant accomplishment of the period was the United States bishops' creation of the National Catholic War Council (NCWC).[3] Originally organized to coordinate wartime relief and ministry to American soldiers serving in Europe, it charted a course for coordinated national initiatives throughout the century and helped convince American Catholics that national responsibilities should outweigh parochial, diocesan, and ethnic concerns.[4] The efforts of American Catholics were becoming increasingly organized, pragmatic, and centralized—the outflow of a solidified national and emerging international consciousness.

"WHAT WILL AMERICA DO?": THE WARTIME APPEAL TO RESCUE THE MISSIONS

America's heightened international awareness that matured during the war became entwined with the Catholic mission impulse. Numerous reports from "front line" missionaries lamented the significant loss of French and German missionary priests as well as mission alms from warring countries. The repatriation of French missionaries, ordered by law, was especially significant as the French accounted for nearly three-quarters of Catholic missionaries prior to the war. The removal of German missionaries, sometimes expelled from colonial territories by the Allied powers, exacerbated the crisis in manpower. Over 500 German Catholic missionaries were expelled from the mission field and over 400 were imprisoned during the war. The emptying of most of Europe's mission schools and seminaries further impacted the shortage, assuring there would be few replacements in the mission field for those returning home. Even after the war, the Versailles Treaty limited the work of German missionaries in their colonies.

Sam at Home, 159–75.

3. The organization was later named the National Catholic Welfare Council and still later the National Catholic Welfare Conference. See Slawson, *The Foundation and First Decade of the National Catholic Welfare Council.*

4. Piper, *The American Churches in World War I*, especially 69–106; McKeown, *War and Welfare.*

The European missionaries themselves, *Propaganda Fide*, and indeed Pope Benedict XV himself implored Americans to relieve "bleeding Europe" of its missionary commitments. "What will America do?" was the question voiced by mission supporters the world over.[5] One author reminded his American readers of their duty to the missions, "For years Europe will have to look to the rebuilding of her own ruined sanctuaries and cannot be expected to contribute either vocations or money in abundance, America must supply both."[6] While Protestant missions experienced a crisis of sorts in the aftermath of the war, for the Catholic missions the conflict was the beginning of a new offensive for global mission initiatives.[7] Just as the Americanists believed that the "design of Providence" had destined America to be converted, they also believed that the United States would lead the world in its turn toward Catholicism. Concern for America's providential role in the Church's missionary enterprise increased drastically after the United States' entry into the war.

The qualities of youth and masculinity, idealized during wartime to gain soldiers and bolster enthusiasm for the war, were easily transferred to the cause of the foreign missions.[8] The soldier had been emphasized as the preeminent form of nationalistic, manly heroism fueled by a strong sense of purpose, the lure of foreign adventure, and appreciation for order. Linking this masculine ideal to expressions of patriotism and chivalry popularized the idea of the soldier crusader. This admiration of manliness and sacrifice met its logical conclusion in the glorification of the fallen soldier: the young man who had given everything for his country and by extension his God, transforming the one-time soldier crusader into a martyr. Popular illustrations showed the fallen soldier in the hands of

---

5. Jedin, *History of the Church*, 9:557–58; *An Appeal to the Catholics of the World*; Freri, "Native Clergy for Mission Countries," 193–201; Ferrer, "Lift Up Your Eyes," 282–83; Cramer, "What Will America Do?" 232–33. For similar reactions to the war and the missions among Irish Catholics see Hogan, *The Irish Missionary Movement*, 147–48.

6. Keeler, "College Sodalities and the Mission Crusade," 104.

7. While the Great War provided motivation and necessity for American Catholic involvement in the foreign missions, the war resulted in ambiguity among Protestant mission supporters: Was the war to be seen a providential means to world evangelization or a fratricidal conflict among Christians? This crisis caused many Protestants to question the placement of their missionary zeal or reject the movement altogether. See Showalter, "Crusade or Catastrophe?" 16. Also, Showalter, *End of a Crusade*.

8. For an analysis of American Catholic assessment of the war, see Halsey, *The Survival of American Innocence*, 44–48.

Christ, intimately connecting the sacrifices of war with those of Christ on the Cross.[9]

This Christian militarism utilized during the war years was transmitted to the foreign mission cause in America. The young Jesuit and early member of the Catholic Students' Mission Crusade, P. J. Sontag, appealed to the boyhood of America to devote themselves to the missions as American soldiers had during the conflict. In his two pamphlets, *America's Answer* and *America Must*, Sontag reminded the youth of America that "a great War still goes on" and for mission-minded young people "with hero-blood in their veins the cry is still 'over there! over there!'" While the smoke of battle lingered, Sontag asked young Catholics to "behold the standard of *your* Leader, the Great Leader and Captain, and listen to His call, the call to His war, Heaven's war!," where victory was as sure as the missionary's "immortal fame and unfading honor."[10] Another article likened the needs of the missions to a warring nation's need for soldiers, munitions, and supplies: "War is in the air, and while missionaries are men of peace, we are borrowing war terms to make known their wants."[11]

In the article, "A Call to Arms," written by Richard J. Sykes, S.J., the author wrote of his hope for the missions: "there seems to be a stirring amongst the dry bones of an almost extinct interest in Foreign Missions." Looking to America to take a foremost part in the missionary awakening, Sykes wrote: "We need the Fiery Cross carried through the length and breadth of the world to arouse the dormant Catholic conscience to the fact that two immense continents are still to be converted; that half the human race still lives in darkness and in the shadow of death. Where are the hands that will hold this torch; whose the life that will inspirit this 'Crusade'?"[12]

THE MISSIONS IN THE AFTERMATH OF WAR

The Church emerging from the ruins of the war found itself shocked to the core, still reeling from a disastrous global war that pitted one Christian nation against another. National antipathy remained throughout Europe despite the signing of the documents assuring peace. The chief lesson of

---

9. Mosse, *Fallen Soldiers*, 7, 58, 74–75.
10. Sontag, *America's Answer*, 12.
11. "Our Soldiers of the Cross," 22.
12. Sykes, "A Call to Arms," 15–16.

the conflict seemed to be the perniciousness of exaggerated nationalism, a refutation of the bonds of Christianity in favor of a higher allegiance to the nation-state. During the war, Catholicism as propagated throughout the world by missionaries had been heralded as the antidote to nationalism: "if every heart was a Catholic heart national boundaries would come to mean very little—indeed, would hardly be noticed."[13] In opposition to the nationalism that was at the root of the war, the missionary movement advocated the fostering of a form of Catholic internationalism.

One of the greatest missionaries of the century, Vincent Lebbe, a Belgian missionary to China, was a pioneer of the Church's critique of colonialism, providing the impetus for Pope Benedict XV's letter on the missions, *Maximum Illud* (1919). Lebbe became convinced of the need for radical change if the missions were to avoid collapse.[14] *Maximum Illud*—termed the *magna carta* of the modern mission movement—supported this fundamental shift, seeking to de-politicize mission work and back away from the standard of European domination in the missions.[15] Benedict reminded missionaries that they were not to devote their efforts to any earthly homeland but only to their heavenly home and that no missionary should attempt to increase the prestige of his native land by his action as a missionary, laboring only for the Church and the good of those he encountered. The missionary should be careful to "seek no other profits but those of souls," the letter concluded.[16]

Benedict hoped that by promoting a "new internationalism," conflict in the missions could be diminished. Internationalism and an end to colonialism in the missions was well received by Americans who had almost no stake in mission lands prior to the war. As the American Cardinal James Gibbons stated, "[T]he strongest response to the new internationalism must come from the Church of the ages. The Catholic Church cannot remain an isolated factor in the nation. . . . The message to the nation to forget local boundaries and provincialism is a message likewise to the Catholic Church. Parochial, diocesan, and provincial limits must be forgotten in the face of the greater tasks which burden our collective

13. *Field Afar* 11.6 (1917) 81.

14. Wiest, "The Legacy of Vincent Lebbe," 33–37.

15. Jedin, *History of the Church*, 9:557–59. For the text of *Maximum Illud* see *Acta Apostolicae Sedis: Commentarium Officiale* 11:440–55. For an excerpted English translation, see Barry, *Readings in Church History*, 1233–42.

16. Quoted in Barry, *Readings in Church History*, 1237–38.

religious resources."¹⁷ The American missionaries walked a fine line between advocating the importance of their nation while condemning the type of nationalism that led to war and division.

Benedict's apostolic letter reminded bishops and religious superiors of the pressing need for worldwide evangelization to reach an estimated one billion non-believers. Benedict articulated a plan for the missionary enterprise calling for Roman centralization of organizations directing missionary work, the division of missionary work between social and spiritual aims, awareness of the political climate in foreign lands, and the importance of not allowing nationalism to corrupt advances in the missions. He introduced reforms including the division of mission territories into vicariates administered by religious orders, and the establishment of mission seminaries to better train clergy for the mission field.¹⁸ The document evidenced a growing awareness of the importance of indigenous civilizations and the potentially damaging nature of political and cultural imperialism. The main function of those in charge of mission territories, according to *Maximum Illud*, was "to raise and train a clergy from amidst the nations among which they dwell."¹⁹ To further these aims the pope encouraged attendance at the Roman *Collegio Urbano di Propaganda* (the Urban College), a seminary to train missionary priests, and advocated the founding of regional seminaries to boost the number of indigenous clergy. The pope assigned a greater role to mission aid organizations directed from Rome such as the Society for the Propagation of the Faith, the Holy Childhood Association, and the Missionary Union of the Clergy.²⁰

One of the fruits of the postwar mission impulse was an increased interest in mission theory and praxis, the advent of missiology as an academic discipline. Josef Schmidlin (1876–1944), founder of the Münster-based school of mission science, is considered the father of Catholic missiology. Though a Church historian by training, Schmidlin was influenced by pioneering Protestant missiologists such as Gustav Warneck (1834–1910). Schmidlin began lecturing in missiology in 1910 and four years later was chosen to occupy the first chair of missiology at a Catholic

17. *Field Afar* 12.12 (1918) 198.
18. Jedin, *History of the Church*, 9:559–62.
19. Quoted in Barry, *Readings in Church History*, 1236.
20. Falconi, *The Popes in the Twentieth Century*, 143–47; Bruhls, "From Missions to 'Young Churches,'" in Aubert, Bruhls, and Hajjar, *The Church in a Secularised Society*, 398–99.

university when a position was created at the University of Münster.[21] He published many important works, developed courses on the study of mission, and edited the journal, *Zeitschrift für Missionswissenschaft*. Perhaps his most important publications were *Catholic Mission History* (*Die Katholischen Missionen*, 1926) and *Catholic Mission Theory*, both translated into English by Rev. Matthias Braun, S.V.D., and published by the mission press at Techny, Illinois, in 1931 and 1933, respectively.[22]

In addition to his scholarly work, Schmidlin was also successful in founding student associations dedicated to missionary work. In 1910 he sparked the formation of the *Akademischer Missionsverein* based in Münster. Soon over 600 students had joined the original association and the movement spread to other German Catholic institutions including the seminaries in Passau, Freising, Baden, Bonn, and Tübingen University. Unfortunately, Schmidlin's work ended prematurely when he was forced to retire in 1934 at the age of fifty-eight, having already come under suspicion of the German government. He died in 1944, tortured to death in the Struthof concentration camp.[23]

It was not long after Schmidlin's founding of the Münster "school" of mission science that interest in the study of mission extended beyond the borders of Germany. By the end of the war, two centers for mission study had been founded in Rome: the Urban College founded a mission institute and the Gregorian University established a chair in missiology. Later chairs were established at Nijeman, Netherlands; Ottawa, Canada; Vienna, Austria; Comillas, Spain; and Fribourg, Switzerland. Dozens of other Catholic universities and seminaries initiated lectures in mission history, practice, and theology.[24]

The era of World War I also witnessed an increased interest by secular clergy in mission work. The Maynooth-Galway mission seminary in

---

21. The study of mission also accelerated within American Protestant circles in the early twentieth century. The Kennedy School of Mission at Hartford was formed in 1911, the *International Review of Missions* began publication the following year, and Union Theological Seminary in New York and Princeton University formed mission departments and professorships in 1914. An International Missionary Council was organized in 1921. See Hans Kasdorf, "Missiology as a Discipline in Historical Perspective," 219–38.

22. Dries, *The Missionary Movement*, 81.

23. Müller, "The Legacy of Joseph Schmidlin," 109–13. See also Müller's larger work, *Josef Schmidlin*, as well as Müller, "Joseph Schmidlin," 402–9; and Jedin, *History of the Church*, 9:571–2.

24. Müller, "The Legacy of Joseph Schmidlin," 112.

Ireland was founded in 1917; Almonte, Canada (1919), Burgos, Spain (1919), Montreal, Canada (1921), and Bethlehem, Switzerland (1921) also established training institutions for missionary diocesan clergy. In 1915 the Missionary Union of the Clergy (*Unio Cleri pro Missionibus*) was founded in Milan and was later elevated to the status of a pontifical missionary society like the Society for the Propagation of the Faith and the Holy Childhood Association.[25]

AMERICAN CATHOLICISM'S ORGANIZATIONAL REVOLUTION

The proliferation of organizations after World War I was indicative of a growing consciousness among American Catholics of their political and social strength. As Archbishop Michael Curley of Baltimore proclaimed in 1921: "the watchword is organization."[26] Ironically, Catholic efforts to organize were in part spurred by anti-Catholic sentiment and an accompanying fear of "Catholic power." Groups such as the Knights of Columbus and the Holy Name Society showcased a form of Catholic militancy that was often paired with patriotic Americanism, seen in the popularity of large public events such as parades and rallies.[27] As mentioned earlier, the institutional power of the Church was also made manifest in the founding of the National Catholic Welfare Council, reconstituted as the National Catholic Welfare Conference in 1922. Established in 1919, the council was envisioned as a coordinated effort to demonstrate Catholic support for the nation. After the war's end, the council, directed by the bishops of the United States, undertook other projects of national interest.[28]

The National Catholic Welfare Council's founding coincided with the American organizational revolution of the early twentieth century. During this period, countless national organizations and movements were founded. Beginning in 1900 with the founding of the American Federation of Catholic Societies, other national organizations included

25. Bruhls, "From Missions to 'Young Churches,'" 389; Jedin, *History of the Church*, 9:562.

26. Quoted in Dumenil, "The Tribal Twenties," 34.

27. Dumenil, "The Tribal Twenties," 21–49; McKeown, "The National Bishops' Conference," 565–83.

28. McKeown, *War and Welfare*; Slawson, *The Foundation and First Decade of the National Catholic Welfare Council*.

professional associations such as the Catholic Educational Association (1904) and the Catholic Hospital Association (1915) to welfare associations such as the National Conference of Catholic Charities (1910) and the National Catholic Rural Life Conference (1923).[29]

The Catholic organizational revolution also included renewed interest in youth activities. The Federation of Catholic College Clubs was organized in 1915 as a national body representing students at Catholic institutions of higher education. Newman clubs aimed at providing religious and social support for Catholic students studying at non-Catholic colleges, leading to the eventual creation of the National Newman Club Federation. These decades of organizational development included an increased interest in athletic and social opportunities for Catholic youth, represented by the founding of the Catholic Youth Organization in 1930, the popularity of Catholic scouting, and inter-parochial athletics.[30]

The American victory in the war and the establishment of the National Catholic War Council accelerated domestic interest in the missions, especially on the part of the hierarchy. The council resolved in May 1919: "Our enormous needs at home in this progressive country have so absorbed our thought and our zeal that we hardly have been able, till very recently, to turn our attention to foreign missions. The new position of our nation as the great world power will surely enlarge our vision."[31] At the time of the establishment of the council, Archbishop Keane of Dubuque, Iowa, asked that a separate committee be established to consolidate various missionary activities of the United States under authority of the hierarchy. The committee was to oversee the collection of funds for both the home and foreign missions while "leaving all present missionary organizations intact."[32] Initial planning began in 1919 for what became the American Board of Catholic Missions (ABCM). While the board

---

29. See Wiebe, *The Search for Order*; McKeown, "The 'National Idea'"; Halsey, *The Survival of American Innocence*, 55–57; Ede, *The Lay Crusade*.

30. Weldgen, "A Brief Look at the Growth of Catholic Youth Work in the United States," 1–9; "Bishop Sheil and 'Muscular Christianity'" in Kantowicz, *Corporation Sole*, 173–88; Hennesey, *American Catholics*, 249, 263; Evans, *The Newman Movement*.

31. *Catholic Missions* 13.8 (1919) 191. Attention to the missions is also significant in the bishops' pastoral letter of September 26, 1919. See Guilday, *The National Pastorals of the American Hierarchy*, 285–89.

32. "Hierarchy Decides to Form American Board of Missions," unknown newspaper clipping, September 29, 1929, NCWC/USCC General Secretary/Executive Department, Box 124, Folder 17, ACUA.

functioned under the National Catholic War Council, its administrative committee was distinct. The members of the committee included Archbishop Henry Moeller of Cincinnati as chairman, Patrick Cardinal Hayes of New York, Archbishop Jeremiah Harty of Omaha, George Cardinal Mundelein of Chicago, and Bishop Regis Canevin of Pittsburgh. Because approval from the Roman congregation *Propaganda Fide* was not immediately forthcoming, the ABCM did not receive official approval from Rome to begin work until the fall of 1924.[33] In authorizing it, the American bishops proposed that it "be the official arm of the Church in these United States to carry out all the missionary activities of the Hierarchy in its name."[34] The missionary efforts of American Catholics, like other movements within the Church, became increasingly centralized and organized.

THE DEVELOPMENT OF CATHOLIC STUDENT MISSION SOCIETIES

Influenced by the example of mission-centered religious orders such as the Paulists who labored in the "home missions" and Maryknoll and the Society of the Divine Word who provided American missionaries to foreign lands, a number of seminaries and colleges first formed independent student mission societies at the time of the war. Among the first educational institutions to align itself with the foreign mission movement was St. Francis de Sales Seminary in Milwaukee, Wisconsin. Students organized the St. Philip Neri Society for the advancement of the missions in 1912. By 1917 the group boasted 220 members and an associated Eucharistic League for the Missions, offering spiritual offerings for the cause.[35]

In 1917 the University of Notre Dame, South Bend, Indiana, established the first mission society among lay students at a Catholic College in the United States. There, at the suggestion of Notre Dame's president, John Cavanaugh, C.S.C., a group of students was formed to offer assistance to the Holy Cross order's mission in Bengal, India. Cavanaugh, in writing to *The Field Afar*, called Notre Dame "the fair flower of the foreign

---

33. For a description of the ABCM's origins and lengthy struggle for Roman approval see Gaffey, *Francis Clement Kelley*, esp. 1:306–29, 332–36.

34. "Minutes of the Annual Meetings of the Bishops of the United States, 1919–1935," Meeting of September 25, 1924, NCWC, Collection 10, ACUA, pages 14–16.

35. *Field Afar* 11.6 (1917) 85, 94.

missionary zeal of the past century." The publication in turn lauded the work begun at Notre Dame and stated that it was a clear indicator that "Catholic colleges have not until now been *Catholic* enough."[36] Similar student mission organizations were formed at Mt. St. Mary's Seminary of the West in Cincinnati, Ohio,[37] St. John's Seminary, Boston, and Trinity College for women in Washington, DC. James A. Walsh (1884–1936), cofounder of the Catholic Foreign Mission Society of America (Maryknoll), had directed the mission organization, "Academia," as a seminarian in Boston.[38]

In the vicinity of New York, the American Catholic Students' Foreign Mission League was formed by 1920. Somewhat different from other mission societies, the league attempted to interest college students in mission work and by their example to promote the missions among elementary students in nearby parochial schools. The student members of the league were to visit local parochial school classrooms three or four times annually to distribute missionary posters and to offer an explanation of missionary themes.[39] While many of these student organizations were short-lived, they represent the vitality and creativity of Catholic students in aiding the missions during and after the war years.

CLIFFORD J. KING, S.V.D., AND THE IDEA OF THE CATHOLIC STUDENTS' MISSION CRUSADE

The idea for the Catholic Students' Mission Crusade originated with Clifford J. King, a seminarian for the Divine Word Fathers studying at St. Mary's Mission House, Techny, Illinois. King had been born on February 23, 1888, in Mineville, New York, one of nine children. At the age of six, King and his family moved to Lowell, Massachusetts to find employment in the local cotton mills. When work became scarce in 1902, the family moved again, this time to Pelkie, Michigan to work in agriculture.[40] Unlike many of his peers who had discerned a vocation to the priesthood while

---

36. *Field Afar* 11.6 (1917) 82.

37. "The Story of a Mission Society, Mt. St. Mary Seminary of the West," 1920, CSMC, box 47, folder 16, Historical AAC.

38. "The Academia of St. John's Seminary," 78. The Academia affiliated with the CSMC in October 1920. See CSMC, box 47, folder 1, AAC, for the Academia's constitution.

39. "The Catholic Students' League," 284. By 1923 the League had joined with the Catholic Students' Mission Crusade. See CSMC, box 49, folder 16, AAC.

40. King, *I Remember*, 1–18.

in their youth, King was working as a lumberman at the age of twenty-one when he decided to pursue life as a missionary. After being denied entry to the Oblates of Mary Immaculate because the maximum age for entry into a preparatory seminary was eighteen years old, King applied to the Society of the Divine Word, a society of largely German-speaking priests headquartered in the Netherlands. King was accepted and arrived at Techny on September 8, 1909, to begin studies at St. Mary's Mission House.[41]

Almost immediately after his arrival, while reading the correspondence of missionary priests in the *Far East*, the periodical of the Society of St. Columban, King found himself drawn to the stories of the Catholic missionaries in China. Influenced by Rev. Bruno Hagspiel (1885–1961),[42] an older confrere in the Society of the Divine Word and later rector of St. Mary's Mission House, King authored several mission-centered poems, "The Master's Message," "Consummatum Est!," and an "Elegy of a Dying Heathen," all appearing in *The Catholic Mission Feast: A Manual for the Arrangement of Mission Celebrations* (1914).[43] On September 8, 1915, King and seven others—the first American novices in the order—received their habits. King's path to priesthood, however, was not without its struggles. The dire financial straits of his family back in Michigan nearly caused him to leave the seminary, but the situation improved when the family moved west to Colorado and King decided to remain in formation with the Divine Word missionaries.[44]

The idea for the Catholic Students' Mission Crusade was birthed one evening as the seminarians were dining in their refectory. As was the cus-

---

41. King, *I Remember*, 33–35. For the history of St. Mary's Mission House, see Brandewie, *In the Light of the Word*, especially 62–66.

42. One of the most significant mission promoters in America, Hagspiel, a native of Poland, took his first vows as a member of the Society of the Divine Word in 1906 and was ordained a priest in 1910. He was among the first Divine Word priests sent to America. In 1915 he founded a monthly missionary magazine for children, *The Little Missionary*, and in 1921 a magazine for adult readers, *Our Missions*. Other publications that Hagspiel authored or edited include Freytag, *The Catholic Mission Feast* ("adapted for America" by Bruno Hagspiel and Cornelius); *Financing a Vicariate in the Foreign Mission Field*; *Along the Mission Trail*; *Father Bruno's Vocation Letters*. See Brandewie, *In the Light of the Word*, 112–13, 117, 379. Hagspiel it seems had contemplated some form of a student missionary confederation as early as 1914. See Schwager, "Mission Movement Among Catholic Students," 290–91.

43. Freytag, *The Catholic Mission Feast*, 112–14, 119–20.

44. King, *I Remember*, 39–47.

tom in religious houses at the time, the reading of some text pertaining to the Church or the spiritual life was read aloud during meals. That evening's text was from an issue of the publication, *The Field Afar*, including a note describing the success of the Protestant Student Volunteer Movement for Foreign Missions. King interpreted the note as a challenge to seminarians and Catholic youth to organize on behalf of the foreign missions. He began to inquire about the possibility of organizing a national student mission society beginning with the student mission society at Techny, known then as *Militia Orans*—the praying army. Assisted by classmate Robert B. Clark (1895–1923), a native of Brooklyn, New York, and Father Hagspiel, King attempted to stir up interest at other educational institutions.

In May 1917 a thirty-page bulletin drafted by King was mailed to educational institutions, both Catholic institutions including colleges and seminaries and Newman clubs operating on the campuses of secular universities.[45] King and his associates received few responses to their initial campaign, but there was a favorable response in the pages of *America* magazine, a weekly periodical sponsored by the Jesuits. Rev. Joseph Husslein, S.J.,[46] in an article, "The Coming Crusade," called the proposed Catholic Students' Mission Crusade "one of the most important events in our Catholic education life," predicting its significance within the Church in America. He added that in view of Protestant efforts in the missions it was essential to join them in this "world-crusade" and to "not be content merely to emulate" but to "surpass them."[47] In October 1917 and May 1918, a second and third bulletin were sent to Catholic institutions and again the response was meager, though more encouraging.[48]

Though planning and publicity had commenced months earlier, the Crusade's founding as a national organization dates to the summer of 1918. At the invitation of the Divine Word Fathers of St. Mary's Mission House in Techny, one-hundred students, clergy, and religious met to draw up guidelines for the movement's structure and function. Attending this "First American Catholic Students' Mission Conference," beginning on

---

45. "The Catholic Students' Mission Crusade," 509–10.

46. Husslein's most significant contribution was to the development of Catholic social thought. See Werner, *Prophet of the Christian Social Manifesto*; McDonough, *Men Astutely Trained*, 51–63; McGreevy, *Catholicism and American Freedom*, 147, 154.

47. Husslein, "The Coming Crusade," 200–201.

48. "The Catholic Students' Mission Crusade," 509–10.

July 27, 1918, were representatives of thirty colleges and universities, eight religious orders, and various mission societies.[49]

As the students met in the midst of the war, the conflict could not have been far from the participants' minds. As Father Husslein had noted, the sacrifice and challenges of war were not unlike the call to the missions: "The same enthusiasm ... which has distinguished our Catholic colleges in filling with blue stars the ample spaces of white enclosed within the red borders of their service flags, should now also urge them on to do their utmost in the supreme work of the world-apostolate." Unless we organize, Husslein cautioned, the Church "may in the future resign herself to total defeat in her own glorious mission fields."[50] The possibility of defeat in armed conflict abroad, rallied those who remained at home to sacrifice for the missions. America's failure—whether in war or in the conquest for souls—did not appear as an option.

Within the three-day meeting at Techny, the basic structure and goals of the movement were formulated and officers were elected. From the very beginning the Crusade would accent its obedience to proper ecclesial authorities as well as its American and democratic character. Though the very idea for a national mission organization of Catholic students stemmed from the vision of then-seminarian Clifford King, it was the desire of the Divine Word missionaries that the organization not be tied to the order and community at Techny. The movement would flourish and be truly national, it was believed, if its leadership came from a variety of educational institutions, dioceses, and religious communities. Bishop Thomas J. Shahan (1857–1932), rector of The Catholic University of America, Washington, DC, was elected as the first president of the Crusade.[51] Rev. Francis J. L. Beckman (1875–1948), rector of Mt. St. Mary's Seminary of the West, Cincinnati, was selected as chairman of the executive board. Two seminarians at Mt. St. Mary's Seminary of the West, Cincinnati, Alphonse L. Schumacher (1894–1966) and Francis A. Thill (1893–1957) were elected, respectively, as treasurer and as secretary of the executive board. The Paulist Rev. John M. Handly was appointed

---

49. "Program of the First American Catholic Students' Mission Conference," and "History of the First American Catholic Students' Mission Conference," both in CSMC, box 1, folder 1, AAC; also see *Catholic Missions* 12.9 (1918) 216.

50. Husslein, "A Catholic Students' Convention," 266–67.

51. See Nuesse, *The Catholic University of America*, esp. 147–93. Also Dixon, "The Catholic University of America, 1909–1928."

field secretary to coordinate the growth of the movement and publicize the cause, though later declined to accept the position in deference to his superior's wishes.[52]

Formulated at the Techny meeting was the movement's three-fold goal: prayer, study, and sacrifice. The movement aimed to encourage "systematic prayer and self-denial," "education of all students in mission facts and ideals," and financial support for the missions, though the Crusade decided not to collect any money itself but to forward it to missionaries and mission-aid societies. The basic structure of the movement would be units composed of students from a given educational institution; the units in turn would be organized into districts to aid in regional cooperation. At the meeting it was initially decided not to involve grade school students in the movement but limit membership to seminarians, collegians, and high school students.[53] Though its membership consisted of less than fifty members at its founding, the CSMC had laid a foundation to establish a successful national movement of mission support and education.

WHY A "CRUSADE"? THE CRUSADER IDEAL AND THE MISSIONS

When King chose to attach the name "crusade" to his proposed organization, he was undoubtedly aware of the lore that surrounded the memory of the crusades in the early twentieth century. The crusades, the well-known attempt by Christians to win back the Holy Land from the Muslims, began in 1095 and are usually considered to have ended by 1271. This sending of Christian crusaders from Western Europe was in response to the Muslim offensive to conquer the Christian world, particularly the Holy Land. The attempt was successful in seizing North Africa, the Middle East, Asia Minor and the majority of Spain, nearly two-thirds of Christendom.[54] The crusaders identified their efforts with the taking up of Christ's cross and hence the cross became the symbol of the crusades, visible on the knights' armor and present in the popular mythology of the crusades well after the

---

52. "The Catholic Students' Mission Crusade," 509–10. Handly could not accept the position because of the critical staffing needs of the Paulists who had committed 1/12 of their manpower to war-time chaplaincies. See John Handly, C.S.P. to Father Hagspiel, August 15, 1918, CSMC, box 9, folder 1, AAC.

53. "The Catholic Students' Mission Crusade," 509–10.

54. See Madden, ed., *The Crusades*; Madden, *A Concise History of the Crusades*; Riley-Smith, *The Crusades*.

fighting had ended. The sacrifices of the crusaders, especially their willingness to fight and if necessary suffer death, were linked in the Middle Ages to the religious life, seeing the march of the crusader as a form of pilgrimage, or a participation in Christ's passion.[55] Despite the crusaders' zeal and the religious significance attached to their cause, the "historical" crusades were largely a failure, though costly in terms of finances and manpower. More importantly than their lack of real success, the crusades birthed a tradition of chivalry that later developed to include the mythic "knight in shining armor." The knight cultivated a reputation for honesty, bravery, virtue, obedience to authority, and self-discipline, one that righted wrongs and defended the powerless.[56]

The modern missionary movement drew readily upon the crusader ideal and the willingness to sacrifice all, even life itself, for the salvation of souls. By the seventeenth century, the "French school" of spirituality inspired by Cardinal Pierre de Bérulle (1575–1629) was contributing to a new theology of apostolic mission rooted in the "Incarnate Word," the reality of God become man, and the association between mission and martyrdom.[57] Interest in the cult of the martyrs and the crusades continued unabated within popular Catholicism until at least the mid-twentieth century. Though in the nineteenth century some began to frown upon the crusades as imperialist wars in which European Christians were seeking to dominate, convert, and colonize their Islamic neighbors, such ideas were little frowned upon by the "Church militant" in Europe and the United States.

The naming of the CSMC and its obvious linking of the foreign missions to the medieval crusades was perhaps influenced by the publication of the booklet, *God Wills It!: A Modern Crusade for an Old Cause: The Mission Work Among the Heathens* (1914). First published by the German Missionary Association of Catholic Women, the original text by Rev. Francis X. Brors, S.J., was translated into English and published by

---

55. See as an example, St. Bernard of Clairvaux, "In Praise of the New Knighthood" 127–45. Bernard exhorted the knights to "repel the foes of the cross of Christ" by waging a twofold war against flesh and blood enemies and spiritual enemies. He told the crusaders, "Why should [you] fear to live or die when for him to live is Christ, and to die is gain?"

56. Huizinga, *The Waning of The Middle Ages*, esp. ch. 4, "The Idea of Chivalry," 56–65.

57. Verstraelen, ed., *Missiology*, 221.

the Mission Press in Techny, Illinois, assuring that the Crusade's founders would have been familiar with the work.[58] *The Catholic Mission Feast: A Manual for the Arrangement of Mission Celebrations* (1914), edited by Father Hagspiel, included a mission poem, "God Wills It!," also connecting the crusades to the modern mission movement.[59]

From its beginning, the Catholic Students' Mission Crusade propagated its message using a medieval motif. The initial choice of the name served to summon images of knights, maidens, castles, and conquest. Among its young members, these images were used to promote the life of the missionary, the modern crusader sent to preach Christianity to foreign lands.[60] The importance of the crusader in the early twentieth century was dependent on medieval nostalgia as well as the martial ideal, an emphasis on physical prowess and manliness. The martial ideal was evidenced by the popularity of athleticism and sports such as boxing and basketball and the prominence of military cadet groups. Organizations founded during the period often adopted militaristic names such as the Knights of Labor, the Salvation Army, and the Knights of Columbus, each adopting "muscular Christianity" as an identifying motif.[61] While the "muscular" impulse in Protestantism waned after World War I, its influence in Roman Catholicism continued unabated. As the medieval crusader was viewed as the epitome of manliness, there were a variety of Catholic "crusades" from which to choose during the 1900s. The Catholic Students' Mission Crusade flourished alongside devotional movements such as Father Patrick Peyton's "Family Rosary Crusade," and the Jesuits' international "Eucharistic Crusade" that promoted frequent reception of communion by the young.

Masculinity and the crusading ideal were translated into expressions of patriotism, strength, and chivalry throughout the movement's early history, especially during the days immediately following the Great War.

---

58. The battle cry, "God wills it!" was introduced by Pope Urban II in 1095 at the Council of Clermont, ushering in the First Crusade. The phrase remained popular in furthering the twentieth century mission movement. Hagspiel recommended the booklet, *God Wills It!* in his article, "The Young Man and Foreign Missions."

59. Freytag, *The Catholic Mission Feast*, 111–12.

60. For a discussion of the metaphors and language of war, crusade, and sacrifice in mission see Hoare, "The Influence of the 'Crusade' Symbol and the 'War' Metaphor," 55–74.

61. For an analysis of the emergence of the martial ideal see Lears, *No Place of Grace*, 98–124; see also Putney, *Muscular*, 8–9.

Formed in the shadow of the war, the Crusade emphasized a nationalistic heroism that built upon a strong sense of purpose and the lure of adventure. Its membership cards featured an image of the Crucified Christ leading the crusaders into battle, emphasizing the missionary as a hero-martyr and combining medieval imagery with militarism and nationalism.[62] P. J. Sontag, S.J., an early promoter of the Crusade, asked in his pamphlet titled *America's Answer*, where chivalry could be found in his own day:

> Is the blood that courses so impetuously through the veins of America's boys less noble, less heroic, than that of the heroes of old? I can not believe it is. I believe that the boys of America are as dauntless, as chivalrous, as their brothers of seven hundred years ago. And the dear Christ, who knows, seems to think so, too. For He is calling America to a Crusade to-day. . . . Christ Himself, the Great Captain and Leader, is sending forth His challenge to America,—"Who will fight *for* Me? Who will fight *with* me?"[63]

Sontag's challenge concluded by advising those who wanted to serve Christ on the "front lines" of the foreign missions to apply to one of the "Officers' Training Camps" such as St. Mary's Mission House, Techny or Maryknoll's seminary in Ossining, New York.[64] Father Hagspiel, who could rightly be called the grandfather of the CSMC, also spoke often of the link between the foreign missions and militarism. In *Father Bruno's Vocation Letters*, he reminded young men of the need for priests and for missionaries. "For Christ the King needs men; He needs, above all, officers. For Christ has a wonderful army of men in our beloved America."[65] For King and members of this generation, the image of the crusader was not only the most prominent and mythically accessible image of Christian bravery, sacrifice, and adventure, it was also the most compelling for young men considering life-long commitments as missionaries.

---

62. Mosse, *Fallen Soldiers*, 58. See *The Shield* 6.2 (1926) 16. For a further analysis of this theme in missionary literature, see Dries, "The Hero-Martyr Myth," 305–14.

63. Sontag, *America's Answer*, 20.

64. Ibid., 38.

65. Hagspiel, *Father Bruno's Vocation Letters*, I, 14–15. The volume contains reprints of Hagspiel's column published in the periodical, *The Little Missionary*, 1919–1923. The use of similar language was employed by Irish Catholics in support of the missions; see Hogan, *The Irish Missionary Movement*, 148–50.

OFF TO CHINA: CLIFFORD KING'S DEPARTURE

Clifford King, the founder of the Catholic Students' Mission Crusade, did not play a significant role in the movement after its initial founding. Only a few months after the Techny meeting, in the fall of 1918, King's life changed drastically when the rector of the seminary, Rev. Peter Janser, S.V.D., informed the seminarians that the German Divine Word missionaries stationed in the Shatung Province of China had been removed from their mission posts by the Chinese government. Janser stated that two or three seminarians from Techny were needed immediately to staff the mission and prevent its confiscation by the Chinese. King volunteered for the mission with fellow seminarian and Crusade co-founder, Robert Clark. They along with Rev. Frederick Gruhn, a German-born American citizen, were selected to embark for China. After an impressive commissioning ceremony, presided over by George Mundelein, Archbishop of Chicago, the three boarded a ship bound for Japan on December 3, 1918, the feast of St. Francis Xavier, patron of missionaries.[66]

Ready to embark for the Far East, King and his companions penned a letter to American missionary supporters. Comparing the missionary vocation to that of the American soldier, they asked,

> How did our soldier boys feel when sailing for France? Didn't they exult in the consciousness of being the chosen defenders of the grandest country on God's earth, sent forth to do battle for the maintenance of the country's honors and ideals? They felt that it was an honor to be called upon to fight and die for the noble cause—"that the world might be made safe for democracy." And so do we exult in our vocation and our mission!

The Divine Word missionaries connected their mission as the first American representatives of their order to China in striking similarity to the "mission" of the United States during the Great War. They aimed to "make China safe for the Catholic Faith" and were prepared "to devote the rest our lives and to shed our blood if needs be." They continued, "We believe China could be made safe for the Faith in this generation by the Catholics of America if they only would undertake it in the right spirit and with an adequate organization."[67]

---

66. King, *I Remember*, 68–71.

67. Letter from Fred Guhn, S.V.D., Robert B. Clark, S.V.D., and Clifford King, S.V.D., Seattle, Washington, December 2, 1919, printed in *The Missionary* 33.2 (February 1920) 93–94.

After a brief stay in Japan, King and Clark entered China on January 8, 1919. King continued his studies of theology and assumed the Chinese name, "Wong Kin-King," meaning King Golden Mirror. On October 10, 1920, King, Clark and three Chinese classmates were ordained to the priesthood. The ordination of the two seminarians from Techny marked the first ordination of an American within the Society of the Divine Word.[68] After ordination, King was assigned to assist the priest in the village of Chucheng. Assisted by a lay Chinese catechist, he ministered to twenty-five missionary outposts as well as continued his study of the Chinese language. Less than a year later, King was chosen the first pastor of a new parish in Kingchih.[69] As pastor he did have some success in winning converts and in founding schools in the area, though local bandits and those who disliked Westerners occasionally threatened him and the fledgling Catholic community, providing him with an exciting tale of missionary adventure to relate to mission supporters back home. In September 1922 King was reassigned to China's Honan province where he joined Father Clark to begin a new mission center staffed by American members of the Society of the Divine Word.[70] Shortly after the transfer Father Clark fell ill and died on July 7, 1923. The following year King returned home to America for the first time in five years. His leaving China was motivated by the necessity of securing financial support for his mission and to attract more Americans to missionary vocations.[71]

THE EARLY SPREAD OF THE MOVEMENT

After the departure of King and Clark for China, the center of the CSMC shifted away from Techny and the Society of the Divine Word, yet the organizing strength of the movement remained with those preparing for priesthood. Of the seventeen charter units of the Crusade founded shortly after the Techny meeting, ten were organized in American seminaries, including Kenrick Seminary, St. Louis, Missouri; St. Francis de Sales Seminary, Milwaukee; St. Meinrad Seminary in Indiana;[72] St. John's

---

68. King, *I Remember*, 67–73.
69. Ibid., 75–84.
70. Ibid., 93–101.
71. Ibid., 110–12.
72. The early role of St. Meinrad Seminary in the movement seems of particular importance. One anecdote credits Jolly Hayden, a student at St. Meinrad, with coining the

University, Collegeville, Minnesota; the Maryknoll House of Studies, Ossining, New York; and Mt. St. Mary's Seminary of the West, Cincinnati. Each school had sent representatives to the first Crusade meeting in Techny.

The participation of American seminarians in activities such as the Crusade indicated a shift in priestly training, an increasing emphasis on the seminarians' participation in the life of the local Church beyond the confines of the seminary. Though still isolated, seminarians in the interwar years were occasionally permitted outside seminary walls. They took part in catechetical and mission work in unprecedented numbers through organizations such as the Confraternity of Christian Doctrine (CCD), National Catholic Rural Life Conference, and the CSMC.[73] It was in these institutions that a new generation of priests—whether they were placed in the foreign missions or not—became acquainted with the Catholic missionary enterprise and the goals of the Crusade. The early proliferation of the Crusade into the seminaries can in large part be attributed to the Divine Word Fathers, particularly Fathers Hagspiel and Janser. Janser, in speaking to the Catholic Educational Association in 1919, recommended that Crusade branches be assembled in every American seminary and school of higher education.[74]

The growing emphasis on foreign missions and the work of the CSMC fit with the educational goals of the early twentieth century Catholic school system. As historians have noted, America's Catholic schools aimed to "appeal to the desires and expectations of an upwardly mobile and increasingly assimilated population. On the other hand its primary goal was to communicate a 'Catholic' ethos and worldview contrary to many accepted social and cultural norms."[75] In the 1920s church leaders maintained that educational separatism was in the best interest of the Church and nation. At the same time they emphasized the American identity of their schools. This dual allegiance was signified by the Catholic

---

name "Catholic Students' Mission Crusade" and drafting the substance of its constitution. See Joseph A. Newman, "An Unwritten Chapter of C.S.M.C. History" (1944) in CSMC, box 46, folder 14, AAC; "Saint Meinrad Seminary Unit C.S.M.C." in *St. Meinrad Historical Essays*, April 1929 (St. Meinrad, IN: Abbey, 1929) as found in CSMC, box 47, folder 16, AAC. See also, Davis, ed., *To Prefer Nothing to Christ*.

73. White, *The Diocesan Seminary*, 345–48.
74. Janser, "The Seminary and Mission Endeavor."
75. Veverka, *"For God and Country,"* 66.

Educational Association's adoption of the motto "For God and Country" at its 1918 meeting.[76] Religion and nation would be key to Catholic education as the CSMC emphasized a strong allegiance to both.

The Crusade had been initially successful in attracting members, especially seminarians, through the publication of bulletins and letter-writing campaigns; however, it soon became clear that if the Crusade were to grow significantly it would require a paid staff member to publicize the movement. At the Techny conference, it was recommended that the Crusade employ a field secretary as a means of expanding membership. The initial choice for field secretary had been Rev. John M. Handly, C.S.P., but his religious superior did not grant permission for him to assume the position. Rev. Peter J. O'Callaghan, C.S.P., director of the Paulist-run Catholic Missionary Union, thought it more appropriate to employ a layman, and suggested that Floyd G. Keeler (1880–1964)[77] be chosen as the Crusade's first field secretary. Born in Mount Vernon, Indiana, Keeler had studied theology and was ordained for ministry in the Episcopal Church. After serving as a minister for more than a decade, he, his wife, and five children entered the Roman Catholic Church in 1916. Following his conversion, he taught for one year at Graymoor Monastery of the Franciscan Friars of the Atonement at Garrison, New York, a religious community comprised of former Episcopalians, before accepting the role as field secretary for the CSMC.

Well acquainted with missionary promotion from his years as a minister, Keeler saw himself as particularly able to expand support for the American Catholic mission movement. Having found a suitable layman to assume the new position, the Crusade's leadership searched for funding and found that though the Paulists could not spare any manpower to devote exclusively to the Crusade, the Catholic Missionary Union offered its financial support. From the fall of 1918 through October 1921, Keeler's salary was provided by the Catholic Missionary Union and the first office of the Crusade was established at the Apostolic Mission House, a house

---

76. Ibid., 70.

77. Floyd Keeler, "Reminiscences of Early Crusade Days" (1934); CSMC, box 46, folder 11, AAC; "Bishop To Ordain 4 Diocesan Priests," *The Catholic Virginian* 28.27 (1953) 1, 13; "Requiem Offered for Great Grandfather, 83, Who Was Ordained in Richmond at Age of 72," *The Catholic Virginian* 39.39 (1964) 1, 4. News clippings courtesy of the Archives of the Diocese of Richmond, Virginia.

of studies for missionary priests located on the campus of The Catholic University of America, Washington, DC.[78]

As the first full-time staff member of the Crusade, Keeler was its chief propagator and spokesman during its first two years. During these crucial years of growth, he was an organized and enthusiastic supporter of the movement, maintaining the Crusade's mailing list, making visits to schools interested in affiliating with the Crusade, and writing dozens of articles. Keeler wrote a monthly column in the Paulists' magazine, *The Missionary*, detailing the work of the Crusade and contributed to numerous Catholic publications, alerting many to the work of the movement.[79] As field secretary, he recalled meeting with Richard Cushing, then a deacon and student at The Catholic University of America. Cushing, who was interested in becoming a member of the Crusade, later became the mission-minded Cardinal Archbishop of Boston and founder of the Missionary Society of St. James the Apostle, a society of diocesan priests sent to minister in Latin America.[80]

Keeler's service to the CSMC ended in 1921 when it was decided that all of the organization's offices, not just the executive board, be located at Mt. St. Mary's Seminary of the West in Cincinnati. Though the Crusade leadership asked him to continue as field secretary, Keeler was unwilling to again relocate with his family and expressed his doubts as to Cincinnati's suitability for the movement's headquarters, noting that it had been proposed that a more fitting location would have been in New York City alongside the American Board of Catholic Missions. Instead of moving to Cincinnati, Keeler decided to direct his missionary enthusiasm in another direction, becoming a professor of Greek and English at the Maryknoll Preparatory Seminary in Clarks Green, Pennsylvania. Later he worked for the National Catholic Welfare Conference's News Service and served as publicity director for the Catholic Near East Welfare Association in New York from 1926 until 1943. Throughout his life he remained committed to

---

78. Founded by the Missionary Society of St. Paul the Apostle (the Paulists) in April 1904, the Apostolic Mission House opened as a residence for priests preparing for missionary work. The house contained the Crusade's first field office.

79. For example, Keeler, "Mission Study in Our Schools," 283–86; Keeler, "Missionary Organization and the Mission Societies," 124–28; Floyd Keeler, "College Sodalities and the Mission Crusade," 103–4.

80. "Text of Eulogy at Requiem for Father Keeler," *The Catholic Virginian* 39.39 (1964) 16. For Cushing's missionary role see Garneau, "'Commandos for Christ.'"

the work of the missions, whether through encouraging membership in the Crusade, teaching Maryknoll seminarians or promoting mission aid associations, once noting, "Work for the Crusade and for the missions is the breath of my life."[81]

Soon after the foundational meeting of the Crusade, King wrote, "In this movement America must set the pace to the world.... Picture what an imposing body the Crusade will be when well organized throughout the country; but do not leave them with the impression that it is to be a *national* institution. That would not be Catholic enough! The Crusade is going to be an international, universal movement."[82] The vision of King and the early crusaders was to form a national movement with a related international structure, forming a worldwide students' mission crusade network.

Crusade bulletins were sent to educational institutions in Canada, England, Ireland, Spain, and Italy. The international response was nearly immediate; student missionary groups in Europe were eager to join with the Crusade. Seminarians at the Maynooth national seminary in Ireland organized a missionary society in 1916 and within two years a mission seminary, St. Columban, in Galway was founded. There the students began publication of *The Student Missionary* in 1919 to spread interest in the foreign missions among students and seminarians in Ireland.[83] By 1920 the Crusade was corresponding with affiliated student organizations in Australia, Austria, Canada, England, Germany, Holland, Ireland, Spain, and Switzerland. In Spain, the movement "Los Doce Apóstoles," literally the twelve apostles, was organized by students to give spiritual and material help to the missions.[84] Despite the initial promise of an international

---

81. After the death of his wife, Keeler studied for the priesthood for the Diocese of Richmond, Virginia, and was ordained May 9, 1953 at the age of seventy-two. After serving as assistant pastor at Holy Cross Church in Lynchburg, Virginia, he was assigned in 1954 as chaplain of Kings Daughters Hospital, Martinsburg, West Virginia, where he remained until his death in 1964. Executive Report, August 1, 1921–August 1, 1922, box 48, folder 2, CSMC, AAC; quote from Floyd Keeler to Francis Thill, June 3, 1921, box 48, folder 1, CSMC, AAC. For background on the Catholic Near East Welfare Association see McGuiness, "The Call of the East," 33–42.

82. Letter from Clifford J. King, quoted in *The Missionary* 32 (1919) 49.

83. *The Missionary* 32.1 (1919) 49; *The Missionary* 31.9 (1918) 509–10. The Maynooth seminary had only months earlier begun a missionary society known as the Maynooth Mission to China, later organized as the Foreign Missionary Society of St. Columban. See Hogan, *The Irish Missionary Movemen*, 91–97.

84. *The Missionary* 32.4 (1919) 222; *The Missionary* 32.8 (1919) 456; *The Missionary*

Coming Crusade

network of mission crusaders, there seems to have been little communication between the Crusade and the European student mission societies after 1920. While King had favored an international Crusade, opposition toward the CSMC as an international organization was voiced at both the 1918 and 1920 Crusade conventions. The general consensus of the members was that the Crusade should foster a decidedly national character.[85] The CSMC, despite is success, would not become known as the "father" of an international student mission movement.

WHO CAN BE A CRUSADER?

The involvement of women in the work of the CSMC seems to have been an afterthought, not having come into the minds of the movement's founders at the time of the inaugural meeting. King and his assistants sent invitations only to men's institutions of higher learning and women did not attend the meeting in Techny in July 1918 nor the regional Crusade gathering held in Jasper, Indiana in July 1919. The first inquiry from a women's college was from the foreign mission society of Trinity College, Washington, DC. In March 1919 the Crusade's field secretary felt it necessary to correct the "misconception" that the Crusade was "entirely a men's affair." Floyd Keeler announced that it was the Crusade's desire that all students, both men and women, be enrolled in the Crusade and that at the national meeting to be held in the summer of 1920 it was hoped that "a sufficient number of women's institutions" would be represented "to enable them to hold a separate conference for the consideration of their own problems and methods."[86] Initially units for women and men were to be separated, establishing two parallel departments within the Crusade. However at the time of the second national meeting of the Crusade held in August 1920 at The Catholic University of America, Washington, DC, a female delegate, Nancy Arnold, of Notre Dame College in Maryland, strenuously voiced her disapproval of the plan for separation. Arnold, who had been selected to address the 300 student delegates on the topic, "Two Departments in the Crusade," was so firm and convincing that the

---

33.4 (1920) 200; *The Missionary* 34 (1920) 20; *The Missionary* 32.12 (1919) 697.

    85. See "Minutes of the Second General Convention, Washington, DC" (1920), CSMC, box 9, folder 14, AAC, 141–47.

    86. *The Missionary* 32.3 (1919) 163.

plan for distinctive departments was "dropped by common consent."[87] While the Crusade would not divide its activities and meetings between men and women, most units were of one gender, reflecting the character of American Catholic education.

Perhaps due to the absence of any roles for women in the founding of the Crusade, there seems to have been little distinction between the activities of men and women in the movement. From the time of their acceptance into the Crusade, women were included on its national executive board, their place being assured by the organization's revised constitution. Two years after women were welcomed into the Crusade, there were at least four women among the fourteen local field secretaries recruiting for the movement.[88]

In addition to broadening the role for women in the movement, at the 1920 general convention a decision was reached to further expand the membership of the Crusade. Henceforth not only seminarians and college-age men but students of women's colleges, high schools and elementary schools, as well as graduates and those who had attended college, so-called "veteran" crusaders, would be invited to take part in the movement.[89] The theme of the meeting, "Spread," was introduced by Maryknoll seminarian John Considine, indicating the members' determination to spread the influence of the organization throughout the country, amidst all levels of Catholic education.[90] Though the founders of the movement were not enthusiastic about incorporating elementary and high school students into the Crusade, within a year the newly organized "Junior Crusade" boasted 171 units comprised of 38,000 members, bringing the total membership to over 60,000, double the number of the previous year.[91]

---

87. *The Missionary* 34.2 (1920) 49.

88. At the 1920 convention Miss Catherine McCarthy was selected to serve on the executive board. See "The 'Spread' Book," 1, no. 1 (November 1920), CSMC, unnumbered box, AAC. This bulletin is contained within the bound volume of "C.S.M.C. Bulletins," numbers 1–3. Also see "Constitution of the Catholic Students' Mission Crusade," undated, CSMC, box 47, folder 16, AAC; "Our Leader Knights—The Crusade's Field Secretaries," *The Shield* 2.3 (1923) 3.

89. These structural changes were represented in a revised constitution. See "Constitution of the Catholic Students' Mission Crusade," undated, CSMC, box 47, folder 16, AAC.

90. "Minutes of the Second General Convention, Washington, DC" (1920), CSMC, box 9, folders 11, 13, 16, AAC.

91. "Address of Msgr. F. J. Beckmann (sic), Third General Convention, Dayton, Ohio,

The founding generation of the Crusade, heavily influenced by the First World War, successfully employed military metaphors to elicit the support of American youth for the missionary conquest. An accent on manliness, bravery, and adventure that lingered from the war was easily converted into the thrust for missionary vocations. The missionary, however idealized, was viewed as a chivalrous modern crusader, converting the pagan world with the cross of Christ. At first limited to seminarians and collegians, the movement spread rapidly throughout the American Catholic educational system to gain a foothold in elementary schools, high schools, and women's academies and colleges. The developing vision of the early members of the Catholic Students' Mission Crusade proved that their undertaking, though not international in scope, would be a truly national endeavor, representing American Catholic men and women from every part of the country and every educational level. Like the American Catholic mission movement, by the end of the twentieth century's second decade, the Catholic Students' Mission Crusade had come of age.

August 18, 1921," CSMC, box 1, folder 8, AAC.

THREE

Knights and Ladies

The Call of the Crusade, 1920–1940

THE FACE OF THE Catholic Students' Mission Crusade was substantially altered during the first few years of its existence, already developing beyond the vision of its founders. During this period of ferment and creativity, the Crusade's leadership hammered out the basic structure and character of the movement. By 1920, the CSMC was no longer seen as the offspring of the Society of the Divine Word as the organization no longer maintained ties to any single religious order. Instead, both the organization's headquarters in Techny, Illinois, and the field office in Washington, DC were relocated to Cincinnati, Ohio where it found support from the bishops and clergy of that diocese. As the Crusade's membership extended demographically and geographically, the majority of the CSMC's members were not seminarians. Instead, women, lay students, and even high school and elementary school students joined the ranks of the Crusade.

The acceptance of younger students and women into the movement resulted in a surge in membership. In 1920 the CSMC counted roughly 10,000 members; two years later that number jumped to 210,000. By 1939, there were approximately 700,000 members.[1] Geographically, the CSMC continued its expansion, crossing the continental U.S. in just a few years. By 1922 the Crusade had units in all but a handful of states: Nevada, Wyoming, Maine, South Carolina, Georgia, Florida, Alaska, and Hawaii. The highest concentration of membership remained in the Mid-Atlantic and Midwestern states with signs of growth in less likely locations such as Nashville, New Orleans, Omaha, Wheeling, San Francisco, St. Paul, Minnesota, and Seattle. Units were formed in most of the major cities

---

1. J. Paul Spaeth to Rev. Michael A. Mathis, C.S.C., September 10, 1940, CSMC, box 46, folder 13, AAC.

in America including New York, Boston, Washington, DC, Pittsburgh, Detroit, Louisville, St. Louis, and Denver.[2] The movement developed in the 1920s as a truly national organization of youthful Catholics.

When in 1920 it was decided to transfer the headquarters of the movement to Cincinnati, the decision was not met with unanimous approval. Not all saw the relocation as an opportunity for growth. The CSMC's field secretary, Floyd Keeler, among others, questioned the wisdom of a move to a location so remote from the urban, Catholic centers of the east coast: New York, Boston, and Philadelphia. Still Cincinnati was considered an appropriate location for the Crusade's center because of its early significance to the CSMC and the American Catholic mission movement. Students and administrators at the seminary in Cincinnati, Mt. St. Mary's Seminary of the West, had been among the first leaders of the Crusade, three being elected officers of the organization at the founding meeting in Techny. In the early years of the Crusade's formation, the CSMC unit at Mt. St. Mary's Seminary of the West was the leader in recruiting and enrolling student units from surrounding schools.[3]

In addition, the Archbishop of Cincinnati, then Henry Moeller, was a fervent supporter of the missions, having been a founding member of the American Board of Catholic Missions, and host of the ABCM meeting in Cincinnati in December 1920. Moeller and his predecessor, Archbishop Elder, had welcomed a variety of missionary initiatives in Cincinnati: apostolates to urban ethnic groups, rural Catholics, and non-Catholics.[4] A number of mission-centered religious congregations also served in Cincinnati including the Passionists, Scalabrini (Fathers of St. Charles), and Comboni (Verona) Fathers. Mission historian Robert Carbonneau, C.P., observed that Cincinnati during the 1920s was the "center of the American Catholic mission experience." Cincinnati's diocesan newspaper, the *Catholic Telegraph*, featured the missions as front-page news. Area Catholics were informed about the missions and responded generously. The mission spirit was alive and well in Cincinnati.[5]

When in 1921 Bishop Thomas Shahan of The Catholic University of America, first executive board president of the Crusade, resigned his post,

---

2. "Crusade 'Spread' Map," *The Shield* 2.1 (1922) 6. Also, CSMC, box 49: "Local Conferences—Minutes and Correspondence," AAC.

3. "Greater Cincinnati's Crusade Attainments." *The Shield* 6.2 (1927) 1–2.

4. See "The Queen City," *The Missionary* 3.9 (1898) 29.

5. Carbonneau, "Life, Death, and Memory," 393–94 (393).

he suggested that Moeller assume his office since he was the American bishops' mission representative. Moeller was elected to the office without opposition and the Crusade consequently found a permanent home in Cincinnati.[6] The temporary headquarters of the CSMC were transferred from Mt. St. Mary's Seminary of the West, Cincinnati to the diocese's Catholic Welfare Building at 129 East Ninth Street, Cincinnati in September 1920, where they remained for the next three years.

EARLY CRUSADE LEADERSHIP

When the movement relocated to Cincinnati it found—in addition to support from the bishops of Cincinnati—an abundance of dedicated priests and laity willing to shepherd its growth. Throughout most of the movement's history, one or two priests directed the movement assisted by numerous paid and volunteer lay workers and local unit moderators throughout the country, most often religious sisters teaching in Catholic schools.

Among the most significant early leaders was Msgr. Francis Joseph L. Beckman (1875–1948), then rector of Mt. St. Mary's Seminary of the West. Born in Cincinnati, Beckman was ordained a priest for the Archdiocese of Cincinnati on June 20, 1902. He became a professor at his alma mater, Mt. St. Mary's Seminary of the West, in 1908 and was elevated to the position of seminary rector in 1913, remaining until 1924 when he was ordained as Bishop of Lincoln, Nebraska.[7] Beckman was noted by many as one of the most influential Catholic youth leaders of the twentieth century, serving the Crusade as chairman of the executive board beginning in 1918. He continued to lead the Crusade as executive chairman while serving as the bishop of Lincoln and later archbishop of Dubuque, Iowa.

Another significant early leader was Francis A. Thill (1893–1957) who was selected as secretary of the CSMC at the Techny meeting in 1918 at which time he was a seminarian in Cincinnati. Born in Dayton, Ohio,

---

6. See "Lecture on the Third General Convention of the Catholic Students' Mission Crusade held at Dayton, Ohio, University of Dayton, August 18, 1921," 20, CSMC, box 56, folder 2, AAC.

7. Six years after his consecration Beckman became Archbishop of Dubuque, Iowa. He resigned as archbishop on November 11, 1946 amidst a diocesan financial controversy and died October 17, 1948, in Chicago. See "Archbishop Francis Beckman Dies in Chicago; Native of Cincinnati was Noted Youth Leader," *Cincinnati Enquirer*, October 18, 1948.

Thill was ordained a priest for the Archdiocese of Cincinnati in 1920. Upon ordination, Thill received permission from Archbishop Moeller to continue his involvement with the movement. In addition to his work with the Crusade, he served as professor at St. Gregory minor seminary and Mt St. Mary's Seminary of the West, both in Cincinnati, and was named chancellor of the Archdiocese after completing canon law studies in Rome. Thill was the first editor of the CSMC publication, *The Shield*, remaining in that capacity until his appointment as chancellor in December 1935. He continued his association with the Crusade as "executive counsel," a position expressly created for him. In 1938, he was ordained bishop of Concordia, Kansas, which later became the diocese of Salina, Kansas.[8]

Edward A. Freking (1899–1970) became a member of the CSMC executive board in 1920 while a college student. Born in Cincinnati, he attended St. Xavier High School and Xavier University. After graduating college, he enrolled at Mt. St. Mary's Seminary of the West and was ordained in 1926. He served as professor at his alma mater, Mt. St. Mary's Seminary, as well as editor of the *Catholic Telegraph*. His affiliation with the CSMC continued throughout his life. In 1935, he was appointed as national secretary of the movement, replacing Thill who had become bishop of Salina, Kansas. Freking soon was named editor-in-chief of *The Shield*. Beginning in 1948, following the death of Beckman, he assumed the role of executive chairman of the board. He remained the national director of the movement until his death.[9]

Among the first officers of the movement was also J. Paul Spaeth (1894–1976). After graduating from Xavier University in Cincinnati in 1917, he entered Mt. St. Mary's Seminary of the West in Cincinnati. While a seminarian, in 1919 Spaeth was appointed national treasurer of the Crusade. After leaving the seminary he continued his association with the movement.[10] He was recognized as perhaps the most knowledgeable and active layman in the American Catholic mission movement, working

---

8. "Monsignor Is Raised to Catholic Bishopric in Ancient Ceremony," *Cincinnati Enquirer*, October 29, 1938; "Domestic Prelate Elevated to Bishop," *Cincinnati Times-Star*, August 26, 1938; "Funeral—To Be Saturday—For Bishop Frank Thill," *Cincinnati Enquirer*, May 23, 1957; "Bishop Frank A. Thill, Mission Crusader," *The Shield* 18.2 (1938) 2–3.

9. "Monsignor Edward A. Freking," 2; "Msgr. Edward A. Freking—Biography," CSMC, box 54, folder 14, AAC.

10. *The Missionary* 32.6 (1919) 337.

on the Crusade staff for more than fifty years. He became director of unit activities in 1923 and was named editor of the Crusade's publications, including *The Shield* in 1935, while continuing as activities director. For decades he was the unsung hero of the Crusade, responsible for most of the day-to-day activities of the movement and the author of hundreds of articles, pamphlets, books, and plays. The chief force behind the Crusade's educational arm, he became editor of the Crusade's "Five Hours" series of mission books.[11]

In 1929 Spaeth married Louise F. Scheuerman (1906–1986) who herself had been active in the Crusade as a student. The two often worked side by side on behalf of the CSMC, coordinating most of the Crusade conventions. Louise Spaeth, like her husband, was an avid writer, contributing to numerous publications of the CSMC as author and editor. Much of her work on behalf of the movement was done without any compensation as a gift to the propagation of the missions.[12] Paul Spaeth, along with the assistance of his wife, was the primary contact between the national office and the local Crusade units for decades, communicating with moderators throughout the nation and mission experts at home and abroad.

Many of these early Crusade leaders, priests and laity, had become active in the movement while they were themselves youth. Remarkably, many were among the first leaders chosen at the Techny meeting in 1918. They remained the core of the movement for several decades, performing the daily administrative work of the Crusade and exercising the most significant influence in terms of the movement's strategies, educational content, and direction. These leaders brought continuity to the Crusade in the midst of much change, assuring that the movement would not lose sight of its founding vision.

---

11. Following the demise of the Crusade, Paul Spaeth retired in September 1972, though he continued as a consultant to the Archdiocesan Mission Office for several years. Spaeth was recognized for his work, receiving the honor of Knight of the Order of St. Gregory from Pope Pius XII in 1948 and the 1959 World Mission Award. See "J. Paul Spaeth, Catholic mission official," *The Cincinnati Post*, December 9, 1976, 18:1; "J. Paul Spaeth, Active in Missions," *The Cincinnati Enquirer*, December 9, 1976, B2; "Spaeth, Joseph Paul," 693.

12. Louise Spaeth was decorated with the papal *Pro Ecclesia et Pontifice* medal in 1954 in recognition of her work for the missions. "2 CSMC Workers Are Awarded Papal Medals by Archbishop," *Catholic Telegraph*, April 2, 1954. See also Louise Spaeth's death notice, *The Cincinnati Enquirer*, January 13, 1986: D3.

POPULAR MEDIEVALISM

The early leaders of the movement helped shape the crusader ethos that emerged in the 1920s. With the relative peace and prosperity of the period and the increasing distance from the events of the First World War, the Crusade attached itself to new images and ideas, finding its inspiration in both American and Catholic ideals. In the Crusade's attempt to attract a new generation of youth, it utilized a worldview that prized nationalism, embraced popular "medievalism," and promoted Catholic idealism.[13]

The leaders of the Crusade during the interwar years were greatly affected by the image of the crusader and the analogy of a "holy war," as was Clifford King, the founder of the CSMC. Yet, unlike King and the first crusaders who connected with the images of modern warfare during World War I, the images of war popularized by the CSMC in the 1920s looked more often to a romanticized past: the medieval age. The crusader image represented a redirection of wartime militarism from guns and tanks to the less bloody and more valiant shield and sword but one that remained attractive to young Catholics eager for adventure, independence, and heroism. Influenced not by international conflict as much as domestic religious turmoil evidenced by heightened anti-Catholicism, the propagators of the Crusade looked to the medieval age as a symbol of the harmony between Church and culture.[14]

The Crusade was not unique in seizing upon medieval imagery to attract members and communicate its ideals during the interwar period. The Catholic worldview of the time was mediated through the lens of medievalism. Catholics of the early twentieth century, as historian William Halsey acknowledged, were "eager to dress in something other than immigrant rags" and by remembering the Middle Ages believed they could participate in "a golden age of Catholic influence and power."[15] Old and young looked longingly to the high Middle Ages and envisioned an era when altar and throne were joined, universities flourished, guilds promoted a just social order, and the highest virtues of men and women were confirmed and extolled.

---

13. Halsey, *The Survival of American Innocence*; Sparr, *To Promote, Defend, and Redeem*.

14. For a discussion of anti-Catholicism during the "tribal twenties" see Dumenil, "The Tribal Twenties," 21–49; Higham, *Strangers in the Land*, 291–95; Curry, *Protestant-Catholic Relations in America*, 6–25.

15. Halsey, *The Survival of American Innocence*, 66.

Interest in medievalism was not purely nostalgia for a bygone era. For some the medieval ideal was a valid and timely witness to the deficiencies, if not evils, of modern life. Catholicism in the early twentieth century saw itself as a faith under attack. As in past ages when the crusaders had waged war to reclaim the Holy Land, modern society brought with it new and pressing dangers to the Church and its members. The ascendant nation state, the apparent triumph of liberalism, and an emphasis on the individual at the expense of the community were all signs of a hostile modern world. The Church feared that in many countries that were traditionally Catholic, atheism may have been gaining the upper hand. Catholics in America consequently strapped on the armor befitting a Church besieged by modern culture. The Church in America, still keenly aware of prejudices against itself, was on guard against the advances of secularism and materialism, ideologies at the root of unbelief.

Related to the surge in medieval interest was the scholastic revival that was seen as an antidote to the errors of modernity. As a philosophical model derived from the teachings of St. Thomas Aquinas, scholasticism affected every educational branch in the Church from seminaries to colleges to primary schools. As a product of medieval thinking, scholasticism was believed to possess the philosophical substance with which to overcome modern intellectual errors. Its notions of the natural law, unity, and order became normative in the Catholic worldview as scholasticism reigned as the primary model taught in every Catholic institution of education. It, perhaps more than any other variable, can be credited with providing for the construction of a separate "Catholic culture."[16] Within the missionary movement, scholasticism merged well with the growing concern for non-Christian peoples. Both movements saw themselves—whether through philosophy, theology, or both—as aiding in the redemption of modern man, a procession of conversion from error to truth.[17]

Combining medievalism with the missionary cause, the crusaders aimed to approve and expound the political, theological and ideological goals of Church and country. Searching for acceptance and approbation, Catholic use of medievalism and nationalism served not so much as a duality but as a complementary method of showing the continuity of the

---

16. Gleason, *Contending with Modernity*, 105–23.
17. Gleason, *Keeping the Faith*, 27.

Catholic faith and the American ideal.[18] The merging of the missionary ethos with dominant religious and nationalist rhetoric produced a synthesis that appealed to the idealistic and youthful Catholics of the interwar years, while articulating a vision consonant with more "mature" scholastic thought and American political ideology.

Founded as a "crusade," the CSMC was linked closely to the neo-medievalism of early twentieth-century America. Medievalism provided a powerful cadre of symbols for use by the CSMC as evidenced in nearly every publication or activity of the CSMC during the interwar years. *The Shield* often pictured CSMC members in medieval garb, whether as participants in mission pageants or as part of various ceremonials of the organization. A striking image of the crusader as hero and martyr was popularized through the Crusade's membership cards, featuring an image of the Crucified Christ leading the crusaders into battle. The card's caption read:

> The old Crusaders had a legend that should their courage fail, Christ Himself would come to lead them. Members of the Catholic Students' Mission Crusade may rightfully cherish a similar confidence. God wills the missionary conquest of the world. The new Crusader may justly believe in his own power to further this most sublime cause, since God is with him.[19]

The cards combined medieval imagery with an image of divine assistance, a powerful image for adventurous and idealistic youth.

As a member of the CSMC during the 1920s, Rev. Daniel A. Lord, S.J. (1888–1955) was largely responsible for connecting the work of the foreign missions with the ideal of the crusader.[20] Lord christened the stately headquarters of the movement in Cincinnati as "Crusade Castle," wrote and directed two mission pageants, *God Wills It* (1922) and *The*

---

18. There have been various attempts by historians to link medievalism and Americanism. See Gleason, *Keeping the Faith*, 11–34; Halsey, *The Survival of American Innocence*, 61–83.

19. *The Shield* 6.2 (1926) 16.

20. Lord, *Played by Ear*, 249–68; Faherty, "A Half-Century with the Queen's Work," 99–114; Dinges, "'An Army of Youth,'" 35–49; Sparr, *To Promote, Defend, and Redeem*, 31–50; Gavin, *Champion of Youth*; McGloin, *Backstage Missionary*. The Lord papers can be found at Georgetown University, Washington, DC, St. Louis University Archives, and Midwest Jesuit Archives, both in St. Louis, Missouri.

Giantkiller (1926), and authored the CSMC's Ritual of Initiation (1924) complete with medieval costumes and characters.

At the time of the Crusade's development the most prominent organization for American Catholic youth was the sodality, which flourished under the leadership of Father Lord. Beginning in America as a loose network of student-based charitable and devotional groups headquartered at Jesuit educational institutions, the sodality spread to parishes, elementary schools and high schools throughout the early twentieth century. Lord became national director of the Sodality in 1925 and editor of its publication, *The Queen's Work*. The sodality experienced a substantial renewal under the leadership of Father Lord who became synonymous with the growth of the movement. By the 1920s the movement counted more than 7,700 affiliated groups, double the number of twenty years earlier.

Lord was also one of the principal participants in the Catholic literary revival of the era, aiming at the development and dissemination of distinctively Catholic literary and dramatic presentations.[21] Prior to his leadership of the sodality and even before his ordination as a Jesuit priest, Lord became associated with the CSMC. St. Louis, Missouri, where Lord was teaching and being formed as a religious, was an early center for the mission movement, eleven local schools having affiliated with the Crusade by 1921.[22]

Lord's attraction to the work of the CSMC was not surprising since the inspiration for his literary and dramatic works often came from the themes and personalities of Christian history. From his youth Lord had been fascinated with the life of St. Francis Xavier, the patron saint of the missions, who he called "a great, romantic, and highly adventurous Jesuit."[23] Though Xavier was not from the Middle Ages, Lord desired to connect his legacy with the modern missionary and apostolic work of the Church.[24] In addition to reading into the life of Xavier a sense of his own mission, Lord envisioned a congruency between his own life and the medieval world,

21. Sparr, *To Promote, Defend, and Redeem*, 31–50.

22. Program for "The Dreamer Awakes: A Musical Mission Masque, The Odeon, February 22–26, 1924," DAL, box 23, folder 11, GUSC.

23. Lord, *Played by Ear*, 118.

24. See "A Missionary Knight," *The Bengalese* 3.12 (1922) 6; "The Great Crusader," *Catholic Missions and Annals of the Propagation of the Faith* 1.12 (1924) 285. These authors connect St. Francis Xavier's missionary work with his "knightly character" and "chivalrous dreams."

stating, for instance, that the Jesuit novitiate that he attended at Florissant, Missouri, resembled "the monastic towns of the Middle Ages" and that he believed he and his Jesuit confreres to be true successors to the medieval scholastic thinkers.[25] While still a theology student, he became interested in the American movement to support the foreign missions and began to promote the Crusade locally.[26]

CALLING FOR A CRUSADE: *THE DREAMER AWAKES*

Among the most popular and important means of recruiting in the early years of the CSMC were performances of Father Lord's mission pageant *The Dreamer Awakes* (also performed under the title *God Wills It!*). Song and dance-style "musical masques" or pageants defined Lord's early career and were influenced by earlier civic pageants such as Percy MacKaye's *Masque of St. Louis* (1914) and Thomas Wood Stevens's *Pageant of St. Louis* (1914).[27] Relying on local talent with minimal rehearsing and not a cast of traveling professionals, Lord's masques blended moral and social lessons with historical themes, often featuring the triumphant medieval crusader. Called by one historian "the multimedia events of the era" the pageants included "Lord pounding away at the piano, spotlights turning from one end of the proscenium to the other, and much flapping of drapery and theatrical gowns."[28]

First performed in St. Louis on February 22, 1922, before a crowd of some 18,000, the production of *The Dreamer Awakes* featured five hundred young crusaders as participants.[29] The pageant was performed before large audiences in Brooklyn; Pittsburgh; Cincinnati; Detroit; Quincy, Illinois; Burlington, Vermont; and Washington, DC between 1922 and 1926. Lord boasted that the pageant was so popular that even at a hefty expense of up to $10,000 per production, the event always netted a profit

---

25. Lord, *Played by Ear*, 121, 151; other medieval references can be found on pp. 118 and 146.

26. See G. Fitzgibbons, "Planning a Local Conference," *The Shield* 1.4 (1922) 5–7.

27. For a list of his early plays and pageants, see Gavin, *Champion of Youth*, 207–8. For influences on Lord's pageants see Glassberg, *American Historical Pageantry*, 187–92; and Lord, *Played By Ear*, 197. These civic pageants often exhibited the crusader in the cause of social progress, especially emphasizing the citizenry's triumph over corruption.

28. McDonough, *Men Astutely Trained*, 86.

29. "St. Louis Shows the Way," *The Bengalese* 3.4 (1922) 13.

for the missions, the bulk of the money coming from ticket sales ranging from a mere twenty-five cents to $1.50 per ticket.[30]

The theme of the production was the awakening of American Catholic youth to the mission ideal and was based on the allegory of "Sleeping Beauty." The chief characters, "Jack America" and "Jane America," representing American youth, were depicted in the pageant's opening at play, merry and cheerful but "wrapped in oblivious slumber while the pagan world passed unheeded by their gates." In one production the students danced around a "maypole" with their friends, an obvious medieval allusion.[31] These playful young people, it later becomes known, had fallen victim to "Indifference," a character analogous to the wicked witch from "Sleeping Beauty."

Later the pitiable "pagans" are introduced, represented by students dressed in Native American, Middle Eastern, Japanese, and Chinese costumes. In the finale, the crusader is able to overcome "Indifference" (played by a young man) with the help of "Religion" (played by a young woman) as the conversion of the pagan world is set into motion.[32] The pageant reached its climax with the lighting of a giant electric cross and the final exhortation of the crusader:

> A heathen world lies at your door. Men cry to you for help, and you have slept. God's work for souls cries for stout hearts and eager hands, and you have dreamed your days away. Up! Take the Cross upon your shoulders. Crusaders all, together we go forward to the conquest of souls! God wills it! God wills it![33]

The aim of the pageant was primarily personal, prompting each student to evaluate his or her commitment to the missions: "Look into your heart and see if perchance you too may not be a Dreamer whom the Crusade must wake."[34] In addition, the communal goal of the pageant was

---

30. Emma L. Fetta, "Mission Finds Home in 'Crusade Castle,'" *Cincinnati Enquirer*, September 2, 1923, 1, 19.

31. "Catholic Students' Mission Crusade, Greater Cincinnati District Rally, May 1–3, 1922," Record Group 25/B-15, CSMC Conference Files, box 42, folder 1, Archives of Xavier University, Cincinnati, Ohio.

32. Daniel A. Lord, *The Dreamer Awakes: A Mission Crusade Masque* (1923), CSMC, box 32, folder 2, AAC. See also "'Dreamer Awakes' Charms as Pageant for Missions," *Washington Post*, February 18, 1924, 5.

33. Lord, *The Dreamer Awakes*, 23.

34. "Program for *The Dreamer Awakes: A Musical Mission Masque*, The Odeon,

to successfully bridge the prominent Catholic boundaries of ethnicity, neighborhood, and parish affiliation.[35]

The pageant embraced both medieval and twentieth-century American themes. Not surprisingly, the crusader acted as the heroic protagonist, calling all to conversion from the waywardness of the world. The youth who had fallen under the spell of "Indifference" were portrayed as basketball players and cheerleaders. Living out their everyday "American" existence, these Catholic young people it was feared could quickly lose sight of the higher "Catholic" ideals of sanctification and evangelization.

Despite seeming to critique certain aspects of modern culture, the play's cultural bias in favor of Western, American ideals cannot be mistaken. Other nationalities were shown with stereotypical "purity"— "turbans" for Middle Eastern people, feathers and headdresses for the Native Americans, and miniature "buddhas" for the Chinese. Native Americans were first seen taking part in a "war dance," playing their "tomtoms."[36] In the written synopsis of the play, Lord wrote that the natives were to be shown in the best possible light: "as seen through the eyes of their guardian angels."[37] From the play's text, however, it is clear that the "pagan world" had rejected the divine, remaining in the darkness of unbelief. Near the play's conclusion, the crusader exhorted the "student world" to "take . . . the torch and carry it to the lands that never saw the light!"[38] It is clear that the participants believed themselves to be heralds not only of the true faith but of a superior culture as well.

THE CRUSADE "RITUAL OF INITIATION"

The second work to bear Lord's imprint was the Crusade's "Ritual of Initiation," the formal rite by which students became members of the movement. Acted out for the first time[39] on the occasion of the elevation

---

February 22–26, 1924," DAL, box 23, folder 11, GUSC.

35. An editorial in Cincinnati's *Catholic Telegraph* in response to the pageant congratulated the Crusade for "shaming the sinners of parochial narrowness." See *The Bengalese* 3.6 (1922) 1.

36. Lord, *The Dreamer Awakes*, 21, 28.

37. Ibid., 5.

38. Ibid., 33.

39. At the previous summer's Crusade convention held at the University of Notre Dame, 1,500 student members participated in the Crusade's "ordinal of admission," an early version of the ceremonial contained in Father Lord's "Ritual of Initiation." Lord

to the episcopacy of Francis Beckman, national chairman of the Crusade, in 1924, the ritual featured more than 250 youthful knights dressed in long white robes with crosses emblazoned on their chests and ladies wearing medieval garb lining the hillside of the Crusade's headquarters.[40]

The ritual began with a questioning of the candidates by "Major Domo" and "Suzerain," the "inquisitors" of the CSMC, perhaps reminding prospective crusaders of the questions and answers contained in the *Baltimore Catechism* or even the questioning of candidates for confirmation by their bishop.[41] However, unlike the affirming quality of the sacrament of confirmation, the inquisitors' role in the ritual was to impress upon the candidates their unworthiness for entry into the Crusade as well as their lack of knowledge of the Church and its missions. Major Domo, asked, for instance, "Have you any idea how many dying infants have been sent to heaven through baptism in all the years of mission work?" When, inevitably, an incorrect answer was given by one of the candidates, Major Domo responded with the correct sum: twenty-eight million. "[Y]ou show that you haven't even *begun* to study mission work," Domo retorted. After the candidates had been sufficiently humbled, Domo exhorted the candidates to action:

> I hope you see now that America—as well as China, Japan, India, Africa, South America, and the South Seas—needs missionaries. That means it needs *your* prayers, *your* sacrifices, *your* pennies, dimes, and dollars, *your* intelligent study—heaven help us! And most of all, it means that America, like China and Africa and all the rest, needs *you* as future priests, mission Brothers, and mission Sisters. Yes, *you*! Who else is there?[42]

---

himself received credit for the revised compilation though another priest seems to have written the earliest text. See Catholic Students' Mission Crusade, *To Defend the Cross*, 208.

40. See "Crusader Bishop Consecrated," *The Bengalese* 5.6 (1924) 8; Daniel A. Lord, "A Ritual of Initiation into the Catholic Students' Mission Crusade, 1924," CSMC, box 47, folder 4, AAC, "Student Crusaders Tender Grand Reception to Honor Their Executive Chairman, Bishop Beckman," *The Catholic Telegraph*, May 1, 1924; "Knights and Ladies Come to Honor Chosen Leader at Crusade Castle," *The Shield* 3.13 (1924).

41. "Major Domo" and "Suzerain" were so-named because of their link to titles with medieval significance. "Majordomo" is a term for a chief minister or officer, literally one who has authority to act as a master of the house. "Suzerain" refers to a feudal lord who holds dominion over others.

42. Lord, "A Ritual of Initiation," 9-B, 9-D.

The CSMC attempted to impress upon the candidates the universal needs of the missions and at the same time individualize the contribution that each member could offer, particularly through a life of service as a priest or religious.

In the next segment of the ritual, "the raising of the three standards," the American flag was raised, followed by the CSMC flag and the mission cross. Here the national character of the movement was apparent. As the Star-Spangled Banner was played or sung, the Suzerain announced:

> Flag of our Country, beneath whose generous folds our land has grown rich and our Church grown strong, we pledge ourselves to share the blessings we have so abundantly received with those who sit in darkness and want. Our wealth shall relieve their poverty; Our Faith shall banish their spiritual night. Great-hearted Americans shall bring to the pagan lands the blessings they have enjoyed beneath the radiant banner of the Stars and Stripes.[43]

America's status as blessed and providential nation was clear; its material and spiritual riches would assure that all nations would have a share in its abundance. In a later episode, the criticism of pagan cultures becomes even more pronounced. The character of Peter the Hermit[44] articulated the backwardness of heathen peoples in bondage:

> Fresh from the lands of the Pagans I come. And what a tale of sin and misery I bring you! ... Slavery lays iron chains on men and women alike. Women weep unnoticed while the hand of savagery crushes out the life of little children. And yet the armies of Christ could march through those lands conquering for God, spreading the glorious light on either hand, crushing the tyrant, freeing the slave, snatching the children from the jaws of living death, lifting women from the knees to their feet, overturning the hideous gods of their temple, and winning new worlds for Christ.[45]

---

43. Lord, "A Ritual of Initiation," 13.

44. According to a legend, Peter the Hermit was visited by Christ and was commanded to go throughout Europe proclaiming the miseries that had befallen Christians living under Muslim regimes. An unofficial crusader, he was erroneously credited with beginning the First Crusade in 1095.

45. Lord, "A Ritual of Initiation," 16.

Such a message had both political and religious overtones: freedom and democracy, the American way, were necessary to the flourishing of both a free citizen and faithful Christian.

In the final episode of the ritual, the "audience with the King," the participants processed to a nearby church or chapel. The men followed the figure of St. Louis while the women processed behind St. Joan of Arc. Benediction was begun in the chapel as the assembly adored Christ present in the Blessed Sacrament of the Eucharist. Kneeling before Christ, the knights and ladies pledged obedience to Christ and His Crusade:

> We, the Knights and Ladies of the new Crusade, consecrate ourselves today to Jesus Christ, our King and Sovereign. We offer ourselves as soldiers in this Holy War, the conquest of the world for the Sacred Heart. We will pray; we will sacrifice; we will labor that the Kingdom of Christ may be spread on earth. We will fight darkness with light, error with truth, paganism with Christianity. Wherever Satan now rules, we will plant the triumphant Cross of Christ.[46]

At the conclusion of the pledge, the *Tantum Ergo* (a traditional song used at Benediction and attributed to St. Thomas Aquinas) was sung and all processed out. The segment in the chapel—meant to be the most solemn and moving portion of the ritual—took on a para-liturgical character that would have been evident to the student participants. Like the sacred moment of the Mass when the priest at the altar elevated the host and bells were rung, the ritual climaxed with an encounter between the Eucharistic Christ and his youthful subjects. The ritual was meant to solidify the resolve of the crusaders to commit themselves to the Church and the spread of its message. One female delegate remarked of the ceremony, "I never felt more thrilled in my life, and I do not think anything I can ever experience again will 'grip' as that did."[47]

---

46. Lord, "A Ritual of Initiation," 31.

47. Eleanore M. Voil, "A Girl's Convention Diary," *The Bugle Call* 3.1 (1923). For an interpretation of the ceremony held at the University of Notre Dame see Dries, *The Missionary Movement*, 90–91.

SLAYING THE MONSTER OF "PAGANISM": *THE GIANTKILLER*

Lord's second dramatic production for the Crusade, coming four years after *The Dreamer Awakes*, was *The Giantkiller*. The pageant was based on the fairytale of Jack the Giant Killer, a Cornish legend in which Jack, a peasant boy, kills a pesky giant who had been terrorizing his neighbors. Jack triumphs over the giant by luring him into a large pit covered with sticks and straw. Jack was portrayed as a youthful mission crusader battling the "giant" of paganism. Written expressly for the Crusade in celebration of the centennial of the Archdiocese of St. Louis in 1926, it was performed at the Odeon Theater before an estimated 13,000 attendees.[48] Unlike *The Dreamer Awakes*, *The Giantkiller* appears not to have been performed throughout the country and made less of an impact on propagating the message of the Crusade.

Similar to the first Crusade pageant authored by Lord, *The Giantkiller* incorporated medieval imagery, being set principally in a medieval village. While set, in part, in the Middle Ages, Lord wished to impress upon his audience that *The Giantkiller* was no "antique affair" and instead was meant to be modern by 1920s standards.[49] The first part of the pageant followed the predictable tale of Jack who slays the giant and returns victorious to the village. Once the audience is familiar with the basic plot of the fairytale, the second part of the play begins, "updating" the fairytale by taking the form of a dialogue between two students, a girl and a boy. In the course of their dialogue the "modern giant" is identified as "paganism" which like the giant of old "destroys whole villages, crushes whole peoples, slays women and children." Like the giant of myth, the giant of paganism is "seated in his cave, only his cave is a dark and ugly temple. His cauldrons are sacrificial fires. His servants are pagan priests and priestesses. His victims are whole nations."[50] In the next scene, the pagan god makes his appearance and his evil intentions are revealed: "Dipping its hands in human sacrifices, blood of its victims poured on altar-stones" he hunts like a "jackal through the lustful groves [of] innocence and purity

---

48. "Program for *The Giantkiller: A Musical Mission Masque*, The Odeon, November 27–December 4, 1926," DAL, MJA.

49. Lord quoted in "'The Giant Killer' Allegorical Pageant at Odeon Tonight," *Giantkiller* publicity folder, DAL, MJA.

50. Daniel A. Lord, *The Giantkiller*, DAL, box 6, folder 13, GUSC, 38–40 (40).

and virtue."⁵¹ Then, as in *The Dreamer Awakes*, the "pagans" under the spell of their vicious god appear—half of who are depicted as Chinese and the other half Indian—to offer a dance. In the forefront is a pagan priest about to execute a mother and her child. As his dagger is raised, "Faith," the "King of all Crusaders" enters.

Medievalism and the purity of faith were viewed as synonymous: the character "Faith" was to be dressed "as a splendid Crusader in gold or silver armor." "Faith" states that he is one of the immortal crusaders who marching "with cross and rosary" has embarked on a new crusade to win the world for Christ the King.⁵² But the audience is told, the immortal crusader, "Faith," cannot be victorious alone; he needs fellow crusaders to join the battle. The first to answer the call is none other than "Jack" who kneels to be made a knight. In the finale, the crusaders and the newly-freed pagans kneel in the direction of a large wooden cross (much like the conclusion of *The Dreamer Awakes*) and in the direction of a large American flag (as in the "Ritual of Initiation"). Kneeling before these two standards, that of the cross and the flag, the entire assembly pledges: "For Christ and humanity!"⁵³

CRUSADE CASTLE

In addition to the dramatic works of Father Lord, the CSMC connected its members to the medieval past through its national center, "Crusade Castle." In September 1923 when the Crusade relocated its headquarters to a six-story villa overlooking the Ohio River valley in Cincinnati, Ohio, Father Lord named the building "Crusade Castle." The building's name and its medieval look were employed to impress upon the Crusade members their connection with the medieval past. Located on twenty-eight acres near Cincinnati's Ault Park, the castle-like home that had been built by a German immigrant and vintner in the 1840s, was offered to the Crusade by Rev. Peter E. Dietz (1878–1947) who vacated the building after the collapse of his short-lived American Academy of Christian Democracy, a school for the promotion of Catholic social teaching.⁵⁴ Dietz, a friend

---

51. Lord, *The Giantkiller*, 43.
52. Ibid., 12, 46.
53. Ibid., 56.
54. In 1917 Dietz relocated his American Academy of Christian Democracy, a school for the promotion of Catholic social teaching, to Cincinnati. After a conflict with

of Beckman's since the time they were both seminarians in Europe, was a leader of Catholic youth in the Newman movement. Dietz also had ties to the foreign mission movement through his brother, Frederick C. Dietz, a missionary to China and the fourth American ordained as a priest for the Maryknoll order. Frederick had studied for the diocesan priesthood before discovering his call to the foreign missions and was one of six Maryknoll priests selected to go to China in September 1920.[55]

Once occupied by the Crusade, the building, according to the wishes of Father Lord, was transformed to fit the Crusade's neo-medieval name and emphasis. The basement of the home, the former wine cellar, was transformed into a chapel and dedicated as the "Oratory of the True Cross" in 1928 after the movement received a large relic of the True Cross sent from Jerusalem's Church of the Holy Cross. The oratory served as a place of pilgrimage for members of the Crusade throughout the country.[56] The chapel was fitted with choir stalls and the walls were adorned with medieval-style banners, representing the various Crusade units. The dining room was refitted with large oak beams to convey the look of a castle's "Great Hall."[57] Lord remained in residence at Crusade Castle, along with the famed European missiologist, Joseph Schmidlin, for one month in the fall of 1923 as an advisor for the CSMC's mission education and leadership program.[58] Crusade Castle became the nerve center for the movement, playing host to mission leadership training events, housing the offices and living quarters for the priests who led the movement, and containing space for the prolific CSMC press, publisher of dozens of mission studies.[59]

Cincinnati Archbishop Henry Moeller, Dietz contacted Rev. Francis Beckman about donating the estate to the Crusade. See Raymond J. Wilson, Jr., "'Truth Will Make You Free' Slogan of Crusade Castle," CSMC, box 46, folder 3, AAC ; Roger Straub, "Crusaders Have a Castle, Not in the Air," *The Shield* 15.5 (1936) 3–4; "National Offices in 'Castle'—Former School Now Crusade Home," *The Shield* 3.2 (1923). For background on Dietz see Browne, "Peter E. Dietz," 448–56; and Fox, *Peter E. Dietz, Labor Priest*.

55. *The Missionary* 29.11 (1916) 616; *Field Afar* 14.7 (1920) 157.

56. See "True Cross Relic Given," *Cincinnati Post*, August 11, 1925.

57. Ben L. Kaufman, "The Surrender of Crusade Castle," *Cincinnati Enquirer*, June 11, 1978.

58. See "Noted Jesuits Arranging Program for Students' Mission Crusade," *Catholic Telegraph*, August 23, 1923; also *Cincinnati Enquirer*, September 2, 1923.

59. After the CSMC dissolved, the Cincinnati Archdiocesan mission office, the Society to Aid the Missions, used the building. In 1977 the Castle was sold by the Archdiocese

Crusade Castle, according to its planners, was to be a center for mission education and leadership.[60] While members of the Holy Childhood Association and other mission aid organizations concentrated their efforts on collecting funds for the missions, the Crusade claimed that its members were not "to rest content with a well-filled mite box or a record of many 'Our Fathers' and 'Hail Mary's' said for the benefit of the missions. They [were] supposed to make an effort to educate themselves about the works which their alms and prayers [were] helping to support."[61] Unlike organizations that merely collected missionary alms, a distinguishing feature of the Crusade was its emphasis on education. Bishop Beckman recognized the importance of education to the movement, writing, "Knowledge is first. Emotional appeals about the romance of the missions will bring a temporary response, but unless our Catholic students understand the mission problems . . . we shall never get the real fruition of our work."[62]

At the 1923 CSMC convention, it was decided to embark on a plan for "serious" study of the missions. After consulting with mission specialists, a plan to implement "round table" discussion groups in each unit of the Crusade was announced.[63] Study booklets with discussion questions (called the "Paladin Series"), focusing on various localities and mission problems, soon followed from the "CSMC Mission Press." This series of textbooks accompanied the organization of "Paladin Study Clubs," a plan for group study of such topics as Africa, China, India, and Korea.[64] Each study "round table" was composed of six to twelve crusaders who agree to meet on a particular mission topic for ten meetings.

---

to a private developer, Donald G. Attermeyer. See Ben L. Kaufman, "The Surrender of Crusade Castle," *Cincinnati Enquirer*, June 11, 1978.

60. "Fifth General Convention, 1926, Dayton," CSMC, box 1, folder 17, AAC, 87–88. Also see "Crusade Round Table Bulletin, October 1933," CSMC, box 1, folder 24, AAC.

61. "What is C.S.M.C.?" *The Shield* 5.4 (1925), 2.

62. Francis Beckman, "Report of the National Executive Board, Tenth National Convention, Cleveland, Ohio," August 17–20, 1937, CSMC, box 48, folder 4, AAC, 3.

63. "The Round Tablers: A New Plan of Mission Education for the Catholic Students' Mission Crusade," CSMC, box 46, folder 12, AAC.

64. Examples of these publications include *Africa* (Cincinnati: CSMC, 1925); *China* (Cincinnati: CSMC, 1925); *India* (Cincinnati: CSMC, 1925); *Korea* (Cincinnati: CSMC, 1925); *The Philippines* (Cincinnati: CSMC, 1925); *Alaska* (Cincinnati: CSMC, 1926); *The Reunion of the East* (Cincinnati: CSMC, 1926). See CSMC, Paladin Series, box 13, AAC.

THE DISPUTE BETWEEN FATHER LORD AND THE CRUSADE

Despite his involvement with the Crusade during its early years and the obvious debt owed to Lord by the Crusade for its early growth, by 1929 some in the CSMC were criticizing Lord and the sodality. At the Crusade's convention held in Washington, DC, in 1929, Lord claimed that "an attack was launched by one of the directors on the Sodality," stating that the sodality was attempting to destroy the Crusade.[65] Among the sodality's detractors was the episcopal leader of the Crusade, Archbishop John T. McNicholas (1877–1950) of Cincinnati, who had abolished Lord's sodality movement within his diocese and cited Lord's work as exemplifying "what happens when Catholic Action passes beyond control of the Bishops."[66]

Msgr. Thill, longtime secretary of the Crusade, who had worked with Lord to promote the Crusade in its early years, tried to smooth over relations between Lord and the Crusade, assuring that there was no conflict between the two organizations and that "the Sodality was friendly to the Crusade." Lord's response to the charge was conciliatory; he lamented the poor attendance of students from Jesuit schools at the Crusade convention and urged sodality directors to promote the Crusade within the sodality by affiliating the mission committee of each sodality with the Crusade. "I believe it would be a very fine thing if the Jesuit schools were taking an active part in [the Crusade]." "We should," he continued, "be playing as significant a part in the Crusade as we did in the beginning of the movement."[67]

The Crusade leadership, who seemed to view the sodality as competing with the Crusade, perhaps found Lord's approach to youth objectionable. The relationship between the sodality and the Crusade had not improved by the time of the sodality's convention of 1932 which resolved that the sodality forward to the Crusade "an expression of the kindly sentiments of the members . . . and their heartiest desire for cooperation between these two organizations for the spread of the kingdom of Christ

---

65. Daniel A. Lord, S.J. to "My dear Director," undated letter but likely 1929, Varia Collection, box 15, folder 1786, GUSC.

66. Gavin, *Champion of Youth*, 106–7 (107).

67. Daniel A. Lord, S.J. to "My dear Director," undated letter but likely 1929, Varia Collection, box 15, folder 1786, GUSC.

on earth."[68] In truth, the relationship between the Crusade and the sodality would never be as amiable as at the movement's beginning.

As Lord's association with the Crusade ended, his interest in the foreign missions appeared to decline even as the medieval motif employed by the CSMC remained strong. Lord's concern for youth continued as did his use of medieval themes, especially as director of the sodality and the lay movement, the Knights and Handmaids of the Blessed Sacrament. Father Lord, however, would not again be a participant in the work of the CSMC.

PAGEANTRY AND POWER: CRUSADE RALLIES AND CONVENTIONS

The interwar years experienced the height of Catholic triumphalism, often demonstrated through public displays of ecclesial pageantry and power. The climax of this mode of civic and religious display perhaps occurred in 1926 when Cardinal George Mundelein, Archbishop of Chicago, hosted the largest public event in the history of the Church in America: the International Eucharistic Congress. Held in Chicago, the event was an unprecedented display of pomp and pageantry. Approximately 150,000 Catholics took part in a Mass at Soldier Field and as many as half a million participated in the Eucharistic procession during the congress.[69] In other cities during the interwar years, Catholics routinely marched in Holy Name Society parades, processed with the Blessed Sacrament through the streets on feasts such as Corpus Christi, and took part in various pilgrimages and festivals with local or ethnic significance. Such displays were viewed by outsiders as attempts by Catholics to control the public sphere, but more often such events were internally instructive: to distinguish Catholics from outsiders and bind them more closely to their own set of values and beliefs.[70]

In light of this impulse, national gatherings were frequent and prominent during the interwar years. In 1926 the sodality movement held its first national conference for students. Other organizations such as the Laymen and Laywomen's Retreat Conferences and the Confraternity

---

68. "Fourth National Students' Spiritual Leadership Convention, June 1932," 1–2, DAL, box 23, folder 11, GUSC.

69. Dolan, *The American Catholic Experience*, 349–50.

70. Kelly, "Suburbanization and the Decline," 311–30; Bodnar, *Remaking America*.

of Christian Doctrine held periodic national conferences during the 1920s. As historian Joseph Chinnici explained, lay Catholics uniquely encountered the Church through such national gatherings. Influenced by Catholic Action, Catholics in the interwar years encountered in Chinnici's words, a "pedagogy of participation," in which they experienced the importance of gathering together as Catholics beyond the usual parochial setting. There they experienced interaction between other laity as well as priests and religious, praying together, sharing in dialogue, and common meals, contributing to a new awareness of equality in Christ as well as the "catholicity" of the Church.[71]

The CSMC joined in the era's emphasis on "public Catholicism," sponsoring Crusade rallies and "mission days." Not surprisingly, the Crusade's public events seized upon medieval and national images to communicate Catholic power and presence to both participants and onlookers. One annual event held in the nation's capital was the CSMC mission rally, held on the campus of The Catholic University of America, Washington, DC, and typically publicized in *The Washington Post*. Like soldiers marching in battle array, the student members of the Crusade marched into the Catholic University football stadium. The demonstrations typically included the attendance of high-ranking dignitaries, often ecclesiastical and secular, as well as religious orders, Catholic fraternal groups and societies. Awards such as the "Grand Cross," the highest honor of the crusade, and the "Paladin Jewels" were given to recognize the most outstanding crusaders.[72] Such events were widely promoted as a means of drawing attention to the missionary efforts of the young. The high point of the day was the celebration of a "pontifical high mass." In Cincinnati, Ohio, near the headquarters of the CSMC, one impressive mission rally held on May 29, 1927 featured a pontifical Mass with a chorus of 11,000 student crusaders.

At these events each CSMC student unit processed into the arena, carrying three flags: the American flag, Crusade flag, and CSMC unit service flag.[73] The service flag was perhaps the most unique visual aspect of the rally. Inspired both by nationalism and medievalism, each local unit of the Crusade carried a service flag, signifying the number of young men

71. Chinnici, "The Catholic Community at Prayer, 1926–1976," 39–43.
72. See for example, *The Washington Post*, May 15, 1933.
73. *Cincinnati Enquirer*, May 22, 1927; May 30, 1927.

and women who had entered the priesthood or religious life.[74] The white flag was adorned with red crosses to show each unit's contribution to the work of the Church and were similar to those used at the time of World War I to signify members of a family who were active in the war effort.[75] Use of the service flag assumed an added dimension with the deaths of the first missionary crusaders in 1929. Chinese bandits murdered Fathers Clement Seybold, Walter Coveyou, and Godfrey Holbein, members of the Congregation of the Passion. Henceforth, gold stars were used for each crusader who met martyrdom.[76] The service flag was a constant reminder of the sacrifices of mission-minded Catholics, further energizing the hero-martyr image used in the Crusade's publicity.

Apart from the visual images utilized in the rallies, the highlight of any gathering of the Crusade was the "rally sermon." In Cincinnati, at the 1927 gathering of the CSMC, Francis Thill, secretary of the CSMC, preached a sermon entitle "The Everlasting Challenge to Youth." The sermon drew upon typical "Americanist" themes: a divinely-instituted Church in a chosen land. Thill began by recalling the American heritage:

> The demonstration in which we are taking part this day exemplifies in a striking manner the idealism and deep religious sense which are the heritage of our land and our church. Everywhere throughout our country are to be found proofs that the character of our nation and the culture which our people enjoy are the developments of a history and a tradition which are eminently religious and essentially missionary ...[77]

Not surprisingly, Thill maintained that the history of America and the history of the Church were one. He downplayed the often-turbulent

---

74. The American sodality movement may have been the first to use a "service flag" to display the number of religious vocations from a parish or school. See Wolff, *The Sodality Movement in the United States,* 53. The CSMC service flag was first used in 1926 in the finale of Father Lord's mission pageant, *The Giantkiller.*

75. Dries, "The Missionary Critique of American Institutions," 68; "The Making of the Service Flag," *The Shield* 4.5 (1930) 8.

76. Carbonneau, "The Passionists in China," 412. See also the larger work, Carbonneau, "Life, Death, and Memory," especially 353–55. Carbonneau notes the participation of all three Passionists in the work of the CSMC. Also "Gold Crosses in the Crusade Service Flag," *The Shield* 8.8 (1929) 5; "In the Service Flag: A New Gold Cross," *The Shield* 17.7 (1938) 11–12.

77. "Plea Made for Missionaries by Crusade Rally Speaker," *Cincinnati Enquirer,* May 30, 1927.

past of the Catholic Church in America to foster belief in a normative and unified national character. Christian America, it seemed, was to be taken as the regnant cultural identity of the period. He continued:

> For our fields are fair beyond the fields of all the world. In the heart of our hills lies treasures more valuable than other lands can boast. And across the mountains and plains of our vast expanse, the spirit of liberty marches with firmer tread and path more sure than may be dreamed of elsewhere beneath the sun. So, too, the heritage of our Christian civilization shines forth with kindly light to the nations which have not felt the benign influence of the teachings of Christ. And yet, with all these blessings at our grasp, we can not know the fullness of happiness in their possession unless we are aspiring to share them with the less favored among the nations....[78]

Thill highlighted the providential character of the United States through its material abundance and political advantage, yet made little mention of exclusively Catholic themes. Again, he sought to minimize divisions and appeal to normative and innocuous notions of liberty, beauty, and civilization.

The tone of the sermon may have been affected by the public nature of the events. Protestants and non-believers were welcome to attend and such events were widely publicized through the religious and secular press. However, non-Catholics were never more than a small minority. In articles released prior to the events the predicted size of the gatherings was often exaggerated. In one case, an expected crowd of 50,000 was estimated at 35,000. The rally in Cincinnati was expected to have over 100,000 attendees, yet there were only 50,000 present for the demonstration (including an estimated three hundred who fainted during the long event due to severe heat).[79] Still the Crusade rallies were impressive outdoor events of great significance to the localities that hosted them.

Another mark of such gatherings was the singing of the CSMC hymn. Its connection to the medieval was explicit: "With joyous note let the earth resound, O'er hill and dale let it rebound; A new crusade do we proclaim with rapturous hearts in this refrain. Our banner to the winds unfurl, Our battle cry to all we hurl; Like knights of old there's no

---

78. Ibid.

79. "Throng of 100,000 to Attend Crusade Rally," *Cincinnati Enquirer*, May 22, 1927; "Thousands at Crusade Rally," *Cincinnati Enquirer*, May 30, 1927.

reprieve until all men this truth receive."⁸⁰ The conquest of the world for the Christian faith was analogous to a medieval battle. The same Catholic militarism was found in the official song of Catholic Action, "For Christ the King."⁸¹ The song was often used at Crusade gatherings so much so that some believed it was expressly written for the Crusade.

The CSMC pledge evidenced similar militant language: "I offer myself as a soldier in this Holy War, the conquest of the world for the Sacred Heart."⁸² For the crusaders, this was not just a pious cheer. In the late nineteenth and twentieth centuries the devotion to the Sacred Heart accented the humanity of Christ, his sanctifying power, and ultimate sovereignty over the world. It was both a symbol of the struggle against modern unbelief as well as the promise of the ultimate triumph of Christ and His Church. Though the Sacred Heart devotion itself was not expressly associated with the Middle Ages, it became closely linked with the anti-modernism strains of the neo-medievalism movement.⁸³

There were many regional and local meetings of CSMC units during the interwar years as well as ten national CSMC conventions held between 1918 and 1938. After the founding convention of 1918 in Techny, Illinois, conventions were held at the Catholic University of America, Washington, DC. (1920, 1929), at the University of Dayton (1921, 1926), at the University of Notre Dame (1923), at Niagara University (1931), in Cincinnati, Ohio (1933), at Loras and Clarke Colleges, Dubuque, Iowa

---

80. John J. Fehring, "CSMC Hymn" (1921) in *New Mission Crusade Song Book*, 1945, CSMC, box 11, folder 18, AAC.

81. The text of "For Christ the King" written by Father Daniel Lord, S.J. in 1933 is as follows: "An army of youth flying the standards of Truth, We're fighting for Christ the Lord. Heads lifted high, Catholic Action our cry, And the Cross our only sword. On earth's battle field/ Never a vantage we'll yield/ As dauntlessly on we swing. Comrades true, dare and do/ 'Neath the Queen's white and blue/ For our flag, for our faith, For Christ the King. || Christ lifts His hands, The King commands: His challenge, 'Come and follow me.' From ev'ry side, With eager stride, We form in the lines of victory. Let foemen lurk, And laggards shirk, We throw our fortunes with the Lord. Mary's Son, Till the world is won. We have pledged you our loyal word. || Our hearts are pure, Our minds are sure: No sin our gleaming helmet taints. No foeman fierce/ Our shield shall pierce,/ We're captained by God's unconquered saints. Yet peace we bring, And a gentle King,/ Whose law is light and life and love. Mary's Son, May thy will be done; Here on earth as it is above."

82. Rivers, *Aphrodite at Mid-Century*, 117–18. The same song is reproduced as the "Crusaders' Hymn" and noted as the song of the CSMC in Crews, *American and Catholic*, 116.

83. See Aubert, *The Church in a Secularised Society*, 118–21; LeBrun, "Politics and Spirituality," 29–43.

(1935), and in Cleveland, Ohio (1937).[84] Perhaps the most notable of these conventions was the 1923 meeting hosted at the University of Notre Dame and attended by 1,500 members. The theme that year, "To Defend the Cross," was chosen for reasons both foreign and domestic. Crusaders were called on to attack "the citadel of modern paganism abroad" and "bigotry at home." In a session on the home missions, the focus was to "campaign against the forces of bigotry now at work in the United States" and to counter the efforts of Protestants proselytizing in America. In the session on the foreign missions, missionaries that had come from Africa, China, and India emphasized the great need for vocations to the priesthood and religious life.[85]

The 1923 national convention featured the first use of the "ordinal of admission" into the Crusade. The ceremony featured a dramatic procession to the Our Lady of Lourdes grotto on the campus of the University of Notre Dame. Once at the grotto, the crusaders knelt to adore their King, Jesus Christ believed to be present in the Blessed Sacrament. Rev. Anselm M. Keefe, O. Praem. (1895–1974), a Norbertine priest, drafted the text of the ordinal.[86] The ceremony was the prototype to Father Lord's "Ritual of Initiation" published the following year and enacted by CSMC units throughout the country for several decades.[87] Like the mission rallies and local demonstrations, the national conferences helped forge a strong group identity and refocus the members of the Crusade according to its ideals.

THE CRUSADE'S APPROVAL FROM ROME

While the Crusade was expanding its influence and membership through regional meetings and national conferences, its very existence was being challenged by the papal-approved Society for the Propagation of

---

84. Frank Thill, "After a Quarter-Century," *The Shield* 23.5 (1944) 6.

85. "Notre Dame—To Defend the Cross," *The Bengalese* 6.5 (1923) 11; "Crusade Hosts Gather in Enthusiastic Conclave at Notre Dame," *The Bengalese* 6.9 (1923) 11.

86. Catholic Students' Mission Crusade, *To Defend the Cross*, 208. Rev. Keefe, born Maynard Eugene Keefe in 1895, entered St. Norbert's Abbey, West De Pere, Wisconsin and was ordained in 1920. He served as an army chaplain during World War II in the southwest Pacific and as dean of St. Norbert College. See *The Milwaukee Sentinel*, 17 October 1974, for Rev. Keefe's obituary.

87. For an interpretation of the ceremony held at Notre Dame see Dries, *The Missionary Movement*, 90–91.

the Faith, Rome's "official" overseas mission-support organization. The American branch of the Propagation of the Faith, which had been largely unsupportive of the Crusade's early work, attempted to centralize mission funding and distribution. This was an apparent aim of Pope Pius XI's 1922 reorganization of the Propagation through the *motu proprio*, "Romanorum Pontificum," in which he transferred its headquarters from Lyon to Rome, assuring that it would be "universal, Pontifical, Roman." According to Pius' wishes, the society would "become the Pontifical instrument to centralize the alms of the faithful intended for the missions."[88]

The enlarged purview of the society seemed contrary to the established structure of the CSMC that allowed for local autonomy within the national organization. The Propagation saw the enlarging Crusade movement as a competitor for mission alms, though the national CSMC office itself collected no money save for membership dues. Any money collected by the individual Crusade units was sent to a missionary or aid organization of the group's choosing. Msgr. Henry Klocker, longtime director of the Crusade, recalled that there had always been "suspicion between the two" and a fear of competition and interference related to the organizations' differing goals. The Propagation existed primarily for alms collecting, while the CSMC for mission education.[89]

The tension between the organizations came to a head in 1923 when the Propagation cautioned the Crusade to end its decentralized collection of funds. In an editorial printed in *Catholic Missions*, the official publication of the Society for the Propagation of the Faith in America, the Crusade was congratulated for its impressive growth but the Propagation cautioned that the Crusade should quickly "take steps . . . to unify the distribution of funds collected. As long as each unit is left free to follow its own desires in bestowing its alms, it must follow that some missionaries will, of necessity, receive duplicated allotments; some none at all." A second editorial in September 1923 cautioned against "indiscriminate giving" and a month later a third editorial stated it was a matter of "justice" that all funds be turned over to "agencies already organized"—meaning the Society for the Propagation for the Faith in the case of foreign missions and the American Board of Catholic Missions for support of the home

---

88. Quoted in William Quinn, "A Plea for United Effort," *Catholic Missions and Annals of the Propagation of the Faith* 1.11 (1924) 241–42.

89. Taped interview with Msgr. Klocker by Christine Kroner, University of Cincinnati, Department of History, February 25, 1991, CSMC, AAC.

missions. In order to persuade the Crusade, the Propagation compiled a brief on "Financial Assistance to the Foreign Missions" and directed it to the CSMC's student members.[90]

As the issue of mission funds was still unresolved, the American Catholic bishops took up the question at their meeting on September 16, 1925. The question put forward was whether all organizations collecting money for the missions, especially Catholic magazines, were compelled to send their funds to the two official collecting organizations: the Propagation for the Faith for the support of foreign missions, and the American Board of Catholic Missions for domestic support. The bishops resolved that "no action ought to be taken" and that any bishop was "free to allow any missionary organization to collect in his diocese." The result was that each missionary society, including the CSMC, was allowed to continue gathering funds in their own ways, provided that they had the support of the local ordinary.[91] Seeing that the bishops were unwilling to legislate any change in the collection of mission alms, the Propagation backed away from their insistence that the CSMC restructure its distribution of funds.

The leadership of the Crusade remained unconvinced that any restructuring was necessary and the Crusade's collecting of funds continued without substantial change throughout the controversy. In 1926 an understanding was reached between the two organizations, the result of meetings between the two organizations. Rev. William Quinn, director of the Propagation, attended the 1926 Crusade convention and members of the Crusade were invited to take part in the Second National Convention of Diocesan Directors of the Society for the Propagation of the Faith held in Cincinnati in January 1926. The meeting of the Propagation directors in Cincinnati included a visit to Crusade Castle and a presentation by Father Thill on the work of the Crusade. The result of the meeting was that a new "bond of interest" between the two groups was forged and was further strengthened when thirty-eight American dioceses agreed to allow their local Propagation directors to assume the additional role of diocesan Crusade directors. As a result, the Crusade continued to operate freely

90. *Catholic Missions* 17.8 (1923) 190; *Catholic Missions* 17.9 (1923) 214; *Catholic Missions* 17.10 (1923) 238; "Our Financial Assistance to the Foreign Missions," *Catholic Missions* 17.10 (1923) 236–37.

91. "Minutes of the Annual Meetings of the Bishops of the United States, 1919–1935," Meeting of September 16, 1925, NCWC, Collection 10, ACUA, 10–11.

with the understanding that the CSMC was to hold fast to its primary aim of mission education, not mission collecting.[92] The threat against the Crusade's existence was apparently real as Bishop Beckman confided in the student delegates at the 1926 Crusade convention that only a year earlier "it was thought the Crusade and all other societies would end."[93]

To clarify the role of the Crusade within the scope of mission promotion and to solicit ecclesial approbation for the movement, Beckman and Thill journeyed to Rome to meet with Pope Pius XI and Willem Cardinal van Rossum, then serving as prefect of *Propaganda Fide*.[94] After explaining to the pontiff the goals of the movement and highlighting its successes, Beckman and Thill requested that the Holy Father grant CSMC members "spiritual privileges" like those that had been granted to the medieval crusaders. Pius XI granted their request: "As our predecessors, the Popes of old, blessed the arms of Crusade warriors who defended the sacred places against the impious infidel, so do We bless the prayers, the works, the sacrifices of the new student crusaders in their spiritual warfare to win the world for Christ." Accordingly, indulgences were granted to those who took part in the Crusade Ritual of Initiation, those who visited the Oratory of the True Cross in Crusade Castle, and those attending CSMC conventions. As a result of the meeting, the bond between the Crusade and Rome was solidified, virtually assuring that the American branch of the Society for the Propagation for the Faith would not assume the Crusade's work.[95]

It is probably no coincidence that the pope who "saved" the Crusade was also the pontiff who made the greatest contribution to the missionary impulse in the Church. Pius XI, known as the "Pope of the Missions," articulated the spiritual themes that would be key to bolstering the Crusade's work.[96] His encyclical letters *Ubi Arcano* (1922), *Quas Primas* (1925), and

---

92. "S.P.F. Directors Join Crusade to Diocesan Work," *The Shield* 5.9 (1926) 1.

93. "Report of the Executive Committee," CSMC, box 1, folder 19, AAC, 11; Fifth General Convention, Dayton, Ohio, 1926, CSMC, box 1, folder 15, AAC, 45–47. See also "Crusade Leader Book, 1930," CSMC, box 14, folder 1, AAC, 11–12.

94. Born in Holland in 1854, van Rossum, was one of the most significant proponents of the twentieth century Catholic mission movement. Ordained as a Redemptorist priest, van Rossum was named a cardinal by Pope Pius X in 1911 and prefect of *Propaganda Fide* seven years later. In 1925, he was named "Cardinal Protector of the Crusade." He served as prefect until 1932.

95. Francis Beckman, "To Rome and Back," *The Shield* 23.4 (1944) 17–20.

96. See Josef Metzler, "Pius XI (1857–1939) The Missionary Pope," 55–61; Jedin,

Miserentissimus Redemptor (1928) emphasized the Church's universal domain and Christ's overarching Kingship while instilling in Catholics a renewed triumphalist vocabulary. The faithful could now claim participation in the potency of Christ the King's reign and the divine dominion of his Sacred Heart. Indeed, the Crusade would take up the new language of the day. In the crusader's Ritual of Initiation, he or she pledged obedience to Christ the King, made real to the crusader through the Blessed Sacrament exposed on the altar. Similarly, the official hymn of the Crusade stated its aim of claiming the world for the Sacred Heart.

Pius XI's emphasis on the universal included the need for mission territories outside Europe to be entrusted to local, native clergy. His encyclical on the missions, *Rerum Ecclesiae* (1926) stated that the goal of the new churches in mission lands was independence and an indigenous clergy and hierarchy. The move toward indigenous clergy in the missions was strengthened by the ordination of six native bishops in China in October 1926. Pius supported the Urban College in Rome, the University of *Propaganda Fide*, for the benefit of seminarians sent from mission countries. In 1922, Pius centralized the pontifical mission societies (Society for the Propagation of the Faith, Society of St. Peter the Apostle, Society of the Holy Childhood, and the Pontifical Missionary Union).

Pius XI during the Holy Year of 1925 prompted the organization of the Universal Missionary Exhibition that became permanent in 1927 with the establishment of the Ethnological Missionary Museum in the Vatican, an effort to further understanding of the Church's missionary activity and the world's cultures. That same year at the request of the Society for the Propagation of the Faith, Pius XI instituted World Mission Sunday, a yearly reminder to Catholics of the Church's unity and universality and request for them to renew their commitment to the work of evangelization.[97] The greatest gains for the CSMC came during a time of heightened mission enthusiasm and the creation of new mission aid organizations and structures under the leadership of Pius XI.

History of the Church, 9:562–69. Also "Pius XI, 'Pope of the Missions,'" *The Shield* 18.6 (1939) 2.

97. Jedin, *History of the Church*, 9:563–64.

CATHOLIC ACTION THROUGH MISSION ACTION

Pope Pius XI, in as much as he became identified with the work of the missions, was also recognized for his support of "Catholic Action," the participation of the laity in the apostolate of the hierarchy.[98] As a reaction to state-supported youth movements, the Catholic Action movement organized youth, not around the goals of the secular nation-state, but according to the demands of Christ and the Church. While Catholic Action stemmed from Pope Pius X's encyclical *Il Fermo Proposito* (1905), which had particular application to the youth of Italy, in practice Catholic Action was an international movement of associations devoted to devotional, charitable, and educational activities.[99] Drawing upon themes especially attractive to youth such as fraternity and conquest, Catholic Action took many forms, including mission work.

In the 1930s, the Crusade was not unlike other national movements that were linked to Catholic Action. The CSMC followed the pattern of other organizations that though not founded by the hierarchy, began by local, grassroots initiatives and were subsequently "domesticated" as part of Catholic Action. As groups like the CSMC flourished, clergy and especially the hierarchy sought to place organizations under their "protection" under the encompassing umbrella of Catholic Action. As in the case of the Newman, Catholic Youth Organization, and sodality movements, the CSMC leadership attempted a difficult balancing act: to be approved by the pope and to receive the benefits of its being tethered to Rome, and to be sanctioned by America's bishops, yet retain its autonomy as a national organization.[100]

The CSMC was successful in striking this balance it seems through deference to the church hierarchy and efforts to insert itself within Catholic Action without abandoning its form of student and clerical leadership. Bishop Beckman acknowledged that in participating in the

---

98. For an excellent introduction to Catholic Action in America, see Chinnici and Dries, *Prayer and Practice in the American Catholic Community*, 115–18, with accompanying documents on pp. 118–79. See also Robb, "Specialized Catholic Action," which analyzes specialized movements within Catholic Action including the Young Christian Workers.

99. See Civardi, *A Manual of Catholic Action*, 15, 21. For an interpretation of Catholic Action in terms of fraternity and conquest see Le Guillou, "Mission as an Ecclesiological Theme," 84.

100. The attempted centralization of Catholic youth work under the National Catholic Welfare Conference is described in Evans, *The Newman Movement*, 87–90, 94.

"wider fields of Catholic Action" there was a danger of the CSMC moving away from its original purpose.[101] Beginning in 1935, the theme "Catholic Action through Mission Action" was constantly voiced and there was a concerted effort to place the work of the CSMC within Catholic Action, especially by emphasizing the movements' shared character.[102] Both relied on the idealism of youth; both Catholic action and mission action were viewed as "struggles between two civilizations"; both had the same goal: the "reign of Christ in the hearts of men."[103]

While some viewed the imposition of the "Catholic Action" name on the work of the Crusade as artificial, the incorporation of the Crusade's mission into Catholic Action broadly defined was instrumental in the CSMC's movement toward domestic causes. While in its early years, the Crusade placed emphasis on foreign missions, especially in the Far East, the mid-1930s evidenced a shift to mission work at home. The reason for this reorientation is somewhat unclear. The Jesuit John LaFarge noted a precipitous decline in foreign mission enthusiasm in the late 1930s as might have been expected during a time of domestic turmoil caused by the Great Depression. In 1939, LaFarge wrote that zeal for the missions was being curtailed by a "growing distaste for insecurity and adventure, coupled with the wearing off of the novelty of the foreign mission field." "The Catholic Students' Mission Crusade which started off as such a powerful auxiliary to the missions has been obliged to take up a variety of home interests—social, religious, etc.,—to keep up interest and obtain members," he stated.[104]

Whatever the reason, it is unmistakable that in the mid to late 1930s attention began to shift to the domestic needs of the Church, especially the cause of the "home missions," evangelization among non-Catholic

---

101. Francis J. Beckman, "Report of the National Executive Board, Eleventh National Convention, Washington, DC," August 22-25, 1939, CSMC, box 48, folder 4, AAC, 2.

102. See Francis J. Beckman, "Report of the National Executive Board, Ninth National Convention, Dubuque, Iowa," August 6, 1935, CSMC, box 48, folder 4, AAC; "Mission Action is Catholic Action," *The Shield* 15.1 (1935) 3-5; "The Crusade Measured by Catholic Action Standards," *The Shield* 13.3 (1933) 2; Bishop James E. Walsh, "Catholic Action and Foreign Missions" in "The Tenth Crusade Convention, Cleveland, Ohio, 1937," CSMC, box 1, folder 29, AAC, 39-43; Bishop William D. O'Brien, "Catholic Action and Home Missions" in "The Tenth Crusade Convention, Cleveland, Ohio, 1937," CSMC, box 1, folder 29, AAC, 45-52.

103. Walsh, "Catholic Action and Foreign Missions," 43.

104. Quoted in Breslin, *China, American Catholicism, and the Missionary*, 111.

Americans, and interracial justice. Initiatives that developed within the CSMC during these years were quite varied, though related to the missionary impulse. One initiative trumpeted the slogan, "a convert for every crusader," recognizing the need for crusaders to be evangelists in their own communities. The organization supported attempts to catechize through efforts such as Catholic Evidence Guilds, "convert-making leagues," and summer schools of religion for Catholic students attending public schools.[105] At the same time other Crusade members devised a study of the "Catholic rural problem" in collaboration with National Catholic Rural Life Conference, which had been founded in 1922. The study utilized the CSMC's *Rural America: A Catholic Source Book*.[106]

"THEY KNOW THAT THE *WORLD* INCLUDES THE NEGRO WORLD"

In addition to evangelization among non-Catholic and rural Americans, interracial justice became an important issue for the CSMC beginning in the early 1930s, well before many in the Church were voicing such concerns.[107] Interest in "social justice," a term introduced by Pope Pius XI's encyclical *Quadragesimo Anno* (1931), was closely linked to the challenge of Catholic Action. The CSMC saw racial issues as an important component to creating a just America. Archbishop McNicholas, president of the CSMC, in articulating the domestic aims of the Crusade stated that it was not to be a "collecting agency" for the foreign missions but "a great power to hold aloft ideals, a power to break down prejudices."[108] In 1933, McNicholas signaled out the "Negro apostolate" as the most

---

105. See Francis J. Beckman, "Report of the National Executive Board, Ninth National Convention, Dubuque, Iowa," August 6, 1935, CSMC, box 48, folder 4, AAC, 3. Also, Edward J. Dever, "Let Us Preach Christ *to* America," *The Shield* 10.4 (1931) 1–2.

106. Bovee, "The Church and the Land," 174; Dolan, "Some Seed Fell on Good Ground"; Joseph P. Donovan, "Catholic Students' Mission Crusade and Rural Problems in its Spiritual Aspect" *Catholic Rural Life Bulletin* 4 (March 1926) 1–2; Francis Thornton, "Activities of the Students' Mission Crusade of St. Paul Seminary in Behalf of Catholic Rural Life," *Catholic Rural Life Bulletin* 4 (April 1926) 1–2; Fortin, *Faith and Action*, 279–80.

107. The CSMC during the 1930s was one of only a few American Catholic organizations voicing interracial concerns. See Southern, *John LaFarge*, 205–6.

108. Address of Archbishop McNicholas, "Official Record of the Fifth General Convention of the Catholic Students' Mission Crusade at the University of Dayton, June 25–28, 1926," CSMC, box 1, folder 14, AAC, 22.

pressing challenge of missionary work in the United States. That same year the CSMC considered its approach to the race problem and adopted a resolution "opposing all un-American and anti-Catholic principles embodied in race prejudice," recognizing that the "Negro, as a human being and as a citizen, is entitled to the essential opportunities of life and the full measure of social justice" and "as a member of a race bearing the heavy yoke of injustice, he (the Negro) needs my kind word, my act of courtesy, my expression of good will" and "above all, as a member of the Mystical Body of Christ, he deserves all the privileges that flow therefrom."[109]

In an era in which Catholic interracial justice was little known and often opposed, the Crusade collaborated with Rev. John T. Gillard, S.S.J. (1900–1942)[110] and Rev. John LaFarge, S.J. (1880–1963),[111] leaders in the interracial movement. Gillard, who had earned his doctorate from The Catholic University of America in 1929, was active in the Crusade, presenting one of the three talks on the black apostolate during the Crusade's 1931 convention. He asked his fellow crusaders to do battle against prejudice: "Let us put to rout first the prejudice in our own hearts, and then the un-American, un-Christian, un-Catholic discrimination in the things of God."[112] A second Crusade-sponsored lecture by Gillard, "The Missionary Apostolate among the Colored," was held at The Catholic University of America on March 2, 1933. Gillard strongly denounced racism to his audience, stating that racism was the greatest obstacle to conversion of African Americans. He implored his listeners: "Bury this prejudice, in the name of the Lord. Christ, hanging on the cross, shed His Most Precious Blood, not merely for the soul of the white man; He died for mankind. The Negro is a man. Treat him accordingly. If Christ made no

---

109. "Proceedings and Addresses of the Eighth National Convention, Cincinnati, Ohio 1933," CSMC, box 1, folder 24, AAC, 41, 48.

110. For background on Gillard see Czuchlewski, "Liberal Catholicism and American Racism," 145–47; Ochs, *Desegregating the Altar*, 301–3. Father Gillard, a Josephite priest dedicated to the evangelization of African Americans, was author of several books including *The Catholic Church and the American Negro* (1930); *Christ, Color, and Communism* (1937); and *Colored Catholics in the United States* (1941). The Gillard papers are housed in the Josephite Archives, Baltimore, Maryland.

111. For background on LaFarge see Southern, *John LaFarge*; and Hecht, *An Unordinary Man*.

112. "Reveille: A Trumpet-Call to Missionary Action, Seventh National Convention of the Catholic Students' Mission Crusade, 1931" in CSMC, box 1, folder 23, AAC, 35–38; quote at 38.

distinction, why should we? Consider the soul, rather than the skin. Go beyond color and you will see an immortal soul, made to the image and likeness of God."[113] Gillard continued his work with the Crusade, authoring the CSMC-sponsored, *The Negro American: A Mission Investigation* in 1935. The book went through three editions in less than six months, evidencing the popularity of the publication's use in classrooms and Crusade study clubs.[114]

Published the year after the founding of the Catholic Interracial Council, the Crusade's advocacy of interracial justice was in the forefront of the movement in the mid-1930s. For the Crusade, interracial support was not only theoretical but also proactive. In 1937 a black seminarian at St. Augustine's Seminary, Bay St. Louis, Mississippi, was elected to the CSMC national executive board, the same year in which the Crusade passed a resolution pressing for the admittance of blacks into institutions of Catholic higher education.[115] In light of the need for black leadership, "where legally possible, Catholic facilities for higher education [should] be made available to Negroes who are able to meet the requirements for such institutions." CSMC delegates were asked to inform their educational institutions that they did not object to the admission of blacks to their schools.[116] The admittance of African Americans to St. Louis University, spearheaded by the Jesuit chaplain, Rev. Claude Heithaus, seems to have been influenced in part by the Crusade's activism.[117]

The Crusade's national interracial efforts were augmented by the work of local units who organized study clubs to educate students about race issues. These clubs proved effective in countering prejudice evidenced by the reaction of participants. One student at Mt. St. Joseph High School in Baltimore reflected, "Before I joined the study club, I was completely unaware of the injustice and sad consequences to the Negro of racial

113. See "Gillard Scores White and Negro Race Prejudice" in the newspaper of The Catholic University of America, *The Tower*, March 9, 1933.

114. Bowling, "Social Implications of the Catholic Students' Mission Crusade," 26.

115. Bowling, "Social Implications of the Catholic Students' Mission Crusade," 12, 83.

116. "The Tenth Crusade Convention, Cleveland, Ohio, 1937," CSMC, box 1, folder 29, AAC, 19.

117. Bowling, "Social Implications of the Catholic Students' Mission Crusade," 81; Czuchlewski, "Liberal Catholicism and American Racism," 150. For Heithaus's contribution to the effort to integrate St. Louis Univeristy see Gleason, *Contending with Modernity*, 235–40.

segregation. But now that I know these facts it is my earnest prayer to God that the sin of segregation be abolished from our country and from the hearts of our people."[118] Other local initiatives included the opening of a mission center for black Catholics in Rochester, New York, the training of lay catechists to minister to African Americans, sponsoring of scholarships for blacks at Catholic high schools and colleges, and the attendance of more than 1,000 crusaders at a racial fellowship dinner.[119] In 1938, Father Gillard wrote of the "tremendous change in opinion . . . in Catholic circles as regard the Negro and Negro missions." "If I were asked," he continued, "to name a single agency which has contributed most to this about-face, I would unhesitatingly name the Catholic Students' Mission Crusade." Gillard concluded, "They know that the *world* includes the Negro world."[120] Gillard, shortly before his death, offered the rather dramatic assertion that "[t]he greatest single influence in interracial relations in the United States is the Catholic Students' Mission Crusade."[121]

By the close of the 1930s, the CSMC had shifted away from the allure of medievalism in favor of the challenge of Catholic Action and the emerging frontiers of social justice, race relations, and the evangelization of non-Catholics. While a combination of medieval and national rhetoric and symbolism had filled a void in Catholic American life in an age with a desperate need for unity, idealism, and order, medievalism had served to create a Catholic subculture that accented its separatism from the modern world. William Halsey has termed this development the "Catholic countersociety," an attempt to "immunize its members from the dominant problems of life without."[122] This cultural separatism provided for the social cohesion of Catholics from a variety of ethnic and economic groups, yet did little to enable American Catholic youth to engage the world and the problems of the mission field.

The need to adopt a new set of images became apparent as crusaders were less likely to don chain mail or red-crossed tunics and more likely

---

118. Quoted in Bowling, "Social Implications of the Catholic Students' Mission Crusade," 32.

119. Bowling, "Social Implications of the Catholic Students' Mission Crusade," 81–83. Also, *The Shield* 24.2 (1945) 21.

120. John Gillard, "New Names for Old Bi-Racial Attitudes," *The Shield* 17 (1938) 3–4.

121. Gillard, *Colored Catholics in the United States*, 246.

122. Halsey, *The Survival of American Innocence*, 57.

to look inquisitively if not fearfully at the present state of the world, not a mythical and idealized medieval setting. The mid to late 1930s witnessed some attempts to break out the "Catholic countersociety" of which neo-medievalism was representative.

By this time the Crusade had taken on a number of domestic missionary causes including the mission to peoples of other faiths, African Americans, and rural peoples. The new causes of the CSMC propelled by "Catholic Action" and an emerging interest in social justice injected the movement with renewed energy and vitality. These new initiatives informed the approach of the Crusade's next generation, one that would neither define itself primarily by a fascination with medievalism nor domestic concerns but by a new struggle: international communism.

FOUR

Ramparts and Shields

Protecting American and Catholic Values, 1940–1960

On the eve of America's entry into World War II, both the domestic and international efforts of the CSMC were gaining momentum. By 1940 membership in student units was spiking toward 800,000 and the Crusade counted seven former members as foreign missionary bishops—all but one serving in China. In total hundreds of former-crusader priests and religious were serving in the foreign missions with hundreds if not thousands more working domestically, laboring as priests or sisters in America's parishes and schools. The CSMC was touted as the nation's largest and most influential Catholic youth movement, a significant force within a rapidly expanding Church.[1]

The growth of the CSMC paralleled the rise of the Church in America. The number of Catholics grew by a remarkable ninety percent between 1945 and 1965, an increase from twenty-four to forty-six million. At the same time, Catholics built more than three thousand elementary and high schools and nearly one hundred new colleges. Enrollment in Catholic schools jumped by more than three million during the period, assuring that the CSMC would have an expanding base from which to recruit its members.[2]

---

1. Bowling, "Social Implications of the Catholic Students' Mission Crusade," 13–14, 74. See also Monica Mary, "Where are the Former CSMCers Now?" *The Shield* 43.3 (1964) 5–6; and Monica Mary, "Home Towns of CSMC Missioners," *The Shield* 43.4 (1964) 13–15 for a sampling of former members serving as foreign missionaries.

2. For the impact of World War II and post-war era on Catholics in America see Gleason, "Pluralism, Democracy, and Catholicism," 208–30; Carey, *The Roman Catholics*, 93–94; Massa, *Catholicism and American Culture*; Wuthnow, *The Restructuring of American Religion*.

While the movement continued its emphasis on "prayer, study, and sacrifice" for the missions, the era of World War II and the ensuing Cold War demanded a distinctive approach to mission promotion. The movement became especially critical of the errors, if not evils, of modernity. At home the Crusade leadership saw modern errors in the form of popular music, movies, and contemporary dress. Abroad they found these expressed in the totalitarianism and brutality of Nazism and communism. The Crusade's concern for public morality at home was tied to concern for the abandonment of moral truths, believing it to be at the heart of communism and other forms of oppression that frustrated the work of Christian evangelization throughout the world. The CSMC saw itself as uniquely qualified to respond to the challenges of the age through its backing by Rome, its connections to the American hierarchy, and its support among the Church's ministers and youth.

The reality of a second large-scale global war refocused the Crusade on the horrifying nature of international conflict and its presumed cause: rebellion from God. The war was blamed on a spiritual and intellectual defect, the unwillingness to submit to the "reign of Christ" over the world. Instead of following Jesus, the "King of Kings," the world had gone terribly astray by succumbing to the quest to obtain power at all costs, even through sheer brutality. The Crusade emphasized the need to return to a society centered in Christ and an abandonment of the enticements of modernity, especially communism and its "Godless" antecedents: secularism and materialism. These were at the root of unbelief, obstacles to spreading the Gospel message.

IN OPPOSITION TO THE "MODERN REBELLION"

While earlier crusaders had attacked the giant of "paganism" abroad, the next generation of CSMC members and leaders offered a scathing critique of emerging "modern" American life. In the name of protecting American and Catholic values—which usually were thought to be one and the same—the Crusade warned youth of such dangers as divorce, birth control, immoral movies, indecent literature, scanty sunbathing, and swing music. Such developments were seen as a form of "modern rebellion" contrary to God's values and those of the Church. If allowed to take root, crusaders believed that America could be "lost" for Christ.

Under the banner of Catholic Action, the CSMC engaged in a form of militant Catholicism, a public and patriotic attempt at the advancement of the Church and protection of the country's welfare. The leaders of the Crusade were the epitome of "militant" Catholics, seeking to infuse public life with Catholic principles. Archbishop John T. McNicholas, Bishop Beckman and Monsignors Freking and Thill—the Crusade's clerical leadership for several decades—were quick to publicly proclaim the Church's stand regarding America's cultural development. These clerics did not envision themselves as pastors for a Sunday-morning-only flock, but rather as appointed spiritual leaders for all times in the various realms of life—private, public, secular, and spiritual. In summing up the message of the Crusade during these years, one writer commented, "On every front where the Church militant lies entrenched, crusaders are fighting under the banner of the Cross. They are sharing in every diocese of our land in the religious offensive which Christ's Vicar has called Catholic Action. The constitutional flexibility of the movement permits every bishop to use his own Crusaders as shock-troops or reserves in any effort to conquer souls for Christ."[3]

The use of these "shock-troops" for Christ by the CSMC took different forms. By the time of the war, Catholics rivaled prim and proper Protestant ministers as protectors of America's public good. Rev. Daniel A. Lord, S.J., who had been instrumental in the early growth of the Crusade, and Archbishop McNicholas, president of the Crusade, led the campaign against the perceived danger of immoral films. Lord helped draft the movie production code in 1929 and solicited the help of the United States bishops to form the Legion of Decency in 1934. The Legion encouraged Catholics to pledge not to view films with questionable content. With the support of countless Catholics who took the pledge, the motion picture industry was forced to censor itself and produce films in accord with Lord's code. McNicholas, serving as the first chairman of the Episcopal Committee on Motion Pictures, supported the Legion and its efforts.[4]

Like Lord and McNicholas, Bishop Beckman of the Crusade also frequently cautioned against American "popular culture." From music

---

3. Eberhardt, "Students' Mission Crusade," 444.

4. For Lord's involvement in the motion picture production code see Vaughn, "Morality and Entertainment," 48–53; Walsh, *Sin and Censorship*; Black, *Hollywood Censored*; Black, *The Catholic Crusade Against the Movies*; Cadegan, "Guardians of Democracy or Cultural Storm Troopers?," 252–82.

and movies to sunbathing, he saw these forms of leisure as leading to social and moral ruin.⁵ In an address to the National Council of Catholic Women in 1938, he called the swing music of Benny Goodman and others "a degenerated musical system ... turned loose to gnaw away the moral fiber of young people." He deemed this new form of music "evil" and "communistic." He stated, "We permit jam sessions, jitterbug and cannibalistic rhythmic orgies to occupy a place in our social scheme of things, wooing our youth along the primrose path to hell."⁶

The conservatism of Msgr. Edward Freking, the Crusade's national secretary, often mirrored that of Beckman. Freking admonished churchgoers for their inappropriate attire at Mass, writing that "Bermuda shorts are not trousers in Cincinnati; sandals showing painted toenails are not shoes; a suntan is not clothing." Those who were improperly dressed he called "spiritually blind" and "so thoughtless of God's presence and their own dignity that what was special for the boudoir has become good enough for back kneelers in church."⁷ As bold and exaggerated as these statements may appear, they were very consistent with a manifestation of public Catholicism aimed at safeguarding morality.

Still the clerical leadership of the Crusade was not primarily a source of criticism of youth and culture. Beckman himself frequently boasted in the virtue and great potential of Catholic young people. When Beckman addressed the movement's national convention held in Dubuque, Iowa in 1935, he exclaimed, "The modern rebellion of youth against authority, especially religious authority, has not received even a moment's consideration from Catholic youth." Beckman took pride in the group's noble aims: the establishment of Christian order and authority. As good Americans and good Catholics, they despised revolution and social upheaval. Instead, the Crusade stood for a distinctively Catholic system of orthodoxy and orthopraxy—right belief and right action—supported by the universal Church and applied in the United States.

---

5. See for example "Archbishop Beckman Attacks Scanty Sun Bathing Attire," *Cincinnati Post*, June 17, 1946. Beckman compared sunbathing to the "paganism of ancient Rome" and its "sun cult."

6. Erenberg, *Swingin' the Dream*, 37, quoting Beckman's address to the National Council of Catholic Women, Biloxi, Mississippi, October 25, 1938.

7. "Dress Up: Suntan Not Clothes, Msgr. Freking Says," *Cincinnati Post*, June 16, 1958.

Even while speaking from a platform imbued with the ideals of religion, the Crusade made it clear that Catholic youth were not to appear as sectarian separatists. They were to counter the prevailing culture while being the leaven of its transformation. One observer commented that the crusaders "were high spirited, but sane young citizens, intent on getting as much as they could out of life, but at the same time, trying to save their own souls and the souls of others. They were normal boys and girls, cultured, well-bred, clever, and alert, but they were not fanatical."[8] The model of engaging culture set forth by the Crusade leadership was one of challenging culture's failings without naively separating its members from the world in which they were living.

ARCHBISHOP JOHN T. MCNICHOLAS AND THE CRUSADE

The Crusade's attempts to turn the tide against modern "rebellion" from God were bolstered by its national president. For nearly a quarter of a century Archbishop John T. McNicholas, O.P. was both Archbishop of Cincinnati and president of the CSMC.[9] When in 1925, the presidency of the movement was left vacant owing to the death of Archbishop Henry Moeller, McNicholas was the obvious choice to lead the Crusade. He was officially elected president of the CSMC in 1926, a position he would hold until his death in 1950. His presidency spanned nearly half of the years of the CSMC's existence. In gaining McNicholas as president, the Crusade could not have been led by a more promising member of the American hierarchy. Intensely devoted to education, youth, the lay apostolate, and the defense of America against secularism, immorality, and the errors of modernity, he was a leading spokesmen for the Church in America.

His own understanding of Church and country was highly influenced by his own intellectual formation. McNicholas, perhaps more so than any other American prelate, embraced the Thomistic, scholastic synthesis based loosely on the works of St. Thomas Aquinas, especially the *Summa Theologica*. Having studied Thomas extensively at the Collegio San Tommaso in Rome, McNicholas believed that Thomism could offer the synthesis needed to restore the connection between tradition and the contributions of modern science and technology. His Thomism brought

---

8. Eberhardt, "Students' Mission Crusade," 444.

9. McNicholas, *Mosaic of a Bishop*; Avella, "John T. McNicholas in the Age of Practical Thomism," 15–25; Fortin, *Faith and Action*, 255–59.

a distinctive approach to his diocese and his presbyterate. He desired that the priests of Cincinnati become Thomists in their own right, sending more than one hundred diocesan priests to Europe's centers for Thomistic thought. At home in Cincinnati, in 1935 he founded the *Institutum Divi Thomae*, an institution for scientific research meant to train Catholic scientists who would view faith and science as allies.[10]

In addition to his thorough grounding in scholasticism and his Roman training, McNicholas' priesthood was marked by his attention to education and lay movements in the Church. Beginning in 1908, McNicholas served as the first national director of the Holy Name Society, a men's confraternity comprising more than 400 American branches. McNicholas increased the strength and visibility of the movement. These parish-based societies, at first connected exclusively to Dominican parishes, grew to encompass a national network. McNicholas established the national headquarters of the movement in New York City in 1909, organized the first national convention in 1911 in Baltimore, and edited the movement's first publication, *The Holy Name Journal*. Through his leadership the movement grew to some 600,000 strong.[11] His experience of leading the Holy Name Society surely informed his own vision for and leadership of the Crusade and related educational and youth movements.

While the leadership of the Holy Name Society marked McNicholas' years immediately after ordination, his years of episcopal service were distinguished by his nationally recognized efforts to strengthen Catholic education and youth involvement in the Church. He served as administrative chairman of the National Catholic Welfare Conference from 1946–1950, was president of the National Catholic Educational Association from 1946–1950, and was episcopal head of the Education Department of the National Catholic Welfare Conference from 1929–1934 and again from 1941–1945.[12]

As a young priest McNicholas himself had desired to be a missionary and as a member of the hierarchy, he was a firm supporter of

---

10. Reher, *Catholic Intellectual Life in America*, 115–16. Reher considers McNicholas an "anti-modernist," but he did not reject modernity outright, especially modern scientific and medical advances. See Heitmann, "Doing 'True Science,'" 702–22.

11. Avella, "John T. McNicholas," 18–19; Tifft, "McNicholas, John T.," 894–95; Concordia, "Holy Name Society in America," 656–57; National Headquarters of the Holy Name Society, *Jesus, His Name*, 23–25, 29.

12. Nason, "Educational Activities of Archbishop John T. McNicholas," 66–68, 102.

the Church's domestic and foreign missions. During his short tenure as bishop of Duluth, he established a mission house for clergy serving rural missions. Later as Archbishop of Cincinnati he was active in the National Catholic Rural Life Conference, sponsoring the 1925 meeting in his diocese. He welcomed the founding of two missionary orders of priests and brothers in Cincinnati. The first, the Glenmary Home Missioners, founded by Rev. William Howard Bishop in 1939, served rural areas with small Catholic populations, popularly known as "no priest land U.S.A."[13] McNicholas' second area of mission concern was the apostolate to urban African Americans. In 1940 he welcomed into the diocese representatives of the Comboni Missionaries (Verona Fathers) who sought an American foundation for their ministry to blacks.[14]

McNicholas' leadership of the Crusade was essential to its growth and firmness of purpose. Like his predecessors who bankrolled the Crusade and prevented financial shortfalls, the Archbishop was the CSMC's most important financier. McNicholas also informed the intellectual outlook of the movement, especially its attempt to offer proof for the philosophical degeneracy of communism, secularism, and some forms of modern thought. In his address to crusaders at the 1937 national convention, he recalled that the Church had always struggled with enemies, both from within and those outside the Church. Every age had its heresies, he claimed, and his age encountered the modern errors of totalitarianism, individualism, emotionalism, and subjectivism. The modern man is "obsessed with the idea of being liberal," he claimed and, still worse, liberalism was accepted without analysis and inquiry. In particular, he outlined the danger of totalitarianism, especially communism, that made man "entirely subservient to civil authority," removing God and the Church from the public sphere.[15]

INTERNATIONAL ANTICOMMUNISM

From the time of the Bolshevik Revolution, Catholics rightly interpreted communism as a potentially mortal enemy of the Church and of religion.

13. Address of Archbishop McNicholas in "Official Record of the Fifth General Convention of the Catholic Students' Mission Crusade at the University of Dayton, June 25-28, 1926," CSMC, box 1, folder 14, AAC, 22; Kauffman, *Mission to Rural America*, 134-35; Fortin, *Faith and Action*, 277-80.
14. Durchholz, *Defining Mission*.
15. McNicholas, *Our Youth of Tomorrow*, 3, 7-10.

As religious persecution of Catholics by communists intensified at the hands of Mexican revolutionaries in the 1920s, during the Spanish Civil War of the mid-1930s and by communists in the Cold War years, American Catholics increasingly rallied for preservation of the faith in countries where it was under siege.[16] Beginning largely as a means of asserting Catholic support for American democracy and identifying with the American mainstream, Catholic anticommunism was often rooted in a distinctively global consciousness, responding to reports of persecution abroad rather than fear of communist infiltration at home. While historians have depicted Catholics in America as preoccupied with building a domestic empire of parishes, hospitals, and schools, a significant number were concerned with the plight of Christians abroad and were determined not to allow the Church to crumble in foreign lands under the weight of totalitarian oppression.

Alongside other Catholic lay organizations,[17] the CSMC occupied an important place within the Catholic anticommunist movement, propagating the global "truth about communism" by exposing the persecution of Catholics under communist regimes. The Crusade's concern for the foreign missions incorporated a visible anticommunist tone beginning with an occasional denunciation in the mid-1930s to a near-obsession with speaking out against communism by 1950. While some within American Catholic anticommunism were preoccupied with "red webs" and the outing of communists at home, the Crusade's efforts were decidedly international in character. The adage to "think globally, but act locally" could be applied to the student members of the Crusade who allowed domestic concerns to be overshadowed by a distinctive missionary consciousness informed by the reality of religious and political persecution abroad. In the case of the Crusade, zeal for the missions and the conversion of "pagans"

---

16. The Church's view of communism was profoundly shaped by the bloody anti-Catholic and anti-clerical repression of the Church during the Mexican Revolution and its aftermath, resulting in the American Catholic tendency "to view the 1917 Bolshevik Revolution in Russia through a Mexican lens and to understand the Russian revolution—almost immediately—as primarily an attack on the Roman Catholic Church." See Powers, "American Catholics and Catholic Americans," 18; Coppa, "Pope Pius XII and the Cold War," 50–66.

17. For a comparison of other American Catholic lay groups' responses to communism, see O'Connor, "Defenders of the Faith." O'Connor details the following: the Catholic War Veterans, Catholic Daughters of America, Blue Army of Our Lady of Fatima, and the Cardinal Mindszenty Foundation.

was often accompanied by anticommunist rhetoric couched in terms of relief, education, and conversion. Consequently, the actions of Catholic missionaries and their youthful supporters were intimately linked to the international movement to combat communism and to show solidarity with Catholics suffering under communist regimes.

The distinctive anticommunist rhetoric of the CSMC differed from both the reactionary counter-subversive form of anticommunism that sought to expose conspiracies and secret networks to legitimate itself, and liberal anticommunism that accentuated personal freedom as the opposite of totalitarianism.[18] Instead, the Crusade sought to promote an intellectual and spiritual alternative to communism that could be accepted at home and promoted abroad, an approach that included support for "God-given rights," respect for order and legitimate authority, and qualified approval of religious freedom as promoted in America. The approach was solidly anchored in scholasticism, a trademark of the Catholic educational system. The anticommunist thrust of the CSMC incorporated spiritual, educational, and activist components targeted at the influence of American Catholic youth.

Defining the Crusade's anticommunist activities was its emphasis on intellectual formation as the antidote to communism. Intellectual arguments against communism were particularly important because the movement was geared toward students: those who were to lead America in the fight against communism. With a strong educational current, the CSMC viewed its efforts in relationship to overcoming competing ideologies of the period: materialism, secularism, paganism, Protestantism, and communism, seeking to supplant these by asserting the primacy of the Catholic Christian worldview.[19]

Though American Catholics had first become aware of communism at the time of the Bolshevik revolution of 1917, Catholic anticommunism became prominent in the 1930s as the Church faced the rise of various forms of aggressive nationalism, manifested in totalitarian dictators such as Stalin, Hitler, and Mussolini. Pope Pius XI's encyclical, *Divini Redemptoris* (1937), helped to awaken Catholics to the dangers of "atheistic communism," though the document's teaching on communism was

---

18. For a discussion of liberal and conservative strains of anticommunism see Powers, *Not Without Honor*, 254–55.

19. As an example see Spaeth, *Perspectives in Religion and Culture*, 11–19.

not new.[20] At home, Francis Cardinal Spellman, Bishop Fulton J. Sheen, and Rev. Edmund A. Walsh, S.J., took the lead in convincing American Catholics of the dangers of the "Red Menace." Walsh worked to oppose diplomatic recognition of Russia in the early 1930s, while Spellman was known for his leadership within the Church hierarchy and his political acumen. Sheen, who has been called the "prophet and philosopher" of American Catholic anticommunism, was often the public face of the movement, authoring many books and pamphlets and giving numerous sermons and speeches on the issue.[21]

The Crusade frequently used its publication, *The Shield*, to report on and often denounce the spread of communism. Unlike organizations such as the youth sodality movement and the Knights of Columbus who targeted the anti-Catholic revolutionaries in Mexico beginning in the 1920s and early 1930s,[22] the first significant references to communism by the CSMC did not appear in *The Shield* until 1936. In January of that year, the cover of the magazine pictured an illustration of a young man carrying a flag showing a cross and the phrase "*Annus Domini*" (the year of the Lord). Beneath him were outstretched hands holding swords, a fiery torch, and bayonets. On the sleeves of their uniforms were the Nazi swastika and the Soviet hammer and sickle. The CSMC graphically depicted that totalitarian regimes were enemies of the Church, taking the form of armed aggressors seeking its destruction.[23]

One of the first anticommunist articles to appear in *The Shield* came in December 1936, near the beginning of the Spanish Civil War. The CSMC was nearly silent on the war itself in which the Spanish Church aligned itself with General Francisco Franco's nationalist forces in opposition to a socialist, communist, and liberal alliance. *The Shield* article examined communism as a "missionary problem," calling it the most "formidable and relentless foe" that the Church faced at that time. The author advised students to differentiate between communism as an economic system and

---

20. Pope Pius IX's *Syllabus of Errors* (1864) had condemned the ideas at the root of communism. See Holmes, *The Papacy in the Modern World*, 93–94.

21. Crosby, "The Politics of Religion," 20–38; Cooney, *The American Pope*, 146–68, 230–36; McNamara, *A Catholic Cold War*; Reeves, *America's Bishop*, 126–48; Riley, *Fulton J. Sheen*.

22. Kauffman, *Faith and Fraternalism*, 287–314; Kauffman, *Patriotism and Fraternalism in the Knights of Columbus*, 89–93; Dinges, "'An Army of Youth,'" 42–45.

23. *The Shield* 15.4 (1936).

communism as a philosophy. The latter, the article advised, was "materialistic and opposed to a spiritual interpretation of life. It is this-worldly in opposition to other-worldly. It denies the existence of God, the spirituality and immortality of the soul, and the necessity of religion, and breaks down all the sacred institutions of society, such as marriage, the family, the home and respect for legitimate authority."[24] From the beginning, the anticommunist rhetoric of the CSMC was decidedly conservative. It spoke not in terms of the liberal notions of freedom and rights but communism as the enemy of institutions, the family, and authority.[25]

Communism, however, appeared to some in the 1930s not so much as a concrete threat but as a distant spiritual, if not philosophical, menace. Articles mentioning communism were sporadic during these years. One article written in March 1937 compared communism to Albigensianism, a medieval Christian heresy that had been successfully stamped out. The writer claimed that the Albigensians were like the Russian communists; both attempted "to stir up trouble for legitimate governments" and were anti-social and anti-Christian. The author, however, assured his readers that the Albigensians had been a greater threat than communism since the medieval heretics were "as efficient and much more convincing than the Communists." With God's help the communist atheists would meet the same fate as the heretics. "What God has done before, He can do again," the author concluded.[26]

The leadership of the Crusade, however, was convinced that communism was more dangerous than a medieval heresy. At a 1937 Crusade convention held in Cleveland, Ohio, Archbishop McNicholas attacked communism in his address to more than 10,000 crusaders. He targeted communism, secularized government education, and large corporations, calling them "usurpers of the family freedom of American homes." These together, according to McNicholas, made "true family life impossible" by restricting freedom and replacing it with national totalitarianism.[27] Speaking to another Crusade gathering in Cleveland, Ohio three months later, McNicholas repeated his charge against totalitarianism, by adding

24. John E. Kuhn, "Communism: A Missionary Problem," *The Shield* 16.3 (1936) 10.

25. Powers, *Not Without Honor*, 254.

26. Arnold Morrison, "Anti-Communism Model: The Albigensian Heresy," *The Shield* 16.6 (March 1937) 18.

27. "50 Felled by Heat as 10,000 Attend Mass at Frederick," *Washington Post*, May 10, 1937: 13.

to his attack on communism an indictment of the government in Spain that had been responsible for the murders of thousands of priests and religious: "a government which has destroyed every vestige of liberty" and the errors of Nazism that had resulted in the usurpation of religious authority by the state. The root of totalitarianism, McNicholas argued, was in the errors of the Protestant Reformation, infecting the world with the belief that the Bible should be the sole rule of faith, that civil authority should be in supreme command of religion within its territories, and that the legitimacy of "a supreme religious authority" (the Church) could be repudiated. From this centuries-old rebellion came the modern rebellion against God, order, and family, McNicholas claimed.[28] At that same convention in 1937, Dorothy Day, editor of *The Catholic Worker*, spoke on "Communism as a Missionary Problem."[29]

In the years before World War II, the Crusade offered a sporadic and ill-defined attack against communism, considering it a vague ideological, though potentially mortal threat. It was a spiritual and intellectual evil, yet one that had made little impact on the life and work of the Church because it was not yet an organized and militant force. The war and its aftermath, however, would convince nearly all American Catholics, including the members of the Crusade, that communism was a formidable foe, capable of ushering in a new world order opposed to Christ and the Church.

MISSIONARY ENGAGEMENT AND AMERICAN ISOLATIONISM

While communism as a "missionary problem" was being discussed in the pages of *The Shield* and Catholic students throughout the country were becoming aware of the war in Europe and the possibility of American intervention, the clerical leadership of the Crusade offered a united front in denouncing American participation in the war and an American foreign policy that could be seen as submitting to the errors of communism. One of the Crusade's founders and long-time chairman, Bishop Beckman, spoke out against American involvement in World War II and was considered by many to be the leading American Catholic isolationist before the Japanese

---

28. McNicholas, *Our Youth of Tomorrow*, 4–5.

29. See "The Tenth Crusade Convention, Cleveland, Ohio, 1937," 61–68, CSMC, box 1, folder 29, AAC.

attack on Pearl Harbor. At the onset of the fighting in Europe, Beckman, then archbishop of Dubuque, Iowa, deemed the war just another imperialist struggle motivated by greed and economic dishonesty. He blamed President Roosevelt for buckling to the demands of communist Russia and denounced the sending of American aid to that country. Beckman was active in the "America First" movement, joining many American Catholics and a majority of the bishops to support nonintervention in the war.[30] At the 1939 Crusade national convention held at The Catholic University of America in Washington, DC, Msgr. Freking, national secretary of the Crusade, and ally of Beckman and of America First, called on the government "not to repeat the mistake . . . made in 1914" by becoming involved in World War I and to instead "stand firm against the slaughter of American youth on foreign fields of battle."[31] Archbishop McNicholas went so far as to call on Catholic young people to become conscientious objectors should the United States enter the war.[32]

The isolationism espoused by the Crusade's leadership prior to the bombing of Pearl Harbor and American entry into the war was motivated primarily by their preoccupation with communism. American Catholic opinion viewed communism as a greater threat than Nazism and fascism.[33] Additionally, as an isolationist country, Beckman believed, America had "a sublime mission" in a world at war to be a voice for peace, remaining resolute as an example to other countries.[34] At the time of the alliance between the United States and the Soviets during the war, Beckman warned Catholics of the "Christ-haters in Moscow and their international brethren."[35] Clearly, Beckman believed that any cooperation with Russia was to compromise America's civic and religious values.

Beckman and McNicholas joined together to oppose Bishop Joseph P. Hurley of St. Augustine, Florida, who in a July 6, 1941 radiobroadcast

30. Doenecke, *In Danger Undaunted*, 138–41, 433–36; Flynn, *Roosevelt and Romanism*, 66, 83, 87, 151.

31. "3,000 Catholic Students Cheer Plea for Peace," *Washington Post*, August 26, 1939, 11.

32. McNeal, "Catholic Conscientious Objection During World War II," 229.

33. A 1939 nationwide poll asked, "If you had to choose between Fascism and Communism, which would you choose?" Sixty-six percent of American Catholics chose fascism, and conversely sixty-seven percent of Jews chose communism. See Dinnerstein, *Antisemitism in America*, 113.

34. Quoted in Flynn, *Roosevelt and Romanism*, 68.

35. Quoted in Allitt, *Catholic Intellectuals and Conservative Politics in America*, 25.

voiced support for American participation in the war and the lending of arms to the Russians.[36] Hurley considered the chief foe of the Church to be Nazism and not communism, though later he would be an ardent opponent of the latter as well. By late 1941, the opinions of Beckman and McNicholas on American intervention in the war had diverged. The archbishop of Cincinnati authored a pastoral letter, at the request of the Holy See, stating that because of certain political and military exigencies, it was necessary to distinguish between the Russian state and the Russian people. The encyclical, *Divini Redemptoris*, was not to be understood as a condemnation of all cooperation with Russia. "We must not . . . identify the Russian people with the Soviet government," McNicholas wrote. "There are millions of poor, simple, God-fearing Russians who hate the atheistic Communism of their government and who pray incessantly for their deliverance."[37]

Beckman, however, could not support what he deemed to be a false separation between the Soviet state and its communist-backed military forces. There should be no "unholy merger of Christianity and communism under the guise of military necessity," he wrote.[38] In early 1942, the Holy See's apostolic delegate to America, Amleto Cicognani, asked Beckman to refrain from public statements opposing the war or the Roosevelt administration because they threatened to create "disunity" among American Catholics.[39] Beckman's anticommunist stance, if not that of the Crusade, showed itself to be more severe than the Vatican and the majority of the United States bishops.

ORDER, GOD-GIVEN RIGHTS, AND DEMOCRACY

Concern for Catholics suffering under communist regimes reached its height in the decade following World War II. The Crusade continued its denunciation of Russia and communism in *The Shield*. By the mid-1940s the magazine was regularly publishing an "Interpretations" section, a series of articles commenting on national and international events, often

36. Fogarty, *The Vatican and the American Hierarchy*, 272–73. For the text of the message see Avella and McKeown, *Public Voices*, 164–67.

37. John T. McNicholas, "Columbus Day Address" (12 October 1942) in Avella and McKeown, *Public Voices*, 174.

38. Francis J. L. Beckman, "Congressmen: Be Warned" (27 July 1941) in Avella and McKeown, *Public Voices*, 168.

39. Flynn, *Roosevelt and Romanism*, 170–71, 189.

choosing topics such as the United Nations and international politics. *The Shield* also reported on the dangers of communism in its "World-Wide Problems of the Living-Church" series.[40] The most frequent contributors of anticommunist articles were Rev. William O. Labodie (1901–1974), a priest of the Cincinnati Archdiocese, and Raymond J. Wilson, Jr., (1918–1976),[41] a layman with a military background. Beyond the articles found in *The Shield*, the Crusade also sponsored the publication of various booklets including Raymond J. Wilson's *Communism: A Catholic Survey* (published in 1949 and later reprinted as *Communism in Five Hours*), and a work edited by J. Paul Spaeth, *Perspectives in Religion and Culture* (1957), aiming to model a Catholic approach to religious pluralism while including a forceful denunciation of communism and other dangerous "isms."

Though at the war's conclusion some American Catholics were hopeful that Russia would not force communism upon its neighbors and the United Nations would be successful in securing a lasting peace, *The Shield* expressed little of that hope. The Crusade leadership still saw storm clouds brewing in the horizon. While celebrating the silver anniversary of the Crusade in 1944, Bishop Francis A. Thill, longtime secretary of the Crusade, commented on America's decline during the period. He stated that America had just witnessed "the period of our national hypocrisy." "Organized atheism, the revival of the ancient paganism that defies the State, the attack on public morality, and the repudiation of private responsibility," Thill continued, "are some of the really bad things for which our world even now is paying a horrid price."[42] Thill later called communism pagan and even satanic: "the devil's gambit being played on the chessboard of contemporary world affairs by the evil men

---

40. See "Apostolate of Printer's Ink," *The Shield* 25.5 (1946) 22, 24 for a discussion of the general aim and format of *The Shield* during this period.

41. Wilson was born in Cincinnati, Ohio, on May 21, 1918. He attended St. Xavier High School and Xavier University, graduating from college in 1940. While there, he participated in ROTC and was commissioned in the U.S. Army as an artillery officer upon graduation. He resigned from the army in 1945 to enter the University of Cincinnati Law School. During his time as a law student, he supported his wife and children by working full time as an assistant editor for the *The Shield*. He died September 2, 1976 in Clearwater, Florida. Sources include an interview with Raymond J. Wilson III, of Dubuque, Iowa (3 June 2004) and Wilson's obituary in *The Cincinnati Post*, September 16, 1976.

42. "Crusade Jubilee," *The Shield* 23.8 (1944) 3.

of the Kremlin."⁴³ Thill saw a world in disarray, not one "saved" through an alliance between Russia and the United States during World War II.

The primary role of the CSMC in battling communism during the mid-1940s was in educating young people about its principles. By 1946, denunciations of communism were frequent and pointed. Rev. William Labodie wrote that finally Americans seemed willing "to deal realistically with Russia." "No more rose-colored glasses," he wrote, after explaining the true totalitarian character of Russia and its program for world domination.⁴⁴ A 1946 article claimed that for at least ten years the Crusade had been studying communism, the teachings of Marx, and the "machinations of communist propaganda." The Crusade recommended "the practice of the spiritual and corporal works of mercy and the exercise of voluntary poverty" as the means of defeating communism.⁴⁵

Catholics reacted so forcefully to communism, in part, because it was a "sin" against one of the most important virtues of Catholicism: order. The Catholic worldview, especially influenced by scholasticism and the neo-Thomistic revival, prized an ordered and integrated culture united through its understanding of nature. Socialism and communism were seen as radical movements and as anti-Catholic if not anti-religious. The Crusade book, *Communism: A Catholic Survey*, opened with the simple phrase: "Communism is incurably revolutionary."⁴⁶ The only logical outcome of communism was the collapse of government, disintegration of security forces and military defense, and the rise of worldwide anarchy.

Rights language was also employed by the CSMC in its battle against communism. Labodie, associate editor of *The Shield*, wrote, "The Russian system does not recognize God and therefore recognizes no God-given rights. Instead of rights, the citizen has only favors, grants, or privileges, conferred on him by the State." The article continued, "[R]ights are not conferred or granted by the Constitution which recognizes and states them—they existed before the Constitution, and they cannot be changed or revoked by the government. Our American freedoms have their source

---

43. Frank Thill, "Light New Candles!" *The Shield* 30 (1950) 5.

44. William Labodie, "Interpretations: America Awakens to the Communist Menace," *The Shield* 26 (October 1946) 15–16.

45. J. Paul Spaeth, "A World to Know," *The Shield* 25.4 (1946) 24. See "Resolutions of The Tenth Crusade Convention, Cleveland, Ohio, 1937," CSMC, box 1, folder 29, AAC, 19.

46. Wilson, *Communism: A Catholic Survey*, 1.

in the God-given rights which the Constitution recognizes."[47] The CSMC portrayed communism as an enemy of order, the Catholic virtue *par excellence*, as well as democracy, the paramount American attribute. "The communist war in China is the same war that communism has waged in other parts of the world—a struggle against established law and government, a war of tyranny against the spread of true democracy," stated one article.[48] According to the Crusade, communism was dangerous because of its degenerate view of the world encompassing God and society.

A BATTLE FOR SOULS: COMMUNISM IN CHINA

The Shield, which had at first attacked communism broadly, soon shifted its focus to particular countries in which the Church was suffering under communist influence. By the late 1940s and early 1950s the communist threat in China captivated the minds of American Catholics. Beginning with the sending of the first American Catholic missionaries to China at the end of World War I, the Far East presented an unusual allure for Catholics. Numerous orders sent American missionaries to China, most notably the Society of St. Columban and the Maryknoll order. As one of the most populous nations in the world, China represented the most important frontier for Catholic foreign missions during the first half of the twentieth century.[49]

A Benedictine priest in China, Rev. Thaddeus Yang (1905–1982),[50] was a frequent contributor to *The Shield*. A convert from Buddhism to Catholicism, Yang saw the situation in China as one of the most important political and spiritual struggles of the twentieth century. As late as 1945, Yang wrote that it was uncertain whether China would become a Christian power or a bastion of paganism. At that time, China was home to 3.5 million Catholics, many of whom were optimistic that China would remain a land fertile for the preaching of the Gospel message.[51]

---

47. William Labodie, "Interpretations: Foreign Policies and Peace," *The Shield* 25.3 (1945) 11.

48. "Peace in the Orient," *The Shield* 25.4 (January 1946) 13.

49. Dries, *The Missionary Movement*, 112–22.

50. Yang came to the United States in 1955 to found a new monastery in the Archdiocese of Los Angeles. See Endres, "The Legacy of Thaddeus Yang," 23–28.

51. Thaddeus Yang, "China's Future and—America's . . ." *The Shield* 25 (1945).

Following the founding of the communist-led People's Republic of China in late 1949, numerous missionaries were expelled, imprisoned, or killed. Nearly all Catholic missionaries were repatriated by 1953.[52] Near the end of 1953, *The Shield* lamented the loss of the Chinese missions, recording the large number killed by the communists: 125 Chinese priests, thirty-seven missionary priests (including two Americans), more than thirty laymen, and numerous brothers, sisters, and seminarians. More than 3,000 missioners had been expelled and more than 850 priests and bishops had been imprisoned. Among those Catholic institutions confiscated were three universities, 200 high schools, and 200 hospitals.[53] The CSMC vivified these statistics by detailing the circumstances of many persecuted missionaries. For instance, in an article, "Prayer Was Their Crime," the magazine described the deaths of Trappist monks beaten and killed by Chinese communists. Thirty-one Trappists out of a community of seventy-five were martyred. The article concluded, "Prayer for these souls, and penance for their sins and our own, are the means we can all use to stop the advance of Communism and to save the world."[54] Such stories were meant to edify the faithful and highlight the sacrifices sometimes demanded of the Christian.

The CSMC employed its spiritual and educational weapons against the communists in China. One appeal for prayer came from Clifford King, S.V.D., the founder of the CSMC and a missionary in China. Father King wrote that the outlook was grim: "Within the last eighteen months the communists have, in fact, succeeded in virtually ruining our Catholic missionary enterprise in more than twenty dioceses." As he saw it, intense prayer was the only possible remedy.[55] Appeals for prayer continued and on October 3, 1948, the CSMC sponsored a national day of prayer for China.[56] *The Shield* highlighted the situation in China in most issues of the magazine published from 1946 through 1953. Despite these efforts the mission to China collapsed abruptly and brutally. Many within the Church, and particularly the Crusade, lamented that the situation in China

---

52. Dries, *The Missionary Movement*, 115.
53. "Panorama of Persecution: China, 1946–1953," *The Shield* 33.3 (1953) 7.
54. "Prayer Was Their Crime," *The Shield* 33.2 (1953).
55. "Red-Plagued China Appeals for Prayer," *The Shield* 26.7 (1947) 9.
56. Catholic Students' Mission Crusade, *Crusade Leader Book* (Cincinnati, Ohio: Catholic Students' Mission Crusade, 1949), 108, CSMC, box 14, folder 5, AAC.

had not been taken seriously until the entire country had succumbed to communism.[57]

BROTHERS, SISTERS, MARTYRS: CATHOLICS BEHIND THE IRON CURTAIN

The second major front of American Catholic concern for communism was in Eastern Europe. The Crusade was deeply concerned about Catholics suffering under communist regimes, especially the imprisonment and torture of foreign missionaries and bishops.[58] A frequent theme in *Shield* articles, particularly from 1944 to 1947, was the need for solidarity with those who were suffering and the need for Americans to object to government persecution of Catholics. In doing so, the CSMC was largely following the path of American Catholic protest that occurred in the 1920s and 1930s at the time of the Spanish Civil War and the church-state conflict in Mexico. Concern for their persecuted co-religionists spread to include Estonia, Latvia, Lithuania, Poland, Romania, Bulgaria, Yugoslavia, and Albania. All of these nations were either absorbed or were controlled through Russian "puppet governments" by 1946. Soviet imperialism also exerted a powerful influence on such nations as Hungary, Austria, Czechoslovakia, and the Netherlands. The CSMC condemned "Russian imperialism" for imposing communism "not by the acceptance of communist doctrines, not by free elections, but by the might of Russian armies, armed minorities, planted fifth columns, forced trade agreements, and one-party elections."[59]

Specific examples of Russian aggression and the mistreatment of Catholics in Eastern Europe abounded. By 1945, it had become clear that Stalin would not allow for free elections in Poland, despite promising it at the Yalta Conference. *The Shield* stated, "Poland's story is one of the greatest betrayals in history."[60] American Catholics felt a keen sense of being deceived by the American government as it became evident that Poland would fall to communist rule. Labodie called the situation in Poland "a

57. See "The Gutting and Destruction of a Battered Church," in Breslin, *China, American Catholicism, and the Missionary*, 89–105.

58. For a comparison, see the Catholic War Veterans' response to communist persecution in Eastern Europe in O'Connor, "Defenders of the Faith," 42–50.

59. William Labodie, "Interpretations: Russia's Policy of Imperialism," *The Shield* 25.4 (1946) 10–12.

60. Ibid., 10.

story of broken treaties, ruthless aggression, and persecution of millions of innocent people." He viewed the Church as the only independent voice for freedom in Poland that could not be silenced through the efforts of secret police, totalitarianism, and the forces of dechristianization.[61]

Tensions flared further when the Yugoslavian archbishop, Alojzije Stepinac, was imprisoned in September 1946.[62] Two years later, the Hungarian prelate Josef Cardinal Mindszenty was arrested, becoming, perhaps, the most notorious Catholic symbol of the evils of communism. New York's Archbishop Francis Spellman was particularly influential in promoting the injustice of Mindszenty's captivity.[63] *The Shield* rallied around Stepinac and Mindszenty as examples of "living martyrdom" and criticized the grounds for their imprisonment and the method of their trials.[64] Through its protest of Soviet intervention in Eastern Europe, the CSMC hoped in some small way to bring about religious freedom for the millions of Catholics in countries behind the Iron Curtain.

SPIRITUAL WARFARE: MARIAN APPARITIONS AND ANTICOMMUNISM

While there were domestic and political motivations at work in battling communism, there were also spiritual reasons for opposing its spread. As historian Patrick Carey has observed, many American Catholics "saw their anticommunism as an apocalyptic religious crusade against a diabolical force that could be driven out only by prayer, fasting, and divine intervention."[65] Marian piety as exhibited in the mid-twentieth century became tied to the struggle against communism and was closely related to the numerous apparitions of Mary that were believed to have taken place throughout the world. There were more than one hundred apparitions reported in the United States and Europe in the decade following World War II. These appearances of the Blessed Virgin shared a common theme: prayer and reparation were needed to overcome the threat of athe-

61. William Labodie, "Interpretations: The Baltic States," *The Shield* 26.5 (1947) 17; William Labodie, "Interpretations: Poland," *The Shield* 26.4 (1947) 17.

62. For the background see Gallagher, "The United States and the Vatican in Yugoslavia," 118–44.

63. Cooney, *The American Pope*, 161–68; Powers, *Not Without Honor*, 194, 227.

64. "Our Brothers Behind the Iron Curtain," *The Shield* 30.2 (1950) 33; James E. Sherman, "You Might Be a Martyr," *The Shield* 30.8 (1951) 6.

65. Carey, *The Roman Catholics in America*, 87.

istic communism. Russia could be converted and universal peace could be achieved or the world could drift into neo-paganism if the Blessed Mother's commands went unheeded.[66]

Nearly every Marian apparition from Lourdes, France to Fatima, Portugal to the American apparition at Necedah, Wisconsin, was appealed to in the rhetoric of Catholic anticommunism. The message of Mary at Fatima, however, served as the centerpiece of the movement's Marian thrust. In 1917 the Blessed Mother appeared to three children near the town of Fatima. According to one of the visionaries, Mary had asked that Russia be consecrated to her Immaculate Heart and that Catholics receive communion on the first Saturday of each month. The Church took this charge seriously. Groups such as the Blue Army of Fatima and the Catholic Daughters of America promoted Mary's message and the importance of spiritual combat against communism.[67] The "Leonine prayers" said at the conclusion of every low Mass beginning in 1934 were offered for the conversion of Russia.

Though the link between Marian piety and anticommunism was not a frequent theme found in *The Shield*, it was occasionally mentioned in the magazine's pages. The CSMC-sponsored publication, *Communism: A Catholic Survey*, encouraged prayer, especially recitation of the rosary, as the primary means of combating communism and asked young people to become familiar with the message of Our Lady of Fatima.[68] An article in *The Shield* in 1950 stressed that the world could only be saved from communism by "prayers, sacrifices, and penances"—all commanded by Mary when she appeared at Lourdes, France (1858), Fatima, Portugal (1917), Lipa, Philippines (1948), and elsewhere.[69]

Among the pamphlets and books listed as suitable for CSMC members to send to the foreign missions were those concerning Marian apparitions: William Thomas Walsh's *Our Lady of Fatima* (1947) and James P. O'Reilly's *The Story of La Salette* (1953).[70] While Walsh only alluded to Russia briefly at the beginning and end of his work, the themes of

---

66. See Cadegan, "The Queen of Peace in the Shadow of War," 1–15, Kselman and Avella, "Marian Piety and the Cold War in the United States," 403–24.

67. See O'Connor, "Defenders of the Faith," 82–83.

68. Wilson, *Communism: A Catholic Survey*, 115.

69. Mary Florence Walsh, "The Holy Year and the Collegian," *The Shield* 30 (1950) 20.

70. *The Shield* 33.6 (1954) 14.

conversion, reparation, and its link to the political situation of Europe is clear. According to Walsh, the Blessed Mother appeared to the children at Fatima in order to change the course of history. Mary foretold the Bolshevik Revolution, the Second World War, and according to Walsh the "menace that Marxism offers to the entire world." She stated that if her wishes were followed Russia would be converted and the world would know peace. Otherwise, Walsh claimed, "every country in the world would be scourged and enslaved" by communism. Indeed, Walsh concluded, "[t]he future of our civilization, our liberties, our very existence may depend upon the acceptance of her commands."[71]

The Crusade's founder, Clifford King, S.V.D., believed the CSMC itself to be an indispensable force in the conversion of Russia as predicted at the Fatima apparitions. King recalled that the founding of the Crusade "almost exactly coincided with that of Our Lady's last appearance at Fatima." King continued,

> From the moment I first realized the remarkable coincidence . . . I have felt an interior certainty that Our Blessed Lady, even at the time of her Fatima appearances, had taken note of our Crusade in embryo and was planning eventually to commission our CSMC as her front-line troops for the purpose of . . . a great campaign of prayer, penance and sacrifice, aimed at bringing about the conversion of Russia.[72]

The Crusade was not unlike other anticommunist Catholic movements of the period, employing the messages of the Blessed Mother to highlight that the battle against communism was a spiritual war, not just a political and ideological campaign.[73]

THE RETURN TO ASIA

By the early 1950s attention by *The Shield* to Eastern Europe began to fade. The magazine began to refocus on communism in Asia, namely in China, Korea, Vietnam, Japan, and India. The campaign against communism in Korea took on renewed importance after communist North Korea invaded South Korea on June 25, 1950. The CSMC national convention held in 1950 included the drafting of a special pledge that crusader members

---

71. Walsh, *Our Lady of Fatima*, v, ix, 226–27.
72. Clifford J. King, "'Russia Will Be Converted,'" *The Shield* 37.4 (1958) 4.
73. Powers, *Not Without Honor*, 276.

"pray daily for the return of peace to the Catholic Church in Korea and for all its leaders and children during the present crisis in that country."[74]

The CSMC was also concerned with the state of Vietnam's 1.5 million Catholics. It supported the Vietnamese Nationalists and Ngo Dinh Diem, a Catholic leader backed by the United States government. In opposition to the communists and their leader Ho Chi Minh, Diem gained control in South Vietnam in 1954 and received strong support from the American hierarchy, especially the powerful Cardinal Archbishop of New York, Francis Spellman. Americans became aware of the situation in Vietnam through the popular book, *Deliver Us from Evil* (1956), written by American Catholic Dr. Thomas Dooley, a medical doctor serving in Southeast Asia, who provided a firsthand account of the struggle of Vietnamese Catholics against the communists.[75]

Unable to influence significant numbers abroad because of communist influence in Asia, the Crusade initiated programs to educate foreign students studying in the United States. One integral component to the Crusade battle against communism in Asia was sponsoring letter exchanges and seminars for foreign students whose home countries were threatened by communism.[76] At the 1952 CSMC national convention, the membership decided to promote a series of "seminars on the Christian apostolate" targeted at students from the Far East. The seminars, lasting for five or six days, were an opportunity for intensive training in the lay apostolate with the goal of sustaining the faith in countries where clergy had been expelled or imprisoned by the communists. The first such meeting was held at Seton Hall University, South Orange, New Jersey and resulted in the formation of the Chinese Catholic Students' Society, the Japanese Catholic Students in America and CSMC affiliation with the already existing Vietnamese Catholic Students in America. By 1954, the seminars had expanded to incorporate African and Latin American students studying in America.[77] The CSMC believed that both Americans

---

74. Peter Ryang, "Korean Catholics Ready for a New Start," *The Shield* 30.3 (1950) 13.

75. Cooney, *The American Pope*, 240–45; Fisher, *Dr. America*, 34–89.

76. "The CSMC Reports on the War Years," *The Shield* 26.5 (1947) 21.

77. Edward A. Freking, "CSMC National Center Reports," *The Shield* 33.4 (1954) 19; "Vietnam to America," *The Shield* 34.1 (1954) 9, 32–33. See also E. A. Freking, "Program for Foreign Students," *America* 98 (March 8, 1958) 659–61; and Edward A. Freking, "A Report on the Apostolate for Foreign Students in the United States," June 14, 1955,

and international students could profit from the exchange by fostering mutual understanding between cultures, discussing the weaknesses of the communist ideology, and preparing for apostolic action in the face of regimes hostile to religion.[78] Convinced that the opposition between the Church and communists in various countries in Asia, Latin America, and Africa would be a lingering reality, the Crusade sought subtle means of influencing the religious-political situation in communist-influenced nations.

WAGING INTELLECTUAL WAR ON COMMUNISM

In the face of communist interference in the work of the Church in Asia and Eastern Europe, the CSMC attempted to battle communism through education and activism both at home and internationally. The anticommunist program was described as "partly intellectual and partly practical action" but all efforts were "essentially apostolic." The CSMC asked that all members "engage in a special kind of apologetics"—not so much a defense of certain theological tenets of the faith but an effort to combat the modern philosophical errors that inspired communism. The end result, according to *The Shield*, would be "a more articulate attitude on the part of the body of educated Catholics, so that they would make their influence felt in the public press, in radio forums, in lecture halls, and wherever it is possible to present truth in opposition to error."[79]

By 1948 the CSMC devoted much of its apologetical efforts to the defeat of communism and its pernicious antecedent: secularism. At the 1948 Crusade convention held at the University of Notre Dame the membership agreed to engage in an intellectual apostolate against communism. Termed the "Intellectual Relief Campaign," the movement sought to

---

CSMC, box 29, folder 1, AAC.

78. A study conducted in 1955–1956 measured the impact of the CSMC in fostering international understanding in one school, St. Mary's High School, Columbus, Ohio. The attitudes of students toward peoples from Africa, India, China, Russia, and the Philippines were measured before and after participation in Crusade educational activities. The study found a slight positive change in attitudes. Not surprisingly the most pronounced and entrenched distaste for any people was seen in American attitudes toward Russia. See Gaffney, "A Study of the Use of the Materials of the Catholic Students' Mission Crusade," 24–26.

79. James N. Lunn, "New Programs for a College Apostolate," *The Shield* 27.7 (1948) 7–8.

defeat secularism and communism through the printing and distribution of Catholic literature, particularly among youth in mission lands.

Issues of *The Shield* often included lists of organizations involved in the distribution of Catholic literature (where either literature or donations could be sent) and an inventory of particular titles that had been requested. These lists reveal that the majority of mission contacts desiring literature were in China, India, Japan, and the Philippines. However, there were also contacts listed for such unlikely places as Denmark as well as in the "home mission" states of Mississippi and Texas. The list of suitable books and pamphlets included a mix of religious materials and those representing the "classics" of Western Civilization. For instance, works by Catholic authors Yves Congar, Etienne Gilson, James Keller, Thomas Merton, and Fulton Sheen were listed alongside the writings of Aquinas, Virgil, Homer, and Shakespeare.[80] The cost of the booklets typically ranged from twenty-five to fifty cents per copy.[81] Few, if any, of the books were expressly anticommunist. Each, however, was geared toward the cultivation of a well-formed intellect, one able to combat the philosophical and political errors of the age.

The greatest concentration of "intellectual relief" efforts was in China. The Catholic Truth Society of Hong Kong was the principal gateway for publications that could be routed into "Red China." By 1949 the Catholic Truth Society had printed 150,000 pamphlets on the Church and social questions and was coordinating the publication of the *China Missionary Bulletin*.[82] However, donations were soon depleted and the Catholic Truth Society was forced to halt its efforts. J. Paul Spaeth, director of activities for the CSMC, wrote that the failure of the society represented the loss of a great opportunity for the Church in China and that if Crusade members had been able to sacrifice to provide only $3,000 for the organization, it could have continued its work.[83]

---

80. See, for instance, *The Shield* 33.6 (1954) 14.

81. Eugene Willging and Raphael Brown, "Small Arms in the Battle of Books," *The Shield* 33.6 (1954) 13. See also Willging, "The Mission Book Apostolate," 77, 89; and Spaeth, "Books for the World," 82–85.

82. Eleanor E. Waters, "Intellectual Relief Campaign: We Can Still Help China," *The Shield* 29.3 (1949) 19–20.

83. J. Paul Spaeth, "Lost: A Great Opportunity in China," *The Shield* 30.7 (1951) 14–15.

By the early 1950s, the "Intellectual Relief Campaign" had been replaced by a nearly identical crusader activity: "The Battle of the Books." Spearheaded by Eugene Willging, director of libraries at The Catholic University of America, the CSMC maintained a master file of suitable literature with contacts in the mission field where materials could be sent. It emphasized that it was not only a question of providing Catholic literature to missionary peoples but a strategic attempt to overshadow and outnumber the propaganda of the enemy. *The Shield* reported, "Communists are flooding Asia and Africa with cheap popular books that are poisoning the minds of millions against Christianity."[84] It was assumed by the crusaders that the message of communist books could be resisted if Christian tracts were only available.

Closely related to the campaign for intellectual relief was a new emphasis on molding the minds of American Catholic youth to resist the lure of modern errors. Beginning in November 1946 *The Shield* initiated a new series of articles called the "Philosopher's Apostolate" written by Vincent E. Smith, professor of philosophy at The Catholic University of America and later at the University of Notre Dame.[85] The series attempted to attack the philosophical underpinnings of communism by highlighting the errors of modern philosophy. In 1950 *The Shield* introduced a series of articles written by Smith as an attempt "to reveal secularism's underpinnings."[86] The goal of the articles was "to give Catholic philosophy students an understanding of the oppositions which they will encounter from various sources of influence." Smith devoted much of his efforts to striking at modern thinkers: Sigmund Freud, Albert Einstein, Vladimir Lenin, Jean Paul Sartre, and John Dewey, among others. In Smith's article on Lenin, he called Lenin a "discontented radical" and "atheist" who "preached his atheism by the sword." His was a flawed philosophy made worse by the coercive force utilized by the Russians.[87] By the end of the

---

84. Willging and Brown, "Small Arms in the Battle of Books," 13.

85. Vincent Edward Smith (1915–?), in addition to being a professor, was president of the American Catholic Philosophical Association and editor of the association's journal, *The New Scholasticism*, from 1948 through 1965. His works include *Idea-Men of Today*, *Philosophical Physics*, and *Footnotes for the Atom*.

86. Vincent Edward Smith, "The Logic of Secularism," *The Shield* 30.1 (1950) 17.

87. Vincent Edward Smith, "Lenin: An Agitator with a Philosophy," *The Shield* 31.3 (1951) 19.

series in 1954, Smith had even taken aim at the "mechanical brain" (known to us today as the computer).[88]

Yet Smith was not only concerned with uncovering error, he also propagated a distinctive intellectual vision for American Catholics: scholasticism. As mentioned earlier, scholasticism was an intellectual system based loosely on the thought of St. Thomas Aquinas that defined for Catholics notions of the natural law, unity, and order. Scholasticism became normative in the Catholic worldview, reigning as the primary model taught in every Catholic institution of higher education.[89] Smith and the CSMC held that if understood properly the scholastic method could equip the mind to defend itself from the lure of communism.

DEFYING THE LIMITS OF MCCARTHYISM

The thrust of the CSMC's anticommunist program coincided with the height of anticommunism in America, yet its emphasis differed sharply from much of American anticommunist rhetoric. While American anticommunism in the early 1950s seemed to be dominated by the figure of Joseph McCarthy, the CSMC seemed to take little notice of the Catholic senator from Wisconsin.[90] *The Shield* contained no reference to McCarthy's focus on the domestic infiltration of communists that led to the push for an investigation of suspected subversives in the federal government. The concerns that dominated this reactionary strand of anticommunism were not those of the Crusade. The CSMC was interested not with conspiracies and secret networks but rather was stirred by a real and vigorous persecution of the international Church. By the mid-1950s, McCarthyism had been discredited in the eyes of many and anticommunism was becoming less of a preoccupation for American Catholics even as the international situation did not improve.

---

88. Vincent Edward Smith, "The Mechanical Brain and Its Limitations," *The Shield* 31.7 (1952) 25.

89. Gleason, *Contending with Modernity*, 105–23.

90. For American Catholic reaction to McCarthyism see Crosby, *God, Church, and Flag*, 228–51; De Santis, "American Catholics and McCarthyism," 1–30. Catholics in general registered slightly higher support for McCarthy than other Americans, though McCarthy had Catholic critics of his anticommunist methods, if not his goals. See Crosby, "The Angry Catholics"; Crosby, "The Jesuits and Joe McCarthy," 374–88, Grant, "Bishop Bernard J. Sheil's Condemnation of Senator Joseph R. McCarthy," 43–50.

During the 1940s and 1950s the anticommunist impulse within the CSMC evolved. What began as an intensely "philosophical" battle had embraced new strategies, promoting direct action more than strictly intellectual or spiritual formation. This activism took the form of letter writing, promotion of political participation, and encouragement for Catholic youth to accept positions of leadership and service within the Church and outside of it.[91] The focus on education of youth, a hallmark of the CSMC's anticommunism activities continued, yet it was increasingly in terms of cultural understanding and even a focus on developing organizations led by foreign students themselves. The Crusade's anticommunist activities indicate that a significant number of Catholics in America were not alarmist McCarthyites influenced by thinly-supported fears of subversives operating in their midst, but instead were chiefly influenced by accounts of the suffering of the worldwide Church.

AN ANTIDOTE TO SECULARISM AND COMMUNISM: CHURCH VOCATIONS

During the 1940s and 1950s, the Crusade increased its efforts to promote vocations to the priesthood and religious life and later vocations as lay missionaries. As a component of its quest to Christianize the world and maintain the strength of the Church at home, vocations had always been a priority. Yet the perception of communist "recruiting" and encroaching secularism, caused the Crusade to rally for leaders who could imbue the world with the sacred. The post-war Crusade sought for and prayed for an explosion in the number of vocations to the priesthood and religious life and its prayers were answered. More seminaries and houses of religious formation were built between 1945 and 1965 than in the entire history of the Church in America previously.[92] Crusaders themselves responded in large numbers. The Crusade Conference of Clerics and Religious at Catholic University was particularly active in the promotion of priestly and religious vocations beginning in 1943. In launching a "Vocations Crusade," the conference members utilized Catholic newspapers and magazines. Members wrote dozens of vocation essays and fictional short

---

91. Wilson, *Communism: A Catholic Survey*, 108–12. Refer to the CSMC's opposition to China's admittance to the United Nations in Edward A. Freking, "No Debate on Red China," *The Shield* 34.2 (1954) 19, 24.

92. Kauffman, "Formation of American Identities," 146.

stories, appearing in three-dozen Catholic publications. Their work included the popular "C.S.M.C. Vocations Corner" that consisted of thirty articles published in *Our Sunday Visitor*.[93] Crusade-sponsored publications included *The Guidepost: Religious Vocation Manual for Young Men*, compiled by the Catholic University Conference of Clerics and Religious (1948), and *A Missionary Index of Catholic Americans*, containing the names of missionary Catholic priests and religious serving outside the country. Six editions of the directory were published during the 1940s.

Beginning in the mid-1950s the Crusade began to expand its vision of the missionary. No longer limited to religious priests, brothers and sisters, the Crusade's view began to include the idea of the lay apostolate in mission work.[94] Prior to the 1950s lay involvement was seen as chiefly a support role for the missions—prayer, study and sacrifice on the home front. Their role as auxiliaries was transformed in the 1950s, influenced by developments in society and the Church. Pope Pius XII's encyclical on missions, *Evangelii Praecones* (1951) and Pope John XXIII's *Princeps Pastorum* (1959) both urged a greater role for laity in mission lands, especially indigenous peoples.[95] By the mid-1950s *The Shield* included occasional articles urging young men and women to chose an extra-ecclesial vocation, yet in the service of Christ and the Church. For instance, the editors encouraged youth to consider the apostolates of teaching, government work, the foreign service, or even work with the United Nations.[96]

NEW FRONTIERS IN LATIN AMERICA AND AFRICA

While Asia and Eastern Europe were the primary focus of the Crusade during the 1920s through 1940s, the mission to Latin America and later

---

93. Brady, "The Clerical Conference and Vocations.".

94. Joe Shelzi, "What Future for Mr. and Mrs. In the Missions?" *The Shield* 35.5 (1956) 7, 29–30; "Lay Auxiliaries," *The Shield* 36.5 (1957) 6, 31; "Lay Auxiliaries Move Forward," *The Shield* 37.3 (1958) 6–7, 31.

95. For the texts of these encyclical letters see "Evangelii Praecones," in Carlen, *The Papal Encyclicals* 4:189–202; and "Princeps Pastorum," in Carlen, *The Papal Encyclicals* 5:43–57.

96. See "The Church at Home in Africa," *The Shield* 35.1 (1955) 37–39; "The Kind of Help Latin America Wants," *The Shield* 35.5 (1956) 34–35; "Africa Needs You!" *The Shield* 37.1 (1957) 3–7, 15; "Opportunities for World Service," *The Shield* 34.5 (1955) 17; "Ways to Help in the Lay Apostolate," *The Shield* 41.2 (1961) 20; Catholic Students' Mission Crusade, *Africa in Five Hours*; Hoffman and Magner, *Latin America*.

Africa became increasingly important.⁹⁷ Though for centuries Catholic missionaries, mainly religious order priests from Europe, had been successfully at work in Latin America, the region was plagued with a chronic need for clergy. In the 1940s Americans arrived to help add to the number of priests in that region and to enact the political goal of preventing the spread of communism. Maryknoll opened its first missions in Latin America in 1942. Interest in Latin America grew among seminarians and priests, resulting in the formation of a society of diocesan priests dedicated to serving the countries of Central and South America. Founded by Archbishop Richard J. Cushing in 1958, the Missionary Society of St. James the Apostle counted more than seventy priests at work by 1962.⁹⁸ Overall the number of American Catholic missionaries climbed from 1,600 in 1950 to 2,400 in 1960.⁹⁹

One of the most important voices in the world mission movement, especially following World War II, was the Rev. John J. Considine, M. M. (1897–1983), an early member of the CSMC. Considine began his long association with the Crusade in 1920 when he was elected to its executive board. Having joined the Maryknoll order in 1915, he was ordained a priest in 1923 and subsequently assigned to a post in Rome within *Propaganda Fide*. Upon returning to the United States in 1934 he began teaching at the Maryknoll Seminary in Ossining, New York and worked with the Mission Education Committee of the National Catholic Educational Association. After a lapse of several years, Considine renewed his association with the Crusade in 1935.¹⁰⁰ Afterwards, he was a frequent contributor to *The Shield* and his other works were frequently cited within its pages.¹⁰¹ Considine helped highlight the need for missionaries in Latin America and Africa through his books, *Call for Forty Thousand* (1946) and *Africa, World of*

---

97. This shift is seen noticeably within the Maryknoll order during the period 1942–1948 in which it rapidly expanded its presence in Latin America. See Breslin, *China, American Catholicism, and the Missionary*, 98.

98. Costello, *Mission to Latin America*, 30–39. For an analysis of the Society of St. James see Garneau, "'Commandos for Christ.'"

99. Costello, *Mission to Latin America*, 39.

100. See Francis J. Beckman, "Report of the National Executive Board, Ninth National Convention, Dubuque, Iowa," August 6, 1935, CSMC, box 48, folder 4, AAC, 6.

101. See, for instance, John J. Considine, "Today's Latin America," *The Shield* 36.2 (1956) 4–5, 14; John J. Considine, "The Church's Global Mission and the Future," *The Shield* 42.2 (1962) 20, 29–31; John J. Considine, "Fighting Fire with Fire," *The Shield* 43.2 (1963–1964) 13, 29–31.

New Men (1954) as well as his work with the Latin America Bureau of the National Catholic Welfare Conference.[102] He popularized the appeal for the Church in America to give ten percent of its priests and religious to the mission in Latin America.

John Considine was a primary advocate of the lay apostolate in the missions, among the chief proponents of the Roman-inspired "Papal Volunteers for Latin America" (PAVLA). Considine worked extensively as a promoter and organizer for the Papal Volunteers as director of the Latin America Bureau of the National Catholic Welfare Conference. It was he who helped introduce the "Papal Volunteers" to those attending the CSMC's national convention in 1960.[103] The Papal Volunteers were meant to expand the work of the lay apostolate in Latin America, augmenting the work of small movements such as The Grail of Loveland, Ohio, Catholics for Latin America, the Association for International Development (AID) based in Paterson, New Jersey, and International Catholic Auxiliaries of Evanston, Illinois. Created in May 1960 by the Pontifical Commission for Latin America, the Papal Volunteers was meant to be an international force of lay men and women serving in teams of three to ten members. The greatest response came from the United States where the Papal Volunteers appeared as a Catholic parallel to the Peace Corps developed under the Kennedy administration, fitting well with the president's call for service: "Ask not what your country can do for you, ask what you can do for your country."[104]

The idea was received well by crusaders who followed PAVLA's activities through *The Shield*.[105] Though the initial response was enthusiastic, the initiative was riddled with problems from the start. Of the nearly one thousand volunteers who in the 1960s committed to two years of service in Latin America, more than half abandoned their commitments early. Poor training, inadequate placements, concern over the clerical oversight of the lay volunteers, as well as confusion over whether the volunteers

---

102. Dries, "The Legacy of John J. Considine, M.M.," 80–84. See also Costello, *Mission to Latin America*, 47–48.

103. "Collegians Accept Challenges of Apostolate," *The Shield* 40.2 (1960) 8–12; "'Papal Volunteers' for the Church in Latin America," *The Shield* 40.2 (1960) 11, 14–15; "The Appeal that Came from Rome," *The Shield* 40.2 (1960) 16–17.

104. Rice, *The Bold Experiment*; "Peace Corps," *The Shield* 40.5 (1961) 23.

105. John J. Considine, "Papal Volunteers: More About Them," *The Shield* 40.3 (1961) 4–5, 21; "PAVLA Progress Report," *The Shield* 40.5 (1961) 7.

were primarily religious missionaries or social workers, frustrated the work of the movement. In May 1971 it was announced that the movement would no longer accept volunteers and its work in Latin America would be phased out over several years.[106] The first large-scale lay mission movement that had attracted volunteers from among the CSMC was officially disbanded.

Despite the difficulties experienced in these missionary efforts, the extension of Crusade concern to Latin America and Africa and efforts to include lay vocations as a valid and needed missionary witness accompanied the highpoint of Crusade activity. The movement counted one million members by the 1950s; its publication, *The Shield,* had a circulation of nearly 30,000 distributed at nearly 1,000 of the nation's Catholic high schools; its national meetings continued to attract upwards of 3,000 participants.[107] The CSMC was experiencing its golden age, well regarded as a seedbed for religious vocations, promoter of the lay apostolate, and fierce foe of communism. The Crusade's agitation with communism and its zeal for "sending" missionaries would yield in the following decade to a new thrust: the quest for renewal and relevance in the Church brought on by the ferment of an ecumenical council, Vatican II.

---

106. Costello, *Mission to Latin America*, 89–102, 138–42, 169–73.

107. James J. Fox to Director of Public Relations, Xavier University, July 15, 1953, Archives of Xavier University, Cincinnati (AXU), box 42, folder 1, RG25/B-15 Catholic Student Mission Crusade Conference folders; "19th CSMC Convention . . . biggest and, maybe, best," *The Shield* 40.2 (1960) 2.

FIVE

Age of Reform

Developments in Mission Theology, 1960–1971

The Catholic Students' Mission Crusade's last decade was marked by the cultural and religious upheaval of the 1960s. The conflict in Vietnam, the civil rights movement and race riots, the beginning of Catholic participation in the ecumenical movement, and the convening of the Second Vatican Council all combined to provide the spark for a dramatic reevaluation of social and ecclesial life. At a time when American Catholics were continuing their cultural trajectory away from a "ghetto-like" existence into the American mainstream, the contours and boundaries of the "mainstream" were becoming more difficult to detect. It seemed perhaps that all was in a state of flux, a dramatic pendulum swing that saw some American Catholics grasping desperately to hang on while others were gleefully enjoying "the ride." Catholic youth were often in the crosshairs of change in the sixties, consciously affected by the draft for Vietnam, the seeds of youthful rebellion, secularist "God is dead" theology, and swift changes within the Catholic educational system.[1]

The mission movement within American Catholicism was affected by these changes. At first glance the 1960s appeared to be the heyday of the Catholic foreign mission movement—the summit of decades of increases in American Catholic money, personnel, and influence. Yet there were obvious signs that divisions in the movement were increasing. Within mission theology and praxis, there was a reevaluation of the missionary ideal brought on by the weakening of colonialism and decline of America's international prestige. In terms of personnel, the number of American

---

1. Gleason, *Keeping the Faith*, 82–96; Ellwood, *The Sixties Spiritual Awakening*; Dolan, *In Search of an American Catholicism*, 191–259; Hennesey, *American Catholics*, 307–31; O'Brien, *Public Catholicism*, 230–42.

Catholics serving in the missions abroad peaked at nearly ten thousand in 1968, up from 6,700 at the beginning of the decade. Yet within four years the number had dropped more than twenty percent—by some two thousand missionaries. Maryknoll, the famed American missionary order of priests and brothers, noted a fifty percent decline in seminary candidates.[2] The number of periodicals published in America for the support of the missions fell from a high of thirty-two to only fourteen by 1971 and many of the remaining magazines were struggling to continue publication.[3] Just below the surface of the booming mission enterprise of the 1960s were serious fissures. As missionaries in the field struggled with their own sense of identity and purpose amid social change, some heralded the age as the "death of the missions," a positive outcome of modernity's progress.

THE FOREIGN MISSIONS REAPPRAISED: CRITICISM AND SELF-CRITICISM

Throughout the nineteenth and early twentieth centuries, the Catholic missionary enterprise was inexorably tied to colonialism. Political hegemony joined with religious zeal to spread the faith among Europe's colonial possessions in Africa and Asia. As the movement for decolonization and self-governance gained momentum between 1945 and 1960, the role of the foreign missions in these countries was reassessed. Though the United States had not been as active in colonization as the European powers, American missionaries abroad and their supporters and contributors shared in the decreasing distrust of missionaries, "foreign" agents representing "the West."[4]

As missionaries were increasingly viewed as suspect, the missionary ideal was reevaluated. The missionary could no longer play the part of the self-righteous and thoroughly patriotic crusader sent to "save souls"

---

2. Dries, *The Missionary Movement*, 273; "Missioners down 20% in 4 years," 5; "The Church in the World," 243. See also Kennelly, "Foreign Missions and the Renewal Movement," 445–63, which claims that a close analysis of mission data "dispels the impression of temporary growth followed by decline" (446). Kennelly notes that in 1990 three mission fields—Africa, Central America, and South America—had larger numbers of American Catholic missionaries than in 1960.

3. Connors, "The Participation of the U.S. Catholic Church in the World-Wide Missionary Effort," 136.

4. For a history of twentieth-century decolonization see Stanley, *Missions, Nationalism, and the End of Empire*; Springhall, *Decolonization Since 1945*; and Holland, *European Decolonization*.

but sought out a more passive role as a somewhat transparent and neutral sojourner charged with preaching the "pure Gospel" with no cultural or national strings attached. Catholics of the 1960s would have been uneasy with the missionary tactics of Father Clifford King, founder of the Crusade, who doled out flood relief in China only to those who planned to convert. Once viewed as healthy paternalism, such ploys were seen at best as religious imperialism or at worst fraud. Driven in part by public opinion toward Americans and foreigners in general, missionaries increasingly saw their role as jumpstarting community development and assisting indigenous churches—not importing an American and Eurocentric faith financed by the contributions of Catholics in America and guided by the unwavering goal to convert as many "pagans" as possible.

The sharp shift in perception of the missions had both concrete social and theological underpinnings. The mission movement had thrived on a Catholic idealism and heroism, especially geared at Catholic youth and capitalized upon by the CSMC. It asked Catholics to make sacrifices for God and country, promising rewards in this life and the next. Missionaries who answered the call to foreign lands received the supreme admiration of their fellow Catholics and were sure to experience the height of adventure as a foreign missioner. By the 1960s the "romance" surrounding the missions had largely depleted as Catholics were quicker to recognize the genuine challenges and hardships of the missionary task. Less confident, idealistic, and romantic, Catholics believed less fervently in the purely sublime mission to convert the nations and often doubted the possibility of missionary success.

While for Europeans the colonial system was wedded to the missionary enterprise, American perceptions of the missions were closely bound to its own form of intervention: political, military, and cultural influence, both covert and less than covert. American opinion of the Catholic foreign mission presence was related to the perception of other American activity abroad, whether under the auspices of the government, religious groups, or others. During the 1950s and 1960s the United States government increased the degree and scope of its international entanglement, attempting to destabilize foreign governments thought unfriendly to American interests, including those in Iran (1953), Guatemala (1954), Egypt (1954), and Laos (1959). As the Cold War between the U.S. and the U.S.S.R. intensified, many throughout the world and at home began to distrust America and its international aims. From nuclear proliferation to the ill-advised invasion of Cuba in 1961, American foreign policy was the subject of intense scrutiny and Americans were increasingly unwilling to defend the actions of their government abroad.

Among the first salvos fired in the attack on American intervention, the publication of *The Ugly American* (1958) by Eugene Burdick and William Lederer exposed what many believed to be the false humanitarianism of the U.S. government.[5] A fictional account with a factual basis, the book exposed the mismanagement of American "aid" efforts in Southeast Asia while painting a picture of some Americans abroad as arrogant and spoiled.[6] The book was wildly popular, going through twenty printings and selling four million copies. The reception of the book was the result of an already high level of popular anxiety about the injurious nature of the United States' foreign policy.

The changing perception of Americans abroad affected the mission movement and the CSMC. It was not a difficult mental step for most to see the "ugly American" as the "ugly missionary"—both sent to propagate a harmful and foreign "doctrine." One *Shield* contributor asked why missionaries appeared as "ugly Americans" to those they were seeking to help. Why did the U.S. "fail to win friends" abroad even as its international aid increased? The author stated that too often foreign aid was not provided out of evangelical motives—love or a sense of true charity—but instead out of national self-interest.[7]

The 1960s witnessed a surge of mission criticism and self-criticism. The missionary enterprise, both Protestant and Catholic, became implicated in the evils of imperialism and cultural violence. Within the same year, 1964, several books criticizing missionary work were published: James A. Scherer's *Missionary, Go Home!*, Ralph Dodge's *The Unpopular Missionary*, and John Carden's *The Ugly Missionary*.[8] Such works illustrated the increasing lack of confidence in the foreign mission enterprise—both its potential for success and its worthiness as a Christian pursuit.[9] As

5. Lederer and Burdick, *The Ugly American*.

6. The "ugly American" himself proves to be an admirable character in the book, though others do not fare as well. See Fisher, *The Catholic Counterculture*, 174–77.

7. Marylyn C. Dolan, "Foreign Relief . . . Love is the Key," *The Shield* 38.5 (1959) 17–18.

8. Bosch, *Transforming Mission*, 2–4.

9. Unlike the Catholic missionary endeavor that seemed unconcerned with "decline" until the 1960s, American Protestants questioned their own mission movement

the decade progressed there was a rising disenchantment with the very idea of the foreign missions.

A 1966 article in *Ramparts* magazine titled "Bishop Sheen and the Great Charity Hoax" took aim at the Society for the Propagation of the Faith and its leader Bishop Fulton J. Sheen. The article claimed that the organization was a fraud and that the funds collected from American Catholics never reached the poor that the society claimed to help. Purporting that the truth about the society was uncovered by a lay missionary serving in East Africa, the article stated that missionary bishops themselves understood that they were being "used": "These prelates are disgusted.... They know that very little of the millions of dollars collected every year by Bishop Sheen's office ever reaches the poor." Claiming that the corruption spanned from top to bottom, including the missionaries, the article stated that some corrupt missionary priests preached about the necessity of the Christian sacraments and then sold "tickets" to be used for the reception of baptism and penance.[10]

Among the most outspoken Catholic critics of the missions was then-Monsignor Ivan Illich, a New York priest, a director of a language school for U.S. missionaries in Cuernavaca, Mexico, and a commentator for *The Shield*. He argued that too many American missionaries were only "apostolic tourists" who were not benefiting those they attempted to serve. Without recognizing that they were "guests" among indigenous peoples, the missionaries were doing more harm than good.[11] His criticism of American missionary practice continued in an *America* magazine article titled "The Seamy Side of Charity."[12] Illich asked his readers to "coldly examine the American Church's outburst of charitable frenzy" which he said had resulted in the misguided efforts of the foreign missionaries. In his scathing critique of American Catholic efforts in Latin America, he harshly described missionaries as those who filled the "role of a colonial power's lackey chaplain." He asked them to "humbly accept the possibility that they [were] useless or even harmful" and that the

---

beginning in the 1920s. See, for instance, Wacker, "The Waning of the Missionary Impulse," 191–205. For a study of the later "decline" of Protestant missions see Lebhar, "Why Did the Yankees Go Home?" 27–43.

10. Colaianni, "Bishop Sheen and the Great Charity Hoax," 6, 8.

11. "Lay Mission Apostles: Are They Getting Anywhere?" *The Shield* 41.4 (1962) 12.

12. Ivan Illich, "The Seamy Side of Charity," *America* 116.3 (1967) 88–91; reprinted in Costello, *Mission to Latin America*, 283–89.

foreign mission movement had actually "wasted the lives of young men and women dedicated to the task of evangelization."[13] In his eyes, American missionaries were paternalistic foreigners and meddlers, not envoys of the Gospel message but heralds of a corrupt political system.

At first the criticism of Illich and others was not taken seriously and was generally rebuffed within the ranks of the Church and its missionaries. The critiques seemed to lack any instructive quality and their approach was seen as non-missionaries taking "cheap shots" at missionaries. Peter Hebblethwaite, S.J., in his 1967 article, "Why Missions?" wrote, "There is no more distressing experience for the men in the front line than to be shot at from behind by their own artillery. Many missionaries, bearing the heat and burden of the day, feel just this way about the efforts of theologians writing from the comfortable seclusion of their studies." In recognizing a certain tension between the missionaries themselves and progressive theologians who often lacked first-hand experience of the mission field, Hebblethwaite wrote, "It is not a simple opposition between the men of action and the men of study, since the theology of the missions is closely related to missionary activity." Criticizing the missions, he wrote, naturally caused missionaries to believe their work was being undervalued and undermined: "He is hurt where it hurts most—in his lifelong commitment to the preaching of the Gospel."[14]

Sometimes, as in the case of Illich, however, the harshest critique of the movement came from missionaries themselves and not the comfortable, "armchair" missionaries. Maryknoll's Rev. Vincent Mallon recalled in 1976 that the backlash against the missions sometimes came in the form of self-criticism:

> It was unfortunate that the initial massive mission effort of the U.S. church ran into unsettled times ... Before 1965, I never ran into laymen who were critical of American mission efforts. The criticism came mostly from American missioners themselves. ... A lot of our own people followed [their] lead and said, yes, let's get out of parishes, out of schools, and everything else. But

---

13. For an analysis of Illich's article and its aftermath see Costello, *Mission to Latin America*, 122–30. For a summary of responses to Illich see Garneau, "'Commandos for Christ,'" 336–42.

14. Hebblethwaite, "Why Missions?" 335.

Age of Reform

did the people who were directly affected ever say that? I don't think so.[15]

When the missionaries lost faith in their own effectiveness and indeed the worthiness of the missionary enterprise, their supporters back home in America followed.

Instead of presenting a new missionary ideal, at first missionary detractors largely attempted to discredit the old methods, without envisioning what could take their place. The result was a genuine crisis in the missions in the mid to late 1960s. Some missionaries questioned their vocations to the missionary field, others exited from the ranks of religious orders and the priesthood altogether, and Catholics in America were unsure whether and to whom they should give their support. It was even suggested that the Roman congregation, *Propaganda Fide*, be abolished in favor of a local approach to mission work. Some suggested that the best approach was to pull out all foreign resources—personnel, money, and influence from mission lands, evidencing disagreement about the most fundamental aspects of missionary theory and practice.

THE SECOND VATICAN COUNCIL AND THE MISSIONS

In the midst of the reappraisal of the missions brought on by social and political factors, the world's bishops were meeting in Rome for the Second Vatican Council to discuss the work of Christian evangelization.[16] The bishops attempted to articulate a positive, scripturally based apologetic for foreign missions. When Pope John XXIII announced on January 25, 1959, that he would convene an ecumenical Council of the Church, known as Vatican II, the CSMC reacted positively to the news, hoping that the council would breathe new life into the mission enterprise.

At the time of the council's opening three years later, it was clear that while there had been numerous ecumenical councils in the history of the Church, this gathering of the world's bishops would be unprecedented. The event was unparalleled in part because the council's participants reflected a truly global Church, not a "Western" entity composed of Americans and Europeans. Two hundred indigenous bishops from Africa and Asia

---

15. Quoted in Costello, *Mission to Latin America*, 136.
16. Latourelle, *Vatican II: Assessment and Perspectives*; O'Malley, *Tradition and Transition*; Alberigo, *The Reception of Vatican II*; Komonchak and Alberigo, *History of Vatican II*; Wiltgen, *The Rhine Flows into the Tiber*.

attended as well as 500 bishops serving in mission lands. The CSMC saw the council as an opportunity for the Church to show its truly universal character and rejoiced in the numbers of missionary bishops attending, calling it a "visible proof of the Church's Catholicity." The Crusade particularly supported the council's goal to foster Christian unity and greater understanding among the world's peoples, applauding the eventual decision to invite observers from a variety of other religious traditions.[17]

As the council unfolded, its exceptional character became more pronounced, marking the advent of a new self-understanding for the Church and its missionary practice. Ecumenist and mission promoter Rev. Thomas Stransky, C.S.P. (1930–),[18] claimed that "no other world church or international confessional body has undergone such an intensive examination of consciousness and conscience about mission as did the Roman Catholic Church during the four years of the Second Vatican Council."[19] This examination was intended from the start. In using the term *aggiornamento*, the Italian word meaning "updating," Pope John XXIII declared that the Church was in need of renewal, including its approach to evangelization.

At first the discussion of a conciliar document on the missions followed the normative notions and language of Western missionaries. America and European countries were "mission-sending" countries that had the express goal of *plantatio ecclesiae,* planting the Church in regions where the message of the Gospel was foreign. This definition of mission that was regnant in the pre-conciliar period largely favored a juridical, institutional understanding of mission over a broader theological or biblical approach.[20]

---

17. "Missionary Meaning of the General Council," *The Shield* 41.3 (1962) 6–7, 28 (7); Ronan Hoffman, "Christian Unity Will Draw People to the True Church," *The Shield* 41.5 (1962) 11–12; "The Council and the Mission Apostolate," *The Shield* 42.2 (1962) 24–25; "The Ecumenical Council and World Unity," *The Shield* 42.3 (1963) 2–3, 25–26; "Second Vatican Council and the Missions," *The Shield* 42.5 (1963) 6–7, 28.

18. Stransky, ordained in 1957, was on the staff of the Secretariat for Promoting Christian Unity (1960–1970) and was a prominent observer at Vatican II. He was president of the Paulist Fathers (1970–1978) and has been on staff at the Tantur Ecumenical Center in Jerusalem since 1988. The Stransky papers are located at the Paulist Archives, St. Paul College, Washington, DC.

19. Stransky, "Evangelization, Missions, and Social Action," 343–51; quote at 344.

20. On the pre-conciliar discussion on the mission see Komonchak and Alberigo, "Commission on Missions," in *History of Vatican II*, Volume 1, 192–6.

Age of Reform

During the third session of the council that began in September of 1964, the schema on the missions was presented to the council fathers.[21] Rooted in earlier mission theology, the document was rather brief, containing only thirteen propositions.[22] Pope Paul VI approved the propositions for distribution on July 3, 1964; however, many found the text lacking in substance and outdated. Among the most outspoken critics was Bishop Donal Lamont of Umtali, Rhodesia (now Zimbabwe). He compared the document to the "dry bones" alluded to by the prophet Ezekiel (see 37:1-14), pleading for the council fathers to flesh out the document. He said of the preliminary document, "We looked for a Pentecostal light and they have lit this candle for us. We looked for modern weapons . . . and they have offered us bows and arrows. We asked for bread and they gave us, I do not say a stone, but a few cold propositions from a tract of missiology."[23] Bishop Lamont was not alone in his objections to the document as the schema was overwhelmingly rejected.

After the rejection of the schema, the council fathers sufficiently broadened their outlook on mission, especially through the participation of bishops from Africa, Asia, and the Americas. When the draft was returned to the commission on missions, the council fathers sent 193 suggestions for amendments totaling 550 pages. The text that was to become the Decree on the Church's Missionary Activity, *Ad Gentes* ("To the Nations"), was improved and lengthened, stressing the universality of the missionary role in the Church. The decree was brought to a final vote on December 7, 1965 and was overwhelmingly approved with 2,394 votes in favor, the greatest number of affirmative votes received by any conciliar document, and only five against.[24]

---

21. The background on *Ad Gentes*, the Vatican II document on the missions, can be found in Komonchak and Alberigo, "The Commission for the Missions," in *History of Vatican II*, edited by Komonchak and Alberigo, 3:390-3; Norman Tanner, "Missionary Church," in *History of Vatican II*, edited by Komonchak and Alberigo, 4:331-45; and Ricardo Burigana and Giovanni Turbanti, "The Commission for the Missions," in *History of Vatican II*, edited by Komonchak and Alberigo, 4:573-84; Rynne, *The Third Session*, 204-8; Rynne, *The Fourth Session*, 135-47.

22. The propositions can be found in Anderson, *Council Daybook: Vatican II, Session 3*, 233-34.

23. The full address can be found in Anderson, *Council Daybook: Vatican II, Session 3*, 238-9.

24. For the text of the document see Flannery, *Vatican Council II*, 813-56. For a commentary on the history, content, and implementation of the document see Brechter, "Decree on the Church's Missionary Activity," 87-181. See also Wiltgen, *The Rhine Flows*

The CSMC's *Shield* contained various commentaries on *Ad Gentes* following the document's promulgation. The assessment of the document was in every way positive, referring to it as the "new 'Magna Charta of missions.'"[25] *Ad Gentes* offered significant insights into the situation of the missions in the modern world. One major development was a shift from a concentration on individual "pagan souls" to a focus on entire groups, the People of God broadly defined, as the proper object of evangelization. By emphasizing the common life of all peoples, it was no longer acceptable to see the missions as a competition for souls between Protestants and Catholics or the missions as an effort to "save pagans."[26]

A second major development was an effort to take the missions out of the realm of specialization. The missions were not only the concern of the "professionals"—clergy and religious committed to mission lands—but the entire Church by its very nature was to be seen as missionary. It reminded Christians that all were called to be "missionary," no matter their location in the world. The Church was defined in spiritual terms rather than juridical terms and consequently, new mission territories were seen as every land and every place in which the Gospel was spread, whether to the previously evangelized or those who had never had the Gospel preached to them. The missionary character of the Church was not to be seen as limited by geography—formerly separated from the rest of the Church by a "missionary ghetto."[27] The emphasis on the common duty of Christians to evangelize others, however, risked a decline in missionary undertakings. In the rush to make missionary evangelization the duty of all and not a select few, it was feared the missions could become the express responsibility of none in the Church.

The language surrounding missions also changed dramatically: from "church" to "People of God," from "saving souls" to "being with"

---

into the Tiber, 193–98, 256–60.

25. See George Eldarov, "Vatican II Gave the Church a Magna Charta for Missions," *The Shield* 45.3 (1966) 1–2, 25; "What Did the Council Say About the Missions?" *The Shield* 45.4 (1966) 6–8; George Eldarov, "'To the Nations,'" *The Shield* 46.1 (1966) 1–2, 29–32.

26. Roukanen, "Catholic Teaching on Non-Christian Religions," 56–61; Yates, *Christian Mission in the Twentieth Century*, 166–75.

27. See Ronan Hoffman, "Problems in Missionary Work Today," in *Reappraisal: Prelude to Change*, edited by William J. Richardson, 39.

people, from "planting" churches to bringing about the "reign of God." [28] Missiologist Donal Dorr has described the older theology of mission as "the crusader model" or "the commando model" of mission. The emerging model of mission used complementary images of "gathering in" and "solidarity" to reflect the new relationship between the missionary and his or her people. There was no longer an emphasis on distinguishing between missionary "sending" countries and "receiving" countries. Some even questioned the goal of "church planting," seeking to move from a concentration on infrastructure (the "edifice complex") toward a theology of mission more concerned with the intangible spreading of the faith. Terminology shifted from "the missions" to "young churches," highlighting their indigenous quality and autonomous nature of communities in which Christianity had taken root.[29] The council elevated the importance of the local churches and the dignity of indigenous languages and manifestations of the faith. No longer was the missionary process seen as a singular, one-directional phenomenon. Churches in mission lands were less and less seen as subordinate to the Westerners that had handed on the faith and more responsive to the distinctive local character of the Church.[30] Mission theology emphasized "walking side by side" rather than "the older churches giving something and the younger churches receiving it." Christ's "great commission" to make disciples of all nations (Matthew 28:19) it seems had been replaced in part by the message of the Gospel of Luke 4:18–19, the prophetic calling to heal the blind and set prisoners free.[31]

In addition to the document devoted to the missions, other conciliar texts touched on and influenced the theory and practice of the missions. Among the most notable was the Dogmatic Constitution on the Church, *Lumen Gentium*; the Constitution on the Church in the Modern World, *Gaudium et Spes*; the Declaration on the Relation of the Church to Non-Christian Religions, *Nostra Aetate*; and the Decree on Ecumenism, *Unitatis Redintegratio*. Together these documents offered a positive assessment of the modern world and both non-Catholic and non-Christian

---

28. Dries, *The Missionary Movement*, 257.

29. Dorr, *Mission in Today's World*, 186–92; Schreiter, "Changes in Roman Catholic Attitudes," 113–25.

30. Schreiter, "Changes in Roman Catholic Attitudes," 378–81.

31. Schreiter, *The New Catholicity*, 123–26.

peoples, emphasizing the great promise of progress through cooperation and understanding.[32]

THE RECEPTION OF VATICAN II

The years after Vatican II were an exciting time for the Crusade. The CSMC grappled with change in the Church, considering the role of the laity and women, how the liturgical movement would impact the Church's worship, and how ecumenical dialogue would affect the role of the missionary. At the same time that the movement assimilated broad changes in theological and cultural outlooks, it was also forced to reassess its own inner-workings, image, and activities, reexamining its place within the Church and American life.

The leader who would attempt to guide the Crusade through this challenging era was Msgr. Henry J. Klocker (1918–2001), one of the prominent leaders of the American mission movement during the latter half of the twentieth century. Born April 5, 1918 in Cincinnati, he prepared for the priesthood at St. Gregory minor seminary and Mt. St. Mary's Seminary of the West, both in Cincinnati. Though he personally desired to become a foreign missionary, his parents dissuaded him. Still he maintained his interest in the missions and served as president of the CSMC units at the seminaries he attended. Klocker was ordained in June 1943 by Archbishop John T. McNicholas and his first assignment was assistant pastor to CSMC leader Msgr. Edward Freking, then serving at St. Stephen Church, Cincinnati as well as working at the CSMC national office. After graduate studies at the Angelicum in Rome and various pastoral and teaching assignments, Klocker was appointed in 1951 as director of the Office of the Propagation of the Faith and as assistant to the Catholic Students' Mission Crusade. He became executive secretary of the CSMC in 1958, serving in that capacity until 1971.[33]

---

32. For the texts of these documents see Flannery, *Vatican Council II*, 350–426, 452–70, 738–42, 903–1001.

33. After the demise of the movement, Klocker became Vicar of the Commission on Missions for the Archdiocese of Cincinnati, continuing to work at the old Crusade Castle until 1978. See "Rev. Henry J. Klocker served as priest, teacher," *Cincinnati Enquirer*, December 30, 2001; "Msgr. Henry J. Klocker, You Will Be Busy in Heaven," *Transmissions: The Newsletter of the Missions Office of the Archdiocese of Cincinnati* (Winter 2002); interview with Mary Fran Walter; interview with Msgr. Klocker by Christine Kroner, University of Cincinnati, Department of History, February 25, 1991, CSMC, AAC.

Age of Reform

After the council, Klocker and the CSMC leadership fought to maintain a difficult balance between the decades-old aims and methods of the Crusade and the new spirit of Vatican II. Within the movement and outside of it, there were differing attitudes toward the conciliar reforms. Some believed that the changes proposed by the council were a radical break from the past, while others did not believe they extended far enough. Though some organizations actively worked against the movement for reform in the Church evidenced by the reception of the Second Vatican Council, the Crusade reacted very positively.[34] The Crusade entered into this phase of fermentation and growth, seeking to both inform and be informed by the issues impacting the nation and the Church. The movement realized that for it to flourish, it could not be content with the *status quo* and had be proactive in shaping its own future. As one crusader wrote, the CSMC was in the midst of a search for "renewal and relevance"—one that would cause some to ask whether the movement "fit the times."[35]

The Crusade's response to change was in the affirmative. When in 1966 the chairman of the Crusade claimed that the spirit of *aggiornamento*, a term made popular by Pope John XXIII, had always guided the organization, Freking could offer numerous examples of the Crusade's response to change throughout its history.[36] However, the Crusade's response to the Second Vatican Council represented an even greater turning point for the movement. Among the changes was a greater emphasis on academic study of the missions, on the value of Scripture in evangelization, and the basic goodness of all peoples, whether Christian or not. The form of activity of the CSMC's student members also began to change. Student members became increasingly involved in the workings and decision-making of the movement. They were invited to contribute to *The Shield* and to other CSMC publications, and were even encouraged to organize and lead discussions at local and national CSMC gatherings. The student board that dated from the movement's founding took on an enhanced advisory role.

---

34. For reaction to the Council see Joseph A. Komonchak, "Interpreting the Council: Catholic Attitudes toward Vatican II," in Weaver and Appleby, *Being Right*, 17–36; Chinnici, "Reception of Vatican II in the United States," 461–94.

35. Robert Rossi, "Renewal and Relevance in the Catholic Students' Mission Crusade," *The Shield* 46.4 (1967) 3. Also, "Does the CSMC Fit the Times?" *The Shield* 47.2 (1957–58) 23–24.

36. Edward A. Freking, "'Aggiornamento' in CSMC," *The Shield* 45.4 (1966) 16–17.

Crusaders focused on active apostolic opportunities, not more passive and remote forms of activity.[37] No longer were crusaders content with cancelled-stamp drives, round table discussions, and mission rallies. Members wanted to experience first hand the part they could play in the mission enterprise. In an era of "rising expectations" in which airplanes, radio, and television revolutionized the ease of communication and travel, crusaders wanted to be on the front lines of the mission apostolate.[38] This new outlook accompanied the call to student action, more often personal rather than collective. Crusaders wanted to experience the missions for themselves, not live vicariously through missionary priests and sisters. With the growing attention paid to the lay apostolate it is not surprising that the CSMC touted such opportunities for mission service as the "Papal Volunteers," the Peace Corps, catechists to rural America, or summertime mission volunteers.

By 1966, the CSMC convention reflected the new ideals of the missions. In answer to *Ad Gentes'* challenge that "all of the Church's children should possess a living awareness of their responsibility to the world,"[39] the convention theme, "The Church in the World," emphasized universal problems of hunger, illiteracy, disease, and poverty instead of focusing on the Church in specific geographic regions. One speaker challenged his listeners, "We are responsible for all men as our brothers as never before in human history." While geographically we are "one world," "we have a long way to go to make it truly one world, humanly speaking," he said. He called the presence of human misery contrary to the will of God, urging crusaders to "protest and action." He urged the CSMC to support efforts for international cooperation such as the proposed creation of a pontifical commission on justice and peace.[40]

Though the Second Vatican Council and the document *Ad Gentes* brought about a change in the language of mission, providing a richer

37. "The Church and Ourselves in the Decade of 60's," *The Shield* 40.1 (1960) 2–3, 22–23; "New Spirit for a New Age," *The Shield* 41.1 (1961) 22–23, 25.

38. Frederick A. McGuire, "The Church and the 'Revolution of Rising Expectations,'" *The Shield* 41.5 (1962) 26–27, 33.

39. *Ad Gentes*, ch. 6, sec. 36; see Flannery, *Vatican Council II*, 850.

40. "CSMC Convention Will Focus on Church's World-Wide Apostolate," CSMC, box 6, folder 22, AAC; "CSMC Claims a First in Following Up Mission Directives of Vatican Council," CSMC, box 6, folder 22, AAC; N.C.W.C. News Service, "CSMC Urged to Aid World Poor," August 20, 1966, CSMC, box 6, folder 23, AAC.

Scriptural and theological framework, much of the change in mission theology flowed from the "spirit" of the documents as interpreted by experts in the study of mission. More often than not, the missiologists and theologians attentive to reexamining the missions were far removed from the missions themselves.[41] In the years immediately following the council, the Crusade emphasized the role of theological study as an aid to understanding missiology, the branch of theology dealing with the Church's mission to evangelize. The CSMC aimed at "action through study" with the goal of equipping its members intellectually and spiritually before they took their places among the missionaries of the world.

The principal shaper of the CSMC's post-conciliar approach to mission study was Rev. Ronan Hoffman, O.F.M. Conv. (1921–2004), the only American Catholic at the time who had earned the Doctor of Missiology degree. He began work at The Catholic University of America in Washington, DC, as an instructor in missiology in the School of Sacred Sciences in 1958, remaining in that post for nearly a decade. Hoffman was a frequent contributor to *The Shield* and author of numerous study guides published by the CSMC press.[42] In 1959 he was appointed chairman of Latin American programs for the Crusade and three years later was selected to occupy the post of CSMC "Coordinator of College and Seminary Mission Studies."[43]

Hoffman, known for his progressive outlook and his rhetorical hyperbole, proved to be a liability for the CSMC. His often sensational remarks about the missions were disturbing, including his assertion that the mission movement had "definitely ended" even as ten thousand

41. Pierson, "Roman Catholic Missions," 166.

42. Ronan R. Hoffman was born 12 April 1921 in New York state. He received a B.A., M.A., and S.T.L. from Catholic University. He studied at the Gregorian University in Rome from 1954 to 1957, receiving the Doctor of Missiology degree. His dissertation was titled *The Mission Theory of Cardinal Brancati DeLaurea, O.F.M. Conv.* A member of the New York-based Immaculate Conception Province of the Conventual Franciscan Friars, Hoffman left the order in early 1969, having relinquished his teaching position at Catholic University the previous year. He died June 30, 2004 in Columbia, Howard County, Maryland. Ronan Hoffman file, Archives of the Catholic University of America; letter from Tabetha Dillon, Immaculate Conception Province Archives, October 1, 2004.

Hoffman's contributions to *The Shield* include "The Tradition of Catholic Universalism," *The Shield* 43.2 (1963–1964), 2–4, 37; "Liturgy and How it Serves the Missions," *The Shield* 44.2 (1964–1965), 9, 29, 35. See also Hoffman, "The Development of Mission Theology in the Twentieth Century."

43. See *The Shield* 41.5 (1962) 12.

Americans served as missionary priests and religious. In 1967 when he debated the future of the Catholic foreign mission movement with Rev. Avery Dulles, S.J. (1918–2008)[44] then a theology professor at Woodstock College in Maryland, Hoffman boldly advanced the idea that not only had the era of foreign missions ended but that its demise was beneficial and even providential.[45]

Hoffman called for a complete reformulation of mission theology and practice. According to Hoffman, the existence of Catholic missions for the sake of making converts was an outmoded and dangerous structure. He wrote that "'the missions' not only *have* problems, they *are* themselves a problem. And that problem is not one principally of finances, nor of more personnel, nor of new methods, but rather the theological problem of understanding properly the new reality facing the missionary Church."[46] He suggested that if properly reexamined, mission theology would emphasize service to the world and would recognize that the entire Church is missionary. The form and structure of mission must allow all the baptized to participate in missionary activity, Hoffman argued, rather than leaving it to the responsibility of relatively few professional missionaries. In addition, the new approach to mission should recognize the providential nature of the movement for Christian unity in relation to mission, and would be aware of the revolutionary changes in the secular world.[47] With these broad shifts in mind, Hoffman stated that the missionaries of the future ought to "go far beyond the traditional goals of propagating the Christian faith" which he saw as entirely inadequate. Hoffman stated that missionaries should devote themselves to presenting the "Gospel in a much more secular fashion" through concern for the poor and humanitarian service, for example.[48]

---

44. Dulles entered the Society of Jesus and was ordained to the priesthood in 1956. He studied at the Gregorian University in Rome, earning a doctorate in theology in 1960. He served on the faculty of Woodstock College, 1960–1974, at Catholic University, 1974–1988, and at Fordham University beginning in 1988. Pope John Paul II elevated him to the rank of Cardinal on February 21, 2001.

45. Conference proceedings were published in Cotter, *The Word in the Third World*.

46. Ronan Hoffman, "The Missionary Church and New Realities," 300. Emphasis is in the original.

47. Cotter, *The Word in the Third World*, 24.

48. Ibid., 92.

Age of Reform

In a later address that received wide coverage in the Catholic press, Hoffman stated that "the era of the foreign missionary movement as we have known it has definitely ended" and that "it would be advantageous to the Church if it voluntarily did away with its present missionary organization and structure."[49] His bold ideas and radical thesis that the world would be better off without Catholic missionary efforts as they had existed before drew many responses, including that of Dulles.

Dulles conversely argued that while missions were in a state of fluctuation, their approach was far from outmoded and could be effectively adjusted to meet the needs of the modern Church. While agreeing with much of Hoffman's assessment about new developments in mission theology, Dulles took the opposing viewpoint in terms of the "end" of the foreign mission movement. He stated that "there are changes and adaptations needed for our times" but there should be no end to the missions. Responding to Hoffman's call to do away with the missionary structure of the Church so that all the baptized could become missionaries, Dulles explained that mission work requires specialists even if they are collaborators with others. Dulles cautioned against a secularization of the Gospel by making social service the sum of the Church's international work, warning that he himself "should be very much afraid of any revolution which attempted to achieve the true good of humanity apart from the knowledge and love of God." Dulles countered Hoffman, concluding that the Church should not dismantle the missions but they ought to be "greatly intensified in a manner suited to the needs of the present time."[50] Hoffman and Dulles, while agreeing on the fundamental shifts in mission theology, differed dramatically in their prescription for future missionary work—whether it ought to be radically changed to the point of abolition or whether the traditional model could be adapted to take into account recent developments in the Church.

---

49. Both Dulles and Hoffman addressed the Mission-Sending Societies, Washington, DC, on September 18, 1967. The entirety of both addresses can be found in McGavran, *The Conciliar-Evangelical Debate*, 69–94. Also, for the text of Hoffman's address see Hoffman, "Conversion and the Mission of the Church," 1–20. For Dulles's text see Dulles, "The Changing Nature of Mission," 366–72. Dulles and Hoffman's ideological divide is further represented by the publications that chose to publish their respective addresses. Quoted in "The Death of the Foreign Missions," *The Shield* 47.2 (1967–1968) 6. See also "Missiologist Marks End of Missions," *National Catholic Reporter*, September 20, 1967.

50. Quoted in "The Death of the Foreign Missions," *The Shield* 47.2 (1967–1968) 7.

One of the chief goals of the Crusade in the wake of the council was to better educate student members about these changes in mission theology. The CSMC press increased its output of study guides. Before the council the press had published such titles as *Fundamentals of Missiology* (1957), *The Lay Apostolate* (1959), and *The Church at Work in the World* (1961). Afterwards, the CSMC continued to embrace new thinkers and methods as its close alliance with Thomistic forms of scholastic thought ceased. The publications attempted to introduce its members to a broader theology of mission that was focused less on specific mission countries, the intellectual errors of modern thought, or mission "problems" such as communism.[51] After the council, the CSMC sponsored the publication of the "Scholia Series," timely missiology and theology studies, many of them authored by Jesuits at West Baden College, West Baden Springs, Indiana. The publications attempted to inform students of new developments in mission theology, especially in light of *Ad Gentes*. In explaining the series, Hoffman wrote that "the missions have commonly been presented in terms of activity, and greater emphasis has been given in missionary writings to the external, visible activity designed to establish visible Christian communities. Less frequently have writers given attention to the internal, invisible, spiritual, and supernatural."[52] Publications in that series included *The Council and the Missions*; *The Ecumenical Movement and its Relation to the Missions*; *Lay Builders of the Church* and *Scriptural Foundations for the Missionary Character of the Church*.[53]

In addition to publications, the movement emphasized the role that conferences could play in education. Hoffman organized a first-ever Mission Theology Institute at St. Mary's College, Notre Dame, Indiana, in 1964, in conjunction with the CSMC convention. The institute was co-directed by Sister Maria Assunta Werner, C.S.C. (1916–1995), theology professor at St. Mary's College and later staff member for the United States

---

51. *The Shield* articles detailing this focus on the method of mission include Henry J. Klocker, "Missiology ... Just a 'Hard Word'?" *The Shield* 39.1 (1959) 19–21; "Missiology on Tape Recordings," *The Shield* 40.4 (1961) 20–21; "Progress in Mission Theology Studies," *The Shield* 42.1 (1962) 13–14; Ronan Hoffman, "Missiology: Educated Catholics Need to Know What It Is," *The Shield* 42.5 (1963) 18–19.

52. Hoffman, *The Council and the Missions*, 538.

53. "Publication of CSMC 'Scholia' on Mission Theology Begun," *The Shield* 44.2 (1964–1965) 39; "First Set of Studies in CSMC 'Scholia Series' Now in Print," *The Shield: Seminary Supplement* 45.1 (1965) 3. For a collection of the "Scholia" titles see CSMC, box 16, AAC.

Catholic Mission Council in Washington, DC.[54] The institute featured a keynote address by Bishop John J. Wright of Pittsburgh on the "new ecumenism" and sessions by the renowned Scripture scholar, Rev. Carroll Stuhlmueller, C.P., on "Old Testament Hopes for Mission Theology" and "New Testament Demands for Mission Theology."[55]

THE ECUMENICAL MOVEMENT

Among the marked changes of the 1960s was the rise of ecumenical dialogue and the softening of denominational identification.[56] While the modern ecumenical movement dates from the time of the first International Missionary Conference held in Edinburgh in 1910 and matured through the Protestant-sponsored Conference on Faith and Order and the Life and Work Movement, Roman Catholic participation within ecumenism did not officially commence until the mid-twentieth century.[57] In 1948 when the World Council of Churches was formed Catholics did not participate in accord with Pope Pius XI's encyclical letter *Mortalium Animos* (1928), stating that is was unlawful "for Catholics to give to such enterprises their encouragement or support." Believing that "error has no rights," official Catholic teaching held that ecumenical discussion would be fruitless since the return of Protestants and the Eastern Orthodox to the fold of Rome was the only option for those outside the Catholic Church. Other faith communities were not referred to as "churches" but as sects or societies. It was argued that Catholic involvement in ecumenism could only lead to confusion about doctrines and revealed truths that were to be held by all without question or debate.

Under Pope Pius XII, the prohibition on Catholic participation in the ecumenical movement was relaxed through Pius' *De Motione Oecumenica* (1949). Still large-scale participation by Catholics in ecumenism did not begin until the 1960s, spurred by Pope John XXIII's establishment in 1960

---

54. Werner also contributed to *The Shield*, authored the *CSMC Study Outlines on the Concilium Library* and contributed to the CSMC-sponsored publication, *The Church at Work in the World*, edited by Edward A. Freking, Henry J. Klocker and J. Paul Spaeth.

55. See "Bishop Wright to Speak Here, Institute to Open on Notre Dame Campus," *South Bend Tribune*, August 23, 1964 in CSMC, box 6, folder 5, AAC.

56. Robert Wuthnow indicates that the decline of denominationalism was not unique to Catholics but was an American phenomenon across various faith traditions. See Wuthnow, *The Restructuring of American Religion*, 71–99.

57. Jay, *The Church*, 2:79–94.

of the Secretariat for Promoting Christian Unity with Cardinal Augustin Bea as its first president. A year later Catholics first participated as observers in the meetings of the World Council of Churches, sending among others the American Jesuit, Edward J. Duff.[58]

While the Church was slowly softening its outlook toward ecumenism, Catholics in America were experiencing the pluralism of religious belief. During the 1950s Catholics had entered the middle class and flocked to the suburbs in shockingly high numbers, largely breaking down the walls of ethnic Catholicism. Still most Americans, and particularly Catholics, identified chiefly with their faith in an environment in which they were frequently interacting with Protestants and Jews. The cultural dynamics of post-World War II America set up the opportunity for a "triple melting pot" in which Protestants, Catholics, and Jews would interact in their neighborhoods and workplaces.[59]

One of the achievements of the Second Vatican Council was a new emphasis on ecumenism.[60] The CSMC harnessed interest in this emerging field within theology and by 1964 ecumenism and the theological insights of Vatican II were a primary focus for the movement. In 1963, the CSMC took its first steps toward ecumenical involvement, organizing Student Ecumenical Research Committees (SERC) at colleges, universities, and seminaries. The goal of the committees was to keep members up to date in the fields of theology and ecumenism by collecting and disseminating literature on the topic of ecumenism as well as official Church documents impacting ecumenism.[61] Nearly every issue of *The Shield* after

58. Aubert, "Stages of Catholic Ecumenism"; René Girault, "The Reception of Ecumenism," in Alberigo, Jossua, and Komonchak (eds.), *The Reception of Vatican II*, 137–67.

59. See Herberg, *Protestant, Catholic, Jew*; Kennedy, "Single or Triple Melting Pot?" 331–39. See the issue titled, "The Fiftieth Anniversary of *Catholic, Protestant, Jew*," *U.S. Catholic Historian* 23 (2005) devoted to Herberg's legacy. On attempts at greater understanding between American Protestant and Catholics beginning in the mid-1950s see Curry, *Protestant-Catholic Relations in America*, 61–89; Greeley, *The Church and the Suburbs*.

60. Histories of the ecumenical movement include Tavard, *Two Centuries of Ecumenism*; Minus, *The Catholic Rediscovery of Protestantism*; Bliss, *Catholic and Ecumenical*.

61. "Student Ecumenical Research Committees," *The Shield: Academic Supplement* 43.2 (1963–1964) 8; "Student Ecumenical Research Committees Report," *The Shield* 43.3 (1964) 17–18, 38; "A Progress Report: What SERC Has Done," *The Shield* 45.1 (1965) 7, 28.

the council included a discussion of ecumenism and the missions.⁶² The publication encouraged crusaders to read widely in the "new theology" and to study the works of Gustave Weigel, S.J., Cardinal Augustin Bea, Frederick McGuire, C.M., and Hans Küng, among others.⁶³ Responding to the growing interest in ecumenical activity, the CSMC press also published two works on the topic edited by J. Paul Spaeth: *Ecumenism and Universalism* (1963) and *Ecumenism, Unity, and Peace* (1963).

The 1964 Crusade convention included three sessions on ecumenism, including a discussion on dialogue with Greek Orthodox, Jews, Jehovah's Witnesses, and Mormons, among other faith traditions.⁶⁴ Archbishop Karl J. Alter of Cincinnati, president of the CSMC, in speaking to the 4,200 plus student crusaders called for a greater "emphasis on the ecumenical movement as a first step in strengthening the missionary role of the Church." Lest students think that ecumenism was an optional addition to the CSMC's aims, he stated that involvement in the movement for Christian unity was not a "personal choice." He stated, "You can't be neutral. You can't be indifferent. Our Lord won't let you be. He wants one Church and we have as a responsibility as Catholics to help along the movement, never making surrender of our own teachings, never making a surrender of our own convictions." He urged them to begin by recognizing what different faiths have in common but without overlooking their essential differences. While recommending that students study the theology of Luther, Calvin, and the Anglican church to better understand the beliefs of their separated brethren, he reminded them that ecumenism is "not based on some sort of compromise or some artificial synthesis of Christian belief and practice." ⁶⁵

---

62. Gustave Weigel, "Ecumenism and the Witness-Bearing of Catholics," *The Shield* 42.1 (1962) 2–3, 15, 30; Calvert Alexander, "Mankind's Urge Toward Ecumenism," *The Shield: Academic Supplement* 43.1 (1963) 1–4, 8; Maria Assunta, "A Program for College Study of Ecumenism," *The Shield* 44.2 (1964–1965) 17–18; "Ecumenism . . . Spirit and Movement." *The Shield* 44.4 (1965) 26–28.

63. "SERC Book Digests," *The Shield* 43.4 (1964) 22, 37–39; "Book Digests," *The Shield* 44.1 (1964) 27–28.

64. "Program: 21st National Convention, August 27–30, 1964," CSMC, box 5, folder 31, AAC, 14–15.

65. Karl J. Alter, "Address, 21st National CSMC Convention, August 27–30, 1964," CSMC, box 5, folder 33, AAC. See also N.C.W.C. News Service, "Archbishop Maps Church Unity Course," August 27, 1964, CSMC, box 6, folder 4, AAC.

The youthful members of the Crusade during the 1960s were also more likely to support ecumenical endeavors, having often interacted with non-Catholic Americans in a far greater capacity than previous generations. Catholic involvement in the ecumenical movement progressed rapidly throughout the decade. In 1966 the University Christian Movement was founded, taking in the major Protestant student organizations and two Catholic student associations: the National Newman Student Federation and the National Federation of Catholic College Students.[66]

The reinvigoration of the mission movement contributed to the rising interest in ecumenism and the cause of Christian unity. More so than others, missionaries were aware of the difficulty that Christian denominationalism represented. Rev. Thomas Stransky, C.S.P., was an extremely influential missiologist after the council who advocated the link between missiology and ecumenism. As one of the first Catholics to genuinely collaborate with Protestant experts in the missions to forge a theology of mission, Stransky worked extensively with Protestant missiologists such as Gerald H. Anderson. In turn, missiologists from various Protestant traditions also became interested in Catholic mission theology and practices reflected in their own publications. Though not blind to their differences, after the council, for the first time missionaries and experts from both Protestant and Catholic backgrounds began to dialogue and collaborate, pointing to a new missionary model of ecumenical cooperation.

SOULS CAN SAVE THEMSELVES: "ANONYMOUS CHRISTIANITY" AND A LESS URGENT MISSION

Not unrelated to changes in the missionary ideal and the rise of ecumenism during the 1960s were shifts in the Catholic view of salvation. The background to the debate on the foreign missions was the larger debate on salvation and how it could be achieved. Here too the shifts were noticeable and the debate fervent. Modern-day missiologist David Bosch has argued that the view that came to prominence after the council saw salvation as primarily interpersonal such that true conversion involved reconciliation with one's brothers or sisters not merely one's relationship with God. In this way sin was chiefly seen as a form of alienation between humans.[67]

---

66. Cavert, *The American Churches in the Ecumenical Movement*, 237.
67. Bosch, *Transforming Mission*, 396.

Age of Reform

A second change was an exploration of whether salvation could be obtained universally.[68] Among those theologians speculating about the possibility of universal salvation were Karl Rahner, S.J., and Edward Schillebeeckx, O.P. One key aspect of theological transformation that joined with changes in missionary theory was popularization of the idea of "implicit Christianity" and the "anonymous Christian."[69] By this theory, it was meant that "an individual can already be in possession of sanctifying grace ... even before he has explicitly embraced a credal statement of the Christian faith and been baptized."[70] This teaching was not an innovation, but was becoming recognized in a more profound way. It was born of the belief that God desired the salvation of all and by consequence would not favor certain individuals who happened to be born in a certain place and time and forsake the majority of humankind born in non-Christian lands. Everyone—regardless of race, class, or gender—was viewed as both equally proximate and distant from God.

This understanding of salvation, while not directly responding to the state of the foreign missions, certainly contributed to a lack of interest in the missions and the work of conversion and "saving souls." The once concrete aim of the missionary was considerably weakened and the urgency of missions evaporated. The shift in thinking also challenged the position that members of the Church, especially those of Europe and America, were a "chosen people" and brought into question the unique and absolute claims that had been made by the Church—namely that in and through it salvation came. However, if salvation could be achieved without visibly belonging to the Church, what was the proper function of the missionary? Stated in another way, "Why should the Church exist anywhere at any time"?[71]

---

68. Sullivan, *Salvation Outside the Church?* 162–81.

69. Rahner's idea of the "anonymous Christian" can principally be deduced from the following works: Rahner, "Anonymous Christians," 390–8; Rahner, "Anonymous Christianity and the Missionary Task of the Church," 161–78; Rahner, "Atheism and Implicit Christianity," 145–64; Rahner, "Anonymous and Explicit Faith," 52–59; Rahner, "Observations on the Problem of the 'Anonymous Christian,'" 280–94.

70. Rahner, "Anonymous Christianity and the Missionary Task of the Church," 165. For a summary of the teaching see "The Theory of the Anonymous Christian," in Kilby, *Karl Rahner*, 115–26.

71. Hillman, "Anonymous Christianity and the Missions," 362. For the modern-day context for this phenomena see Dave Shiflett, "Uncertain Crusaders: Christians no longer worry much about converting 'heathens,'" *Wall Street Journal*, November 14, 2003. Shiflett

Some missionaries accepted the theological formulation while others claimed to have been "deeply disturbed," "perplexed and baffled" by Rahner's writings. His conception of salvation, they argued, "far from urging us to zeal, constitutes, as the author himself frankly confesses, 'a considerable obstacle to our apostolic élan.'" By consequence, the missionary apostolate was "slowed down, if not paralysed by different ideological trends which create doubts and uncertainty, and shake convictions that were a great source of apostolic zeal." One missionary criticized the effect of this idea on the movement:

> Awareness of the grave danger to which non-Christians were exposed in regard to their eternal salvation, was not only the source of the magnificent missionary zeal of St. Paul and all the great missionaries in past ages, it has also been one of the principal mainsprings of the apostolate of those of us who have been sent by the Church to the pagans in the world today. It was the idea that we could 'save' them that sustained our effort.[72]

Rahner himself questioned whether "anonymous Christianity" and foreign missionary work could thrive together or whether this notion of salvation might deprive the Church of the force of its missionary task. However, Rahner maintained that "anonymous Christianity" was prior to explicit Christianity and that the first did not render the latter superfluous. Instead it was a first step, a form of preparation for a deeper life in Christ through the Church.[73] Others argued that explicit Christianity was better than anonymous Christianity because grace was more available and more assured in the former and could be extended through the work of missionaries.

Following these theological shifts, still it was seen as less important to convert anyone to a particular Church—Protestant, Catholic or otherwise—if grace could be received outside of the Church. As such the aim of the missionary was left in question. If Catholicism, indeed even

---

wrote, "Americans don't seem much interested in converting the 'heathen,' as it was once put. Indeed, they decreasingly believe there is such a thing as 'the heathen' at all or that Christian belief is necessary for salvation."

72. "A Modern Conception of the Salvation of the Infidels," 421–28. For a sympathetic reading of the impact of "anonymous Christianity" on the mission to non-Christian peoples, see Pasquini, *Atheism and Salvation*, 55–62.

73. Rahner, "Anonymous Christianity and the Missionary Task of the Church," 168–71.

Christianity, was not seen as necessarily superior, unique, and culturally beneficial in comparison to other faith traditions, what could the missionary hope to accomplish? This form of relativism cut at the missionary's *raison d'être*, weakening missionary zeal.[74] Missiologist David Bosch perceptively located the difficulty inherent in the shifting theology of the missions: "How do we maintain the tension between being both missionary and dialogical?" How can the Church affirm "God's universal salvific will and the possibility of salvation outside the church *versus* the necessity of the church and of missionary activity?"[75]

Caryl Rivers, a member of the Crusade in its heyday, who attended one of the CSMC conventions held at the University of Notre Dame, reflected back on the theological certainty that permeated the gatherings: "There was, of course, no question in the mind of anyone at the CSMC convention that it was the Will Of God that everybody in the world ought to be Catholic, and that converting them was the noblest way of doing God's will here on earth." Only later did she discover that "incredible as it may have seemed to us, there were a great many people in the nations of the world, who—despite our invitation—did not really want to be part of Our Crowd." Reflecting back through the lens of the post-conciliar Church of the 1970s on the mission of the Crusade made her uneasy: "[T]he reason for it all, as presented to us, was so detached from human compassion as to be almost mathematically abstract. All those people who were served by the missionaries for whom we saved our nickels and dimes were only silver fish in the sea of possible salvation. They were souls, as indistinguishable from one another as the numbers in a giant computer that might have been sitting in a corner of the office of the Society for the Propagation of the Faith."[76]

By the early 1970s the increased challenges to the missions were evident. Within the Church, theological variants such as "secular theology" and "death of God" theology burst onto the scene. While most of these

---

74. See the contemporary extension of this thinking in Knitter, *No Other Name?*. Knitter's thesis is that religions ought to exhibit a "unitive pluralism" and that each is more complementary than contradictory. See also the Congregation for the Doctrine of the Faith's 2000 instruction, *Dominus Iesus: On the Unicity and Salvific Universality of Jesus Christ and the Church*. For the historical context of this discussion see Dries, "American Catholics and World Religions," 31–50.

75. Bosch, *Transforming Mission*, 488–89.

76. Rivers, *Aphrodite at Mid-Century*, 145–46.

forms of radical theology quickly withered, their often unsettling attempts to reinterpret fundamental Christian doctrines and paradigms were not without effect. When in 1973 a meeting of Catholic bishops drafted a document, *The Evangelization of the Modern World*, they were surprisingly aware of the modern difficulties efforts at evangelization faced, both from within and outside the Church. Among a variety of obstacles, the bishops highlighted "certain currents of thought" such as "'death of God and 'religionless Christianity,'" an "uncertainty of faith" that was evident in scriptural interpretation and even the questioning of central teachings of the Gospel. They also noted a faulty emphasis on pluralism, "badly understood ecumenism," and a disordered ecclesial view that saw the Church as an institution that "conceals rather than reveals the Gospel."[77]

"Anonymous Christianity" not only had an effect on the foreign mission movement. At home, the mission to convert non-Catholic America was in the midst of transformation, if not retreat by the 1960s. The once active apostolate to rural peoples and African Americans that had resulted in mass baptisms during the 1940s and 1950s had declined to only a trickle of converts. Parents of non-Catholics attending parochial schools were no longer expected to attend religious instruction and weekly Mass. Historian John McGreevy cited a new generation of younger clergy who did not view conversion to Catholicism as necessary to the creation of an authentic Christian community, wary of so-called "theological imperialism."[78]

While the CSMC did not respond directly to the advance of "anonymous Christianity," its effect was apparent. The pages of *The Shield* were less likely to mention "conversion" and more likely to discuss modern problems such as poverty, disease, racial justice, and illiteracy.[79] The "problems of the world" were not limited to those of particular localities or religious traditions. Instead, crusaders discovered that these problems would persist even if one were to convert to Christian belief.

77. Synod of Bishops, *The Evangelization of the Modern World*, 5, 6, 13.

78. McGreevy, *Parish Boundaries*, 163–66, 241–42.

79. See, for example, Rene Maheu, "Illiteracy: A Crucial World-Wide Problem," *The Shield* 44.1 (1964) 26.

DEVELOPMENT, HUMANITARIANISM, AND UNIVERSALISM: MISSIONARY IDEALS TRANSFORMED

Despite the difficulties experienced by the mission movement, still theologically, spiritually, and intellectually the Christian foreign missions were reinvigorated in the late 1960s. The Church clearly experienced an unprecedented theological and intellectual ferment in relationship to the missions, evangelization, and ecumenism. Particularly after 1964, dozens of articles and books reappraised the work and future of the missions. A new generation of theologians and scholars took up this new and expanding field. Among these missiologists and missionaries were Albert J. Nevins, M.M. (1915–1997), editor of *Maryknoll Magazine*,[80] Frederick A. McGuire, C.M. (1905–1983), head of the National Catholic Welfare Conference's Mission Secretariat,[81] and John J. Considine, M.M., noted already for his contributions to the CSMC and the mission to Latin America. Along with Hoffman and Stransky, this new generation bolstered the new missiology of the 1960s, bringing fresh ideas and a new approach to the missionary task of the Church.

Nevins was quick to discern the demise of the old missionary ideal in his 1965 article, "End of an Era: The Missions Reappraised." However, unlike Illich and others, Nevins contrasted the old missionary model with a new emerging one. He began, "The orderly, simple, and uncomplicated life that these missioners once knew has disappeared. All of them sense they are witnessing the end of an era. They comprehend in varying degrees that they are caught up in a social, political and technological revolution that undermines the very foundations of their vocations and which challenges the existence of the Church itself."[82] Nevins lamented that in the past when the missionaries brought the Gospel to foreign lands they also "built little islands of their homelands on the outposts of the world." The previous generation of missionaries sometimes unconsciously patronized the people they had come to serve, seeing themselves as righteous, sure

---

80. Nevins, ordained as a Maryknoll priest in 1942, was active in writing and publishing, authoring works such as *Away to Mexico* (1966) and *Away to Central America* (1967). He worked with the Catholic Press Association and was editor of *Maryknoll Magazine* from 1968–1980.

81. McGuire was particularly active in the CSMC. A student crusader himself, McGuire was a frequent contributor to *The The Shield* and participated in every national meeting of the movement after 1950.

82. Nevins, "End of an Era," 32.

that paganism had nothing to offer, and convicted that ecumenism was "formal cooperation with heresy." Then colonialism crumbled: "Almost over night, this world was shattered as a great wind, generated in the heat of atomic explosion and carrying the seeds of rebellion, spread over the lands." The naïve, pagan "children" of the colonies "suddenly became presidents and prime ministers, ambassadors and archbishops." The result was that the missionary "questioned the validity of all his traditional patterns of life." He was accused of paternalism, cultural imperialism, and subservience to colonial powers, for "deliberately helping to train an army of clerks but no leaders." [83]

Nevins was critical of the passing methods: "Certainly the missioner as the Great White Father, the administrator and guardian, can no longer exist . . . and the sooner he disappears, the better." But even as Nevins saw the missionary as outdated, he saw the need for a new type of missionary.[84] This missionary would be focused on humanitarian work, not just saving souls. Additionally the missionary would be seen as a servant of the people, not a superior authority. Nevins related that the "mission of every Christian is not to extend the Church as an institution but to extend the fullness of Christ in His Mystical Body."[85] Nevins clearly saw that the new mission model was extra-ecclesial and more practical and human-centered in its approach yet retentive of its spiritual aims.

With the benefits of the mission enterprise in doubt, missionaries increasingly focused on humanitarian concerns, looking to issues of human rights, illiteracy, poverty, disease, social development, and world peace. Mission priorities centered less on saving souls and more on sustained humanitarian relief. This "temporal" model for the missions dated back as far as the 1930s with an increased emphasis on health care and educational work within the missionary movement.[86] By the 1960s the humanitarian thrust was synonymous with the missions. The missionary was envisioned as a servant of the community, a Westerner charged with material assistance, economic development, and conflict resolution—

83. Ibid., 34.
84. Ibid., 35.
85. Ibid., 37.

86. Hogan references this "temporal" model in his *The Irish Missionary Movement: A Historical Survey*, 129. An American example of this emerging model was Dr. Anna Dengel's Society of Catholic Medical Missionaries, a religious congregation of health care providers, founded in 1936.

likened to a Catholic version of a Peace Corps volunteer.[87] The missionary's new ideal was to be the servant-leader of a pragmatic Catholicism centered on the progress of peoples as popularized in Pope Paul VI's 1967 encyclical letter, *Populorum Progressio*.[88]

Mirroring worldwide concern for human rights and societal advancement, domestic programs took precedence in America. President Lyndon B. Johnson's (1963–1969) "Great Society" initiative aimed at easing poverty, providing medical care for the elderly and poor, and improving the environment. The Civil Rights movement peaked in the late 1960s and the U.S. Catholic bishops began their own social justice initiative, the Campaign for Human Development, to aid minority groups and the poor in gaining economic strength and political power while educating Catholics about the need for solidarity with the poor. The 1960s witnessed a new optimism in human capabilities—a rising expectation that peace, justice, and plenty could be achieved apart from an exclusively religious approach. Correct government and international cooperation it was believed could lead to a new era for the human family. Thus "humanitarianism" and witnessing to the Gospel often became more important than conversion.

The CSMC's work reflected this humanitarian emphasis. Its national conventions included sessions on poverty, including addresses by Catholic Relief Services' Msgr. Joseph A. Gremillion and James J. Norris, the only American layman to address the Second Vatican Council. As a visual reminder of the Church's obligation to the poor, the coronation tiara of Pope Paul VI, who had donated it for the benefit of the poor, was placed on display at the 1966 convention.[89] Convention sessions focused on particular socio-economic problems experienced by those in Appalachia and the "inner city," pledging to collaborate with various civic and religious

---

87. See James J. Berna, S.J., "Peace Corps—or Lay Mission Work: Is there a difference?" (Davenport, IA: Latin American Bureau, National Catholic Welfare Conference), CSMC, box 38, folder 13, AAC.

88. See "Populorum Progressio," in Carlen, *The Papal Encyclicals*, 5:183–201.

89. "Papal Coronation Tiara to Form Backdrop for Poverty Discussions at CSMC Convention," CSMC, box 6, folder 22, AAC.

groups responding to these needs.[90] *The Shield* often explored poverty and its solutions, detailing poverty at home and globally.[91]

This new optimism for solving humanity's ills was short lived, however. As David Bosch argued, "It was perhaps only to be expected that the almost complete identification of the church and its calling with the world and its agenda would eventually lead to such embarrassment and frustration with the inability of the church to carry out the world's agenda that many people despaired of the church and regarded it as expendable."[92] Many lost confidence in the Church, part of a wider cultural attack upon institutions.

For many, the life of the Church had shifted dramatically during the 1960s—from a preoccupation with doctrines and decrees to an emphasis on communal and personal improvement and social empowerment. Its function was no longer only personal holiness and sanctification but the intended elevation of the entire human family, largely in a social, humanitarian sense. The mission movement was not immune to these changes. Spurred by changing perceptions of foreign involvement by Western nations as well as the theological ferment surrounding Vatican II, the mission enterprise was completely reappraised during these years. A new pluralistic understanding of the world and its many faith traditions, the advent of Catholic participation in ecumenism, and a diminishment of a sectarian and separatist ethos contributed to a period of confusion regarding the proper task of the Church abroad. Yet the mission movement of the late 1960s did not remain orphaned, but experienced a revived discussion of mission theology and praxis. A new missionary model emphasizing the missionary as a servant leader on the forefront of humanitarian and ecumenical concerns replaced the former ideal. While many of these changes were positive, the theological and cultural shift of the 1960s was the unrecognized death knell for the Crusade, bringing about the eventual decision to terminate the work of the movement.

90. "22nd General CSMC Convention Program," August 25–28, 1966, CSMC, box 6, folder 8, AAC; NCWC News Service, "CSMC Convention to Study World Poverty," August 13, 1966, CSMC, box 6, folder 23, AAC; "CSMC Golden Jubilee Convention," August 22–25, 1968, CSMC, box 7, folder 3, AAC.

91. Ronan Hoffman, O.F.M. Conv., "World Poverty and Christian Responsibility," *The Shield* 45.2 (1965-1966) 10–12, 24; "The 'Inner City,'" *The Shield* 46.2 (1966-1967) 15; Peggy O'Connell, ". . . For I Was Hungry and You Gave Me to Eat . . .," *The Shield* 47.3 (1968) 23–24.

92. Bosch, *Transforming Mission*, 384.

SIX

The Final Generation

"LET TRADITIONS FALL," PROCLAIMED an article in *The Shield* outlining the need for a new approach and "look" for the Crusade.[1] The end of traditions and the repackaging of the mission movement was seen as essential to assuring the CSMC's continued existence. In the years following the council, its members and leadership diligently worked to ensure that the organization would not appear as an archaic remnant of the pre-conciliar Church, but as a reinvigorated, youthful movement stamped with the new outlook of the mid to late 1960s. The Crusade's response to change was validated by changes throughout the Church, including the liturgy, adaptations within parish and school structures, and the new approaches of Church-affiliated organizations and religious orders. Everywhere there were signs that the old Catholic subculture had given way; older images, structure, and language were replaced. Historian John McGreevy described these competing notions: at odds were "two languages—an older, highly structured communalism and a new attempt to build a 'community without walls.'"[2] When the walls of the earlier Catholic subculture were found wanting, a new vision of the Church arose. The CSMC's traditional mission of religious conversion, its language of Catholic triumphalism and centralized authority, and its reliance on a belief in Western cultural superiority could not adequately adapt nor be assumed by the emerging model of the Church. The new vision for the CSMC emphasized prophetic

---

1. "'Let Traditions Fall,' Mind of Student Execs. In Xmas Week Meet," *The Shield* 48.3 (1969) 11–12.

2. McGreevy, *Parish Boundaries*, 173; Portier, "From Historicity to History," 65–72. Portier argues that the "dissolution of the subculture"—"the demographic point, some time in the mid-1960s, at which immigrant Catholics finally became indistinguishable from other Americans—"and not the council itself is the defining event of twentieth-century American Catholic history" (68).

witness, action, and advocacy, not passive piety or merely a study of mission activities and problems.

The shifts and tensions inherent in this process of reevaluation and discovery were obvious. Historian Joseph P. Chinnici argued that the American Catholic community in the sixties "experienced the shock of tremendous mutations in their public conception of themselves and their relationship to American society."[3] He cited many of the modes of change experienced during that era including new speech patterns, new ritual actions, new symbol-making activities, new groupings and affiliations, and new distributions of institutional power. The Crusade's last years evidenced these new patterns as the language of the missions was reformulated, its symbols and rituals were reexamined, and student members vied for more control of the organization. This process eventually resulted in the movement's very existence being challenged.[4]

NEW IMAGE FOR THE CRUSADE

The CSMC's effort to break down the walls that represented earlier "traditions" included a reevaluation of the movement's name and its publication, *The Shield*. In a December 1968 meeting of the national executive board, the students noted that image had been a drawback to the CSMC's growth. To counter the negative image that some had, the board members recommended that the name of the movement be changed and that its objectives be better clarified to emphasize service and leadership not just study. They also recommended that the format of *The Shield* be substantially altered. *The Shield*, according to the board, lacked appeal, especially to teenagers, and gave the impression of a "magazine written by adults for adolescents." Instead, the students argued, "The teenager of today wants something of and for himself. Something which is geared toward his way of thinking." The recommendation was that the publication be replaced by a student-produced newspaper that would serve to make "teenagers more aware of the universal world around them" and "more open-minded and tolerant of all opinions."[5]

---

3. Chinnici, "Changing Religious Practice and the End of Christendom in the United States," 75.

4. Ibid., 76–77.

5. "'Let Traditions Fall,' Mind of Student Execs. In Xmas Week Meet," *The Shield* 48.3 (1969) 11–12.

In response to the recommendations of the student board, *The Shield*, which had been the official publication of the Crusade for almost fifty years, ended publication with the April/May 1969 issue. Because of the high cost of printing one periodical for all Crusade members, it was decided to replace *The Shield* with three shorter age-specific newsletters: the *Centric* for college/seminary members, the *Cosmic* for high school members, and the *Compass* for junior members. The subscription price was reduced in order to place the publication in the hands of as many students as possible. The newsletters were published less frequently than *The Shield*, were less expensive to produce and less flashy, appearing as a student-produced publication with little or no oversight from their moderators. While in the past, foreign missionaries and the clerical leadership of the Crusade had been the most frequent contributors to *The Shield*, the new publications showcased and celebrated the initiative of the youth themselves. Students often wrote the articles and sections were set aside for letters to the editor and a student opinion poll.[6]

With the increased role of the students in selecting content, the language of the publications changed drastically, perhaps evidencing the mentality of youthful rebellion common during the period.[7] A 1969 editorial written by a high school crusader crassly defended mission work: "The mission club is *not* an institution for weak-kneed asses, but a place for vital, intelligent people who are able to "give-a-damn" even about people with whom they have had no direct personal contact." His was a somewhat aggressive apologetic serving to highlight the tenuous position on which the mission ideology was seen to rest.[8] Through these new publications, CSMC members felt a greater sense of ownership of the movement, controlling for the first time the chief publication of the organization.

The perception that the CSMC suffered from an image problem caused many to question the very name of the movement. The use of the term "crusade" appeared particularly archaic by the late 1960s. Flowing

---

6. For extant issues of the publications see CSMC, box 54, folder 11 (Cosmic, Compass, Centric), AAC. See also "Letter to CSMC moderators," August 14, 1969, CSMC, box 54, folder 11, AAC.

7. Histories of the youth response to the 1960s include DeGroot, *Student Protest*; Erlich, *Student Power, Participation and Revolution*.

8. Hannigan, "What Kind of Love?" 2. Despite his rhetoric, Hannigan styled himself an "anti-student rebel" during an era of youth protest.

from the militarism of the interwar years, the term "crusade" had long been perceived as a badge of Catholic honor, representing the best of virtue, courage, chivalry, and respect. However, in an age that birthed the Catholic peace movement and was highly critical of the war in Vietnam, arms proliferation, and nuclear weapons, distaste for military language, especially when employed by religious causes, increased dramatically. In 1969 the executive board discussed striking the words, "crusade" and "Catholic," renaming the movement the "Confederation of Student Mission Conferences." The board agreed to wait to propose the name change until those meeting for a general convention could consider it.[9] Unofficially, however, use of the movement's full name was falling out of use. Most units preferred to use only the acronym "CSMC" while other groups chose to remain affiliated with the national organization while choosing a distinctive name like "Shalom."[10]

CRISIS WITHIN THE CRUSADE

As the Crusade launched a series of student-produced publications and discussed changing the name of the movement, its members increasingly branched out into various social concerns including urban decay, the plight of migrant workers, human rights, racial justice, and world poverty. The movement's expanding emphasis on the social apostolate inadvertently contributed to the movement's loss of focus. The movement's quick diversification and the splintering of its activities uncovered a general lack of agreement on the future of the movement and of the missionary enterprise.

The spring of 1970 ushered in swift changes within the CSMC leadership. Msgr. Edward A. Freking, long time chairman of the executive board, died suddenly on March 1, 1970. His death was followed by the resignation of Karl J. Alter (1885–1977), archbishop of Cincinnati and national president of the Crusade since 1950, who asked to be relieved of the CSMC presidency following retirement from his episcopal office the previous year.[11] Within the span of a few weeks, the movement's two

9. The next general convention convened by the CSMC in 1970 did not take up the issue of a name change because it had been decided in advance that the meeting would be the last for the organization.

10. "Memorandum for Executive Board Members' Meeting," Easter week, 1969, CSMC, box 48, folder 7, AAC; *Cosmic* 1.3 (December 1969) 3.

11. Alter, *The Mind of an Archbishop*; Fortin, *Faith and Action*, 256, 263–64.

most important offices had been vacated. Rev. Clifford King, founder of the movement, had died the previous summer, August 24, 1969, leaving the movement devoid of its symbolic "father."

An emergency meeting of the executive board was convened on April 18, 1970. It was at that meeting that several important changes came about: Msgr. Klocker was selected to fill the position of executive chairman left vacant by Freking's death; Archbishop Paul F. Liebold (1914–1972),[12] Alter's successor as archbishop of Cincinnati, was selected as national president of the CSMC following the acceptance of Alter's resignation. Lastly, the board members took up the most important and thorny issue of all: the proposed "phase out" of the Crusade's educational programs. With the participation of Archbishop Leibold, who met with Klocker and the students over two hours, the board outlined the Crusade's dissolution.

The end of the Crusade had been contemplated prior to Freking's death when Freking and Alter initiated discussions with Bishop William G. Connare (1911–1995), chairman of the U.S. Bishops' Committee on Missions and bishop of Greensburg, Pennsylvania.[13] It seems Connare was the first to propose the dissolution of the Crusade in favor of the work of the pontifical mission societies. By 1970 the talks had expanded to include the leadership of the societies: Msgr. Edward T. O'Meara, national director of the Society for the Propagation of the Faith and Rev. Augustus O. Reitan, national director of the Holy Childhood Association. Connare, O'Meara and Reitan were each supportive of the proposal.[14] Leibold, who had inherited the leadership of the Crusade from Alter, voiced his support for the path initiated by Freking, Alter, and Connare. Leibold wrote to Connare in December 1969, "With the death of its venerable founders, we feel more freedom in permitting [the CSMC's] missionary thrust to be channeled through other instruments with a view to efficiency of

---

12. Fortin, *Faith and Action*, 358–60.

13. Alter wrote to Connare on September 17, 1969, advising him that the diocesan mission appeal had been less successful "because of the emphasis that has been placed on ecumenism and the new approach to mission work." He informed Connare that he would approve whatever arrangements Freking worked out with him and the pontifical mission-aid societies regarding the future of the CSMC. See Karl J. Alter to William G. Connare, September 17, 1969, CSMC, box 48, folder 7, AAC; also William G. Connare to Karl J. Alter, February 3, 1970, CSMC, box 48, folder 7, AAC.

14. "Official Program 24th General CSMC Convention," CSMC, box 8, folder 1, AAC; "24th General CSMC Convention, August 1970, Supplement to Continuity for Meeting No. 20: Business Section," August 29, 1970, CSMC, box 48, folder 7, AAC.

operation, greater economics, avoiding duplication of effort and even better accomplishment of our common Missionary cause."[15]

The idea of "phasing out" the Crusade was not a unique one as the CSMC was not alone in seeking a cessation of its activities in the midst of a swiftly changing cultural and religious climate. As historian Philip Gleason observed, "By 1970 virtually every Catholic organization had agonized over whether it had any business existing."[16] When student members of the Newman movement met in 1967 at the Maryknoll Seminary in Glen Ellyn, Illinois, they voted to dissolve their national board of directors in favor of a decentralized structure consisting of diocesan leadership. With the historic vote, the Newman movement "virtually passed out of existence." Like the CSMC, the Newman movement cited various reasons for the change: a shift away from national organizations to diocesan initiatives, a greater emphasis on "collegiality" and the role of the local bishop coming out of the documents of Vatican II, financial problems, and a loss of membership.[17] In 1969 the student board of the University Christian Movement, the successor of the Student Volunteer Movement for Foreign Missions, voted itself out of existence, declaring that it ceased to "exist as a national organization."[18] The similarly timed demise of the Student Volunteer Movement for Foreign Missions indicated that the collapse of the CSMC was impacted by broader changes in the mission world and Christianity in general.

At the time the movement's leadership contemplated its dissolution, the CSMC appeared numerically strong, counting one million dues-paying members. However, the commitment and enthusiasm of these members seemed to wane in its later years. Klocker admitted that the membership of one million students, representing some 3,100 American educational institutions, was "somewhat loose" as the number of students paying dues determined membership. Each student member enrolled at a rate of twenty-five cents per year; older students were encouraged but not required to give more. Some dioceses such as Detroit, Michigan, enrolled all of the students who attended Catholic schools in their diocese, thus

---

15. Archbishop of Cincinnati (Paul Leibold) to Most Rev. Wm. Connair (sic), December 19, 1969, General Files, Catholic Students' Mission Crusade folder, C-9, AAC.

16. Gleason, *Keeping the Faith*, 87.

17. Evans, *The Newman Movement*, 159–65; quote at 164.

18. Howard, *Student Power in World Evangelism*, 95–96.

artificially inflating the numbers.[19] In fact, many of the students enrolled were not active in the movement and may not have known of their membership in the CSMC.

At the beginning of the 1960s one unit moderator had noted that many Crusade groups were no longer fulfilling the mission of the movement, that of "prayer, study, and sacrifice" for the missions. Their membership was marginal at best. She claimed that the CSMC was weakened by its lack of membership requirements and insufficient leadership from the national office. "The National Center," she wrote, "assumes that each school is doing what it has pledged to do. But the fact of the matter is that *many* units are failing to do anything substantial for the missions or the Church."[20] Reaching the one million member mark—of which the Crusade was rightly proud—was, however, in theory rather than reality.

One reason for stagnant membership in the later years of the organization's history was that the Crusade failed to incorporate the significant and growing number of Catholic students attending public schools. Though the founding vision of the CSMC included a place for students enrolled in public schools and college students active in Church-sponsored Newman clubs, the CSMC had never attracted substantial numbers of students attending non-Catholic schools. The need was perhaps recognized too late. In 1962 when the CSMC launched its "New Spirit for a New Age" campaign, its leadership discussed the need to initiate "new efforts to reach *all* Catholic students in *all* schools," especially the estimated fifty percent of Catholic students attending public schools.[21] If there were any efforts to include those in non-Catholic schools, they did not appear to be successful.

Membership problems contributed to financial difficulties for the Crusade. Rising costs, especially for printing and postage, exceeded the payment of student dues as convention costs skyrocketed to more than

---

19. Taped interview with Msgr. Klocker by Christine Kroner, University of Cincinnati, Department of History, February 25, 1991, CSMC, AAC.

20. Mother Mary of the Presentation, R.J.M. to Rev. John J. Considine, M.M., May 6, 1962, NCWC/Office of the General Secretary, Latin American Bureau, box 186, folder 10, ACUA.

21. "A New Spirit for a New Age, Suggested Topics for Discussion," March 5, 1962, NCWC/Office of the General Secretary, Latin American Bureau, box 186, folder 10, ACUA.

$75,000 by 1968.[22] The costs of continuing the CSMC's massive educational outreach were increasing and the prospect was one of further increases, the national office reported. Those who attended the 1970 convention were told that the movement had been plunged into financial difficulty through the closing and consolidation of many Catholic schools, decreasing the number of affiliated schools.[23]

While appearing as a thriving national organization, the leadership of the Crusade recognized the increasing difficulties in maintaining the movement. In addition to membership and financial troubles, the movement suffered from the era's general deemphasizing of national organizations. The reexamination of ecclesial life and structure spurred on by the Second Vatican Council resulted in a rediscovery of the local church. *Lumen Gentium*, the Dogmatic Constitution on the Church, contributed to the changing missionary consciousness through a reformulation of ecclesiology. The document affirmed the local church, stating, "The Church of Christ is really present in all the legitimately organized local groups of the faithful."[24]

This shift in ecclesiology led to an emphasis on local governance. For instance, diocesan efforts began to take prominence over national efforts. Parish councils and diocesan synods were convened, leading to a less "top-down" and more grass roots approach. When the CSMC announced its impending dissolution, it often articulated a preference for local mission initiatives, claiming that "Catholic mission leaders in the U.S. believe the time has come for the CSMC to turn over the responsibility for promoting 'mission awareness' to local direction—diocesan mission directors, schools, and school mission units," one publication reported.[25] At the last CSMC convention Bishop Connare reiterated this theme, saying that the

22. "Convention Budget, 1968," CSMC, box 7, folder 18, AAC.

23. "CSMC Convention-goer, Bulletin no. 5, August 27–30, 1970," CSMC, box 8, folder 3, AAC.

24. *Lumen Gentium*, Chapter 3, Section 26; see Flannery, *Vatican Council II*, 381; Bosch, *Transforming Mission*, 371–72. For an exploration of Vatican II's emphasis on local or particular churches see Joseph A. Komonchak, "The Local Realization of the Church," in Alberigo, Jossua, and Komonochak (eds.), *The Reception of Vatican II*, 77–90; Komonchak, "The Local Church and the Church Catholic," 416–47; Adrien Nocent, "The Local Church as Realization of the Church of Christ and Subject of the Eucharist," in Alberigo, Jossua, and Komonochak (eds.), *The Reception of Vatican II*, 215–29.

25. "CSMC Convention-goer, Bulletin no. 5, August 27–30, 1970," CSMC, box 8, folder 3, AAC.

"CSMC will live in another form ... attuned to and strong at the diocesan level."[26] Many, including the leadership of the CSMC, believed that the Church would be more effective and faithful to its mission if its structures were local and diocesan, not national.

The watchword of the late 1960s was "freedom." Aspects of the Second Vatican Council, the peace movement, and the civil rights movement had been anti-authoritarian in purpose and method. Within American Catholicism, clerical culture and the hierarchical structure of the Church seemed to have risen to new heights in the first half of the twentieth century. Clergy and religious were venerated and trusted, almost without exception. In the 1960s, however, these sacred seats of power were criticized vociferously, becoming the lightning rods for protest and scorn. Organizations with a strict hierarchical structure such as the CSMC could not avoid feeling the distrust of power structures.

Institutions that had been revered in the past were seen as the enemy of a modern and progressive human fulfillment. Time-honored parochial institutions including parishes, schools, colleges, and groups such as the Holy Name and St. Vincent de Paul Societies could be suspect. Underground churches and experimental non-territorial parishes developed in response to unfashionable geographical parochial structures. Some questioned whether institutions were outmoded, relics of an earlier time of ghetto Catholicism, or at worst even obstacles to the building of authentic communities.[27]

Those organizations that were able to thrive during this period were "indigenous Catholic Action movements" such as the Grail, Dorothy Day's Catholic Worker movement, Catherine de Hueck's Friendship House, and the Christian Family Movement. These forms of Catholic activism that survived the 1960s were often not national movements but non-traditional, grass-roots communal movements, often small and organized by laity.[28] As such these often lacked "official" status within the Church and were not seen as connected to the hierarchy.[29] The CSMC, which had prided itself

---

26. William G. Connare, "Speech to CSMC National Convention, August 27, 1970," page 9, CSMC, box 8, folder 5, AAC.

27. McGreevy, *Parish Boundaries*, 245–46.

28. On the opposite end of the spectrum were organizations with international backing such as the Society for the Propagation for the Faith and the Holy Childhood Association, both of which remained stable through broad international support.

29. Debra Campbell, "Reformers and Activists," in Kennelly, *American Catholic*

on both the approval of Rome as well as the American hierarchy, did not enjoy such "outsider" status.

"ORDERLY DISSOLUTION": THE 1970 CRUSADE CONVENTION

The Crusade prepared to conclude its more than half a century of mission education and promotion at its final national convention held at the University of Notre Dame, August 27–30, 1970. There some 450 delegates met, a drastic decrease from earlier conventions that had attracted in excess of 4,000. The entire convention aimed at preparing the way for a final vote by the delegates on the cessation of the movement at the end of the 1970–1971 academic year. It fell to Bishop Connare on the first full day of the convention to explain to the membership the "CSMC phase-out," followed by an "open mike" discussion by which students could voice their concerns with the proposal. Seeking to avoid serious discussion on the matter, Bishop Connare exhorted the students in advance of the vote that "this is pre-eminently the moment to 'hang loose.'"[30]

This led up to the adoption of resolutions by the participants urging the present members of the Crusade and all American Catholic youth to continued action on behalf of mission awareness even in the absence of the movement. At the time of the meeting, it was proposed that the Holy Childhood Association continue the work of the CSMC among grade school students. The continuance of programs for college and seminary students was not agreed upon.[31] It was hoped that student activities might also be organized under the lay section of the United States Catholic Mission Council that had been formed near the time of the CSMC's demise.

Women, 175–76. For additional background see Robb, "Specialized Catholic Action in the United States" and two journal issues dedicated to the topic: "Labor and Lay Movements: I," *U.S. Catholic Historian* 9.3 (1990); and "Labor and Lay Movements: II," *U.S. Catholic Historian* 9.4 (1990).

30. William G. Connare, "Speech to CSMC National Convention, August 27, 1970," page 3, CSMC, box 8, folder 5, AAC.

31. "Official Program Twenty-Fourth General CSMC Convention," page 8, CSMC, box 8, folder 1, AAC. The pontifical mission-aid societies wished to continue the mission education programs of the CSMC but did not commit to continuing such programs "'in toto,'" but with the understanding that they could accommodate them as they wished with their own programs. See William G. Connare to Karl J. Alter, February 3, 1970, CSMC, box 48, folder 7, AAC.

Those in attendance approved the student board's resolution that provided "final authority" to the executive board of the CSMC "to provide the orderly dissolution and termination, in the course of the coming year, of the structures and activities of the CSMC."[32] However, the student vote on dissolution held on the first evening of the convention, August 27, 1970, was anything but democratic. A student member of the executive board was asked to read the resolution dismantling the Crusade. According to the notes for that meeting, at the conclusion of the resolution's reading, the chairman was to wait a few seconds and say: "Will all in favor of the adoption of the resolution signify in the usual way by saying 'Aye'?" After waiting a few seconds for the "ayes," the notes commanded the chairman: "DO NOT ask for nays."[33] He then went on to say, "The resolution seems to have received your unanimous approval. The Chairman will see that it is dispatched to our Holy Father."[34] Quietly and "unanimously" the CSMC's own members voted it out of existence.

The convention attempted to put a positive spin on the demise of the movement, calling it an opportunity for "new approaches to mission awareness" through the pontifical mission-aid societies. One CSMC publication stated, "These developments do not mean that programs of action developed by individual CSMC groups must be abandoned. On the contrary, leaders of these groups should make powerful efforts to keep alive the spirit of mission awareness through continuance of these programs."[35] At the conclusion of the "vote" for dissolution, the chairman asked that "there be no note of sadness" but instead "notes of confidence and joy as we face the future of continuing activity for the salvation of the world."[36]

---

32. "CSMC General Convention, Draft of Final Resolution," CSMC, box 8, folder 6, AAC.

33. Emphasis in original. The "chairman" here is presumed to be Rev. Henry J. Klocker, Executive Chairman of the CSMC Board, thought the notes themselves do not indicate his identity.

34. "24th General CSMC Convention, Keynote Meeting Continuity," CSMC, box 8, folder 5, AAC.

35. "CSMC Convention-goer, Bulletin no. 5," August 27–30, 1970, CSMC, box 8, folder 3, AAC.

36. 24th General CSMC Convention, Keynote Meeting Continuity," page 11, CSMC, box 8, folder 5, AAC.

THE CRUSADE'S FINAL GENERATION

While there may not have been any evident sadness or disagreement regarding the movement's demise at the final convention of the Crusade, the leadership of the CSMC harbored doubts about the need to dismantle the movement. Msgr. Henry Klocker, though seemingly supporting the dissolution of the CSMC in 1970, claimed later to be an unwilling participant in its demise. In a 1978 interview, Klocker lamented the end, asking, "Did it really have to close? Couldn't we have fumbled along?" But he admitted, "I was the one holding on . . . I was doing my best to preserve what was here."[37] Still disenchanted with the movement's end in a 1991 interview, Klocker acknowledged that the "sixties were bad years" for the CSMC. Declining interest in the missions, financial difficulties, and a drop in membership were indicative of what he believed was a more general "weakening of faith" which he blamed on secularism and materialism. He did not attribute the decline to the Second Vatican Council as some might have, but instead to the cultural and social changes seen in the 1960s.[38] The decline of the CSMC did not seem to be caused by its inability to adapt to a changing religious and cultural milieu, but the very changes it attempted to navigate rendered its very purpose less urgent. More specifically, the framework of ideas that had buoyed the missionary work of American Catholics—sacrifice, idealism, saving souls, and church planting—were shifting in the wake of new challenges.

The organization's entire life spanned several generations of Americans, suffering its demise at the same time that America's "baby boomers" were graduating from high school and college. The movement appealed less to the generation of youth that matured in the mid to late 1960s. Catholic students educated during the time of the World Wars and the Cold War could easily accept a top-down model of religious organization. Based on the structures of Catholic Action, ecclesial decision-making proceeded from bishop to priests and only then to the laity and student members—if it trickled down to the students at all. Students educated after this time demanded a new model of governance that would allow for independence from authority, particularly from clerical control. Students,

---

37. Quoted in Ben L. Kaufman, "The Surrender of Crusade Castle," *The Enquirer Magazine* (June 11, 1978) 39.

38. Taped interview with Msgr. Klocker by Christine Kroner, University of Cincinnati, Department of History, February 25, 1991, CSMC, AAC.

consequently, sought out membership in other organizations, often secular ones, that could satisfy their requirements for involvement.

Detailing these changes, especially those experienced by America's youth, Andrew Greeley's *Strangers in the House: Catholic Youth in America* assessed the widespread apathy and hopelessness of young people that had replaced an earlier idealism: "There are no more battles to fight, no more mountains to climb, no more crusades to go on, nothing more important to be done. The romantic, exciting, adventurous things are part of the past." For young crusaders, adolescence had provided the opportunity to assist with the greatest, most noble endeavors guided by Church and country. Confident, idealistic, and romantic, they believed strongly in the mission to convert the world to Christ as well as the possibility if not likelihood of its success. The public idealism and the heroic ideal that had previously sustained the CSMC's growth were seemingly lost. According to Greeley, many believed that the youth of the 1960s felt that economic gain and occupational success were the only goals for which to strive. Both could be achieved, Greeley wrote, "without undue spiritual commitment and undue emotional excitement." As he observed, "the bright Catholic world-vision [had grown] dim and hazy."[39]

The culture of the times also resulted in a void of clerical and religious leadership interested in the mission movement. The generation that had guided the movement through the Second World War and the Cold War years was quickly declining. Due to death and retirement longtime Crusade leaders such as Msgr. Freking and Archbishop Alter were no longer active in the movement. The generational "passing on of the torch" found too few willing hands to carry on its distinctive work. The Crusade, which had been a stepping-stone for clerics toward the episcopacy, lacked episcopal patronage in its last years. Those being ordained and entering religious life during and after the council were more likely to seek out forms of social and racial activism at home—involvement in urban ministries, rural mission bands, and Catholic Interracial Councils. The new frontier involved a return to the domestic and the realization that America's own house would best be put into order before it set its sights on rescuing others.

---

39. Greeley, *Strangers in the House*, 9 and 155.

REMEMBERING THE CRUSADE

In its fifty-plus years of existence, the Catholic Students' Mission Crusade represented a dynamic movement of American Catholic youth. Perhaps with the exception of the sodality movement, the CSMC was the most pervasive organization within the vast Catholic educational system in the United States. Peaking at one million members strong, its program of "prayer, study, and sacrifice" contributed to a culture of "mission mindedness" that introduced students to multiple worlds of geographic, linguistic, and ethnic experience. As a form of public Catholicism, the CSMC energized and invited youth to consider the work of the global Church, not only their own neighborhood-based domestic brand of Catholicism.

Spanning several generations, its student members were influenced by World War I, World War II and the Cold War, and finally the Vietnam conflict, Vatican II and the "sixties." Far from being stagnant the movement responded uniquely to each age. At one time its mission of evangelization required it to harness the military imagery coming out of World War I; in the interwar years it utilized a form of popular medievalism. Still later during the time of World War II, the movement became a fierce foe of communism; during the era of Vatican II the organization again reinvented itself to respond to a new theological and social vision of the mission ideal. The four generations of the movement show the dynamism of the CSMC and its ability to respond to change, challenging the notion that pre-conciliar American Catholicism was necessarily monolithic and parochial.

Since the dissolution of the CSMC forty years ago, the spirit of the movement has lived on through its former members. Hundreds of present-day missionaries representing religious orders such as Maryknoll, the Jesuits, Franciscans, Comboni, and Glenmary, were one-time members of the CSMC. Countless priests and religious, at work at home and abroad, can credit the movement for helping to ignite in them the recognition of a religious vocation. Catholics in parishes throughout America still give generously to annual mission appeals, remembering the spirit of sacrifice inculcated by the movement. Catholic elementary students continue to study the Church's efforts at evangelization through missionary works and weekly worshippers routinely recall through prayer the need for unity, reconciliation, and conversion among nations and peoples. The vision of the youthful seminarian, Clifford King, and those who followed him appears less remote today if we recall the missionary spirit that remains alive in the Church, a reminder that much has been accomplished yet much remains unfinished in the Christian effort to evangelize the world.

Bibliography

ARCHIVES AND LIBRARIES

Archives of The Catholic University of America, Washington, DC (ACUA): National Catholic Welfare Conference Collection (NCWC); The Catholic University of America Rector/President Papers; Bishop Thomas Joseph Shahan Papers.

Archives of the Diocese of Richmond, Virginia: Rev. Floyd Keeler File.

Archives of Xavier University, Cincinnati, Ohio (AXU): Catholic Student Mission Crusade Conference Files.

Georgetown University, Lauinger Library, Special Collections Division (GUSC): Rev. Daniel A. Lord, S.J. Papers (DAL); Varia Collection

Historical Archives of the Chancery, Archdiocese of Cincinnati, Ohio (AAC): Catholic Students' Mission Crusade Collection (CSMC).

Midwest Jesuit Archives, St. Louis, Missouri (MJA): Rev. Daniel A. Lord, S.J. Papers (DAL).

INTERVIEWS

Walter, Mary Fran. Interview by David Endres. July 13, 2006. Cincinnati, OH.

Wilson, Raymond J., III. Interview by David Endres. June 3, 2004. Dubuque, IA.

NEWSPAPERS AND PERIODICALS

America (New York, New York)
The Bengalese (Notre Dame, Indiana)
The Bugle Call (St. Mary-of-the-Woods College, St. Mary-of-the-Woods, Indiana)
Catholic Missions (New York, New York)
Catholic Rural Life Bulletin (St. Paul, Minnesota)
Catholic Telegraph (Cincinnati, Ohio)
Cincinnati Enquirer (Cincinnati, Ohio)
Cincinnati Post (Cincinnati, Ohio)
Cincinnati Times-Star (Cincinnati, Ohio)
Field Afar (Boston, Massachusetts and Maryknoll, New York)
The Missionary (Washington, DC)
The Shield (Cincinnati, Ohio)
The Tower (The Catholic University of America, Washington, DC)
Washington Post (Washington, DC)

Bibliography

OTHER

"The Academia of St. John's Seminary, Brighton." *Catholic Missions* 15.4 (1921) 78.

Acta Apostolicae Sedis: Commentarium Officiale. Volume 11. Rome: Typis Polyglottis Vaticanis, 1919.

Alberigo, Giuseppe, Jean Pierre Jossua, and Joseph A Komonchak, editors. *The Reception of Vatican II*. Translated by Matthew J. O'Connell. Washington, DC: The Catholic University of America Press, 1987.

Allitt, Patrick. *Catholic Intellectuals and Conservative Politics in America, 1950–1985*. Ithaca, NY: Cornell University Press, 1993.

Alter, Karl J. *The Mind of an Archbishop: A Study of Man's Essential Relationship to God, Church, Country, and Fellow Man, as Expressed in the Writings of the Most Rev. Karl J. Alter*. Edited by Maurice E. Reardon. Paterson, NJ: St. Anthony's Guild, 1960.

An Appeal to the Catholics of the World to Save the German Foreign Missions. Techny, IL: Mission Press, [1919].

Anderson, Floyd, editor. *Council Daybook: Vatican II, Session 3*. Washington, DC: National Catholic Welfare Conference, 1965.

Anderson, Gerald H., editor. *Mission Legacies: Biographical Studies of Leaders of the Modern Missionary Movement*. American Society of Missiology Series 19. Maryknoll, NY: Orbis, 1994.

Appleby, R. Scott. "Missions and the Making of Americans: Religious Competition for Souls and Citizens." In *Minority Faiths and the American Protestant Mainstream*, edited by Jonathan D. Sarna, 232–78. Urbana: University of Illinois Press, 1998.

Aubert, Roger, J. Bruhls, and J. Hajjar. *The Church in a Secularised Society*. Translated by Janet Sondheimer. The Christian Centuries: A New History of the Catholic Church 5. New York: Paulist, 1978.

———. "Stages of Catholic Ecumenism." In *Renewal of Religious Structures*, vol. 2 of *Theology of Renewal: Proceedings of the Congress on the Theology of the Renewal of the Church: Centenary of Canada, 1867-1967*, edited by L. K. Shook, 183–203. New York: Herder and Herder, 1968.

Avella, Steven. "John T. McNicholas in the Age of Practical Thomism." *Records of the American Catholic Historical Society of Philadelphia* 97 (1986) 15–25.

Avella, Steven, and Elizabeth McKeown, editors. *Public Voices: Catholics in the American Context*. Maryknoll, NY: Orbis, 1999.

Barr, William R. "Introduction: Re-forming Theology in the Global Conversation." In *Constructive Christian Theology in the Worldwide Church*, edited by William R. Barr, 1–10. Grand Rapids, MI: Eerdmans, 1997.

Barry, Colman J., editor. *Readings in Church History*. Westminster, MD: Christian Classics, 1985.

Beaver, R. Pierce. "Mission Motivation Through Three Centuries." In *Reinterpretation in American Church History*, Essays in Divinity 5, edited by Jerald C. Brauer, 113–51. Chicago: University of Chicago Press, 1968.

Bender, Thomas, editor. *Rethinking American History in a Global Age*. Berkeley: University of California Press, 2002.

Bernard of Clairvaux. "In Praise of the New Knighthood." In *Bernard of Clairvaux: Treatises*, Volume 3, Cistercian Fathers Series 19. Kalamazoo, MI: Cistercian Publications, 1977.

Bevans, Stephen. *Models of Contextual Theology.* Faith and Culture Series. Maryknoll, NY: Orbis, 1992.

Black, Gregory D. *The Catholic Crusade Against the Movies, 1940-1975.* New York: Cambridge University Press, 1998.

———. *Hollywood Censored: Morality Codes, Catholics, and the Movies.* Cambridge Studies in the History of Mass Communication. New York: Cambridge University Press, 1994.

Bliss, Frederick M. *Catholic and Ecumenical: History and Hope: Why the Catholic Church Is Ecumenical and What She Is Doing about It.* Franklin, WI: Sheed and Ward, 1999.

Bodnar, John E. *Remaking America: Public Memory, Commemoration, and Patriotism in the Twentieth Century.* Princeton, NJ: Princeton University Press, 1992.

Bosch, David J. *Transforming Mission: Paradigm Shifts in Theology of Mission.* American Society of Missiology Series 16. Maryknoll, NY: Orbis, 1991.

Bovee, David. "The Church and the Land: The National Catholic Rural Life Conference and American Society, 1923-1985." PhD diss., University of Chicago, 1986.

Bowling, M. Lenore. "Social Implications of the Catholic Students' Mission Crusade." MA thesis, The Catholic University of America, 1947.

Brady, Gordon. "The Clerical Conference and Vocations." *The Orb* 1.1 (1946) n.p.

Braisted, Ruth E. *In This Generation: The Story of Robert P. Wilder.* New York: Friendship Press, 1941.

Brandewie, Ernest. *In the Light of the Word: Divine Word Missionaries of North America.* American Society of Missiology Series 29. Maryknoll, NY: Orbis, 2000.

Brechter, Suso. "Decree on the Church's Missionary Activity." In *Commentary on the Documents of Vatican II, Vol.4, Declaration on Christian education; Declaration on religious freedom; Decree on the church's missionary activity; Decree on the ministry and life of priests,* edited by Herbert Vorgrimler, translated by Hilda Graef, W. J. O'Hara, and Ronald Walls, 87-181. New York: Herder and Herder, 1967.

Breen, William D. *Uncle Sam at Home: Civilian Mobilization, Wartime Federalism, and the Council of National Defense, 1917-1919.* Contributions in American Studies 70. Westport, CT: Greenwood, 1984.

Breslin, Thomas A. *China, American Catholicism, and the Missionary.* University Park: Pennsylvania State University Press, 1980.

Brors, Francis X. *God Wills It! A Modern Crusade for an Old Cause: The Mission Work Among the Heathens.* Techny, IL: Mission Press, 1924.

Browne, Henry J. "Peter E. Dietz, Pioneer Planner of Catholic Social Action." *Catholic Historical Review* 33 (1948) 448-56.

Burke, B. Ellen. "The Missionary Movement Among the Children." *The Missionary* 23.2 (1909) 56-59.

Butler, Jon. "Religion in New York City: Faith That Could Not Be." *U.S. Catholic Historian* 22 (2004) 61.

Cadegan, Una M. "Guardians of Democracy or Cultural Storm Troopers? American Catholics and the Control of Popular Media, 1934-1966." *Catholic Historical Review* 87 (2001) 252-82.

———. "The Queen of Peace in the Shadow of War: Fatima and U.S. Catholic Anticommunism." *U.S. Catholic Historian* 22.4 (2004) 1-15.

Carbonneau, Robert. "Life, Death, and Memory: Three Passionists in Hunan, China and the Shaping of an American Mission Perspective in the 1920s." PhD diss., Georgetown University, 1992.

Bibliography

———. "The Passionists in China, 1921–1929: An Essay in Mission Experience." *Catholic Historical Review* 66 (1980) 392–416.
Carey, Patrick W. *The Roman Catholics in America*. Westport, CT: Praeger, 1996.
Carlen, Claudia, editor. *The Papal Encyclicals*. 5 vols. Wilmington, NC: McGrath, 1981.
Carpenter, Joel A., and Wilbert R. Shenk, editors. *Earthen Vessels, American Evangelicals, and Foreign Missions, 1880–1980*. Grand Rapids, MI: Eerdmans, 1990.
"The Catholic Students' League." *Catholic Missions* 14.12 (1920) 284.
"The Catholic Students' Mission Crusade." *The Missionary* 31.9 (1918) 509–10.
Catholic Students' Mission Crusade, U.S.A. *Africa in Five Hours*. CSMC Five-hour Series. Cincinnati, OH: Catholic Students' Mission Crusade, U.S.A., 1961.
———. *To Defend the Cross: The Story of the Fourth General Convention of the Catholic Students' Mission Crusade at the University of Notre Dame*. Cincinnati, OH: Catholic Students' Mission Crusade, 1923.
Cavert, Samuel McCrea. *The American Churches in the Ecumenical Movement, 1900–1968*. New York: Association Press, 1968.
Chidester, David. *Christianity: A Global History*. San Francisco: HarperSanFrancisco, 2000.
Chinnici, Joseph P. "The Catholic Community at Prayer, 1926–1976." In *Habits of Devotion: Catholic Religious Practice in Twentieth-Century America*, edited by James M. O'Toole, 9–87. Ithaca, NY: Cornell University Press, 2004.
———. "Changing Religious Practice and the End of Christendom in the United States 1965–1986." *U. S. Catholic Historian* 23.4 (2005) 61–82.
———. "Reception of Vatican II in the United States." *Theological Studies* 64 (2003) 461–94.
———, and Angelyn Dries, editors. *Prayer and Practice in the American Catholic Community*. American Catholic Identities. Maryknoll, NY: Orbis, 2000.
"The Church in the World." *Theology Today* 25 (1968) 243.
Civardi, Luigi. *A Manual of Catholic Action*. Translated by C. C. Martindale. New York: Sheed and Ward, 1943.
Cohen, Robert. *When the Old Left Was Young: Student Radicals and America's First Mass Student Movement, 1929–1941*. New York: Oxford University Press, 1993.
Colaianni, James F. "Bishop Sheen and the Great Charity Hoax," *Ramparts* 5 (1966) 6–8.
Concordia, George L. "Holy Name Society in America." In *The Encyclopedia of American Catholic History*, edited by Michael Glazier and Thomas Shelley, 656–57. Collegeville, MN: Liturgical, 1997.
Connors, Joseph M. "The Participation of the U.S. Catholic Church in the World-Wide Missionary Effort: Problems, Projections, and Programs." In *Mission in the '70s: What Direction?*, edited by John T. Boberg and James A. Scherer, 129–46. Chicago: Chicago Cluster of Theological Schools, 1972.
"Converting the Old World" *The Missionary* 8 (1903) 27.
Cooney, John. *The American Pope: Life and Times of Francis Cardinal Spellman*. New York: Times Books, 1984.
Coppa, Frank J. "Pope Pius XII and the Cold War: The Post-war Confrontation between Catholicism and Communism." In *Religion and the Cold War*, edited by Dianne Kirby, 50–66. Cold War History Series. New York: Palgrave Macmillan, 2002.
Costello, Gerald M. *Mission to Latin America: The Successes and Failures of a Twentieth Century Crusade*. Maryknoll, NY: Orbis, 1979.
Cotter, James P., editor. *The Word in the Third World*. Washington, DC: Corpus, 1968.

Bibliography

"A Cradle of Future Missionaries." *The Bengalese* 4.1 (1923) 17.

Cramer, George N. "What Will America Do?" *Catholic Missions* 12.10 (1918) 232–33.

Crews, Clyde F. *American and Catholic: A Popular History of Catholicism in the United States*. Cincinnati, OH: St. Anthony Messenger, 2004.

Crosby, Donald. "The Angry Catholics: Catholic Opinion of Senator Joseph R. McCarthy, 1950–57." PhD diss., Brandeis University, 1973.

———. *God, Church, and Flag: Senator Joseph R. McCarthy and the Catholic Church, 1950–1957*. Chapel Hill: University of North Carolina Press, 1978.

———. "The Jesuits and Joe McCarthy." *Church History* 46 (1977) 374–88.

———. "The Politics of Religion." In *The Specter: Original Essays on the Cold War and the Origins of McCarthyism*, edited by Robert Griffith and Athan Theoharis, 18–38. New York: New Viewpoints, 1974.

Curry, Lerond. *Protestant-Catholic Relations in America: World War I through Vatican II*. Lexington: University Press of Kentucky, 1972.

Czuchlewski, Paul E. "Liberal Catholicism and American Racism, 1924–1960." *Records of the American Catholic Historical Society of Philadelphia* 85.3–4 (1974) 144–62.

Davis, Cyprian, editor. *To Prefer Nothing to Christ: St. Meinrad Archabbey, 1854–2004*. St. Meinrad, IN: Saint Meinrad Archabbey, 2004.

De Groot, Gerard. *Student Protest: The Sixties and After*. London: Addison Wesley, 1998.

Delaney, Joan. "From Cremona to Edinburgh: Bishop Bonmelli and the World Missionary Conference of 1910." *Ecumenical Review* 52 (2000) 418–31.

De Santis, Vincent P. "American Catholics and McCarthyism." *Catholic Historical Review* 51 (1965) 1–30.

Desmond, Jane C. and Virginia R. Domínguez. "Resituating American Studies in a Critical Internationalism." *American Quarterly* 48 (1996) 475–490.

Dinges, William D. "'An Army of Youth': The Sodality Movement and the Practice of Apostolic Mission." *U.S. Catholic Historian* 19.3 (2001) 35–49.

Dinnerstein, Leonard. *Antisemitism in America*. New York: Oxford University Press, 1994.

Dixon, Blase. "The Catholic University of America, 1909–1928: The Rectorship of Thomas Joseph Shahan." PhD diss., The Catholic University of America, 1972.

Doenecke, Justus D., editor. *In Danger Undaunted: The Anti-Interventionist Movement of 1940–1941 as Revealed in the Papers of the America First Committee*. Hoover Archival Documentaries/Hoover Press Publication 384. Stanford, CA: Hoover Institution Press, 1990.

Dohen, Dorothy. *Nationalism and American Catholicism*. New York: Sheed and Ward, 1967.

Dolan, Jay P. *The American Catholic Experience: A History from the Colonial Times to the Present*. Garden City, NY: Doubleday, 1985.

———. *In Search of an American Catholicism: A History of Religion and Culture in Tension*. New York: Oxford University Press, 2002.

Dolan, Timothy Michael. *"Some Seed Fell on Good Ground": The Life of Edwin V. O'Hara*. Washington, DC: Catholic University of America Press, 1992.

Dorr, Donal. *Mission in Today's World*. Maryknoll, NY: Orbis, 2000.

Dries, Angelyn. "American Catholics and World Religions, Theory and Praxis: 1893–1959." *American Catholic Studies* 113 (2002) 31–50.

———. "The Foreign Mission Impulse of the American Catholic Church, 1893–1925." *International Bulletin of Missionary Research* 15.2 (1991) 61–66.

Bibliography

———. "The Hero-Martyr Myth in United States Catholic Foreign Mission Literature, 1893–1925." *Missiology: An International Review* 19 (1991) 305–314.

———. "The Legacy of John J. Considine, M.M." *International Bulletin of Missionary Research* 21.2 (1997) 80–84.

———. "The Missionary Critique of American Institutions: From Catholic Americans to Global Catholics, 1948–1976." *U. S. Catholic Historian* 17 (1999) 59–72.

———. *The Missionary Movement in American Catholic History*. American Society of Missiology Series 26. Maryknoll, NY: Orbis, 1998.

———. "Whatever Happened to the Catholic Students Mission Crusade." *The Living Light* 34.3 (1998) 61–64.

———. "'The Whole Way into the Wilderness': The Foreign Mission Impulse of the American Catholic Church, 1893–1925." PhD diss., Graduate Theological Union, 1990.

Dulles, Avery. "The Changing Nature of Mission." *American Ecclesiastical Review* 157 (1967) 366–72.

Dumenil, Lynn. "The Tribal Twenties: 'Assimilated' Catholics' Response to Anti-Catholicism in the 1920s." *Journal of American Ethnic History* 11 (1991) 21–49.

Durchholz, Patricia. *Defining Mission: Comboni Missionaries in North America*. Lanham, MD: University Press of America, 1999.

Eberhardt, Auleen Bordeaux. "Students' Mission Crusade." *Commonweal* 22 (1935) 444.

Ede, Alfred J. *The Lay Crusade for a Catholic America: A Study of the American Federation of Catholic Societies, 1900–1919*. The Heritage of American Catholicism. New York: Garland, 1988.

Edwards, Wendy J. Deichmann. "Forging an Ideology for American Missions: Josiah Strong and Manifest Destiny." In *North American Foreign Missions, 1810–1914: Theory, Theology, and Policy*, edited by Wilbert R. Shenk, 163–91. Grand Rapids, MI: Eerdmans, 2004.

Ellwood, Robert S. *The Sixties Spiritual Awakening: American Religion Moving from Modern to Postmodern*. New Brunswick, NJ: Rutgers University Press, 1994.

Endres, David J. "The Legacy of Thaddeus Yang." *International Bulletin of Missionary Research* 34 (2010) 23–28.

Erenberg, Lewis A. *Swingin' the Dream: Big Band Jazz and the Rebirth of American Culture*. Chicago: University of Chicago Press, 1998.

Erlich, John, and Susan Erlich, editors. *Student Power, Participation and Revolution*. New York: Association Press, 1970.

Evans, John Whitney. *The Newman Movement: Roman Catholics in American Higher Education 1883–1971*. Notre Dame, IN: University of Notre Dame Press, 1980.

Faherty, William B. "A Half-Century with the Queen's Work." *Woodstock Letters* 92 (1963) 99–114.

Falconi, Carlo. *The Popes in the Twentieth Century*. Translated by Muriel Grindrod. Boston: Little, Brown, 1967.

Farrell, John T. "Archbishop Ireland and Manifest Destiny." *Catholic Historical Review* 33 (1947) 269–301.

Ferrer. "Lift Up Your Eyes." *Catholic Missions* 11.12 (1917) 282–83.

Fischer, Hermann J. *For Christ's Kingdom*. Techny, IL: Mission Press, 1913.

Fishburn, Janet F. "The Social Gospel as Missionary Ideology." In *North American Foreign Missions, 1810–1914: Theory, Theology, and Policy*, edited by Wilbert R. Shenk, 218–42. Studies in the History of Christian Missions. Grand Rapids, MI: Eerdmans, 2004.

Fisher, James T. *The Catholic Counterculture in America, 1933–1962.* Studies in Religion. Chapel Hill: University of North Carolina Press, 1989.

———. *Communion of Immigrants: A History of Catholics in America.* Religion in American Life. New York: Oxford University Press, 2002.

———. *Dr. America: The Lives of Thomas A. Dooley, 1927–1961.* Culture, Politics, and the Cold War. Amherst: University of Massachusetts Press, 1997.

Flannery, Austin, editor. *Vatican Council II: The Conciliar and Post Conciliar Documents.* New revised ed. Vatican Collection 1. Dublin: Dominican Publications, 1992.

Flynn, George Q. *Roosevelt and Romanism: Catholics and American Diplomacy, 1937–1945.* Contributions in American History 47. Westport, CT: Greenwood, 1976.

Fogarty, Gerald P. *The Vatican and the American Hierarchy from 1870 to 1965.* Wilmington, DE: Michael Glazier, 1985.

———. *The Vatican and the Americanist Crisis: Denis J. O'Connell, American Agent in Rome, 1885–1903.* Miscellanea historiae pontificate 36. Rome: Università Gregoriana, 1974.

Forman, Charles W. "Evangelization and Civilization: Protestant Missionary Motivation in the Imperialist Era: The Americans." *International Bulletin of Missionary Research* 6.2 (1982) 54–56.

Fortin, Roger. *Faith and Action: A History of the Archdiocese of Cincinnati, 1821–1996.* The Urban Life and Urban Landscape Series. Columbus: Ohio State University Press, 2002.

Fox, Mary Harrita. *Peter E. Dietz, Labor Priest.* Notre Dame, IN: University of Notre Dame Press, 1953.

Freking, Edward A., Henry J. Klocker, and J. Paul Spaeth, editors. *The Church at Work in the World.* CSMC Five-hour Series. Cincinnati, OH: The Crusade, 1961.

Freri, Joseph. "Native Clergy for Mission Countries." *Catholic Missions* 11.9 (1917) 193–201.

Freytag, Anthony. *The Catholic Mission Feast: A Manual for the Arrangement of Mission Celebrations.* Techny, IL: Mission Press, 1914.

Gaffey, James P. *Francis Clement Kelley and the American Catholic Dream.* Bensenville, IL: Heritage Foundation, 1980.

Gaffney, Mary Felicitas. "A Study of the Use of the Materials of the Catholic Students' Mission Crusade to Achieve International Understanding." MA thesis, De Paul University, Chicago, 1958.

Gallagher, Charles R. "The United States and the Vatican in Yugoslavia, 1945–1950." In *Religion and the Cold War*, edited by Dianne Kirby, 118–44. Cold War History Series. New York: Palgrave Macmillan, 2003.

Gallup, George. *The Gallup Poll: Public Opinion, 1935–1971.* Vol. 3, *1959–1971.* New York: Random House, 1972.

Gamble, Richard M. *The War for Righteousness: Progressive Christianity, the Great War, and the Rise of the Messianic Nation.* Wilmington, DE: ISI Books, 2003.

Garneau, James. "'Commandos for Christ': The Foundation of the Missionary Society of St. James the Apostle and the 'Americanism' of the 1950s and 1960s." PhD diss., The Catholic University of America, 2000.

Gavin, Thomas F. *Champion of Youth: A Dynamic Story of a Dynamic Man, Daniel A. Lord, S.J.* Boston: St. Paul Editions, 1977.

Bibliography

Gillard, John T. *Colored Catholics in the United States: An Investigation of Catholic Activity in Behalf of the Negroes in the United States and a Survey of the Present Condition of the Colored Missions.* Baltimore, MD: Josephite, 1941.

Glassberg, David. *American Historical Pageantry: The Uses of Tradition in the Early Twentieth Century.* Chapel Hill: The University of North Carolina Press, 1990.

Gleason, Philip. *Contending with Modernity: Catholic Higher Education in the Twentieth Century.* New York: Oxford University Press, 1995.

———. *Keeping the Faith: American Catholicism Past and Present.* Notre Dame, IN: University of Notre Dame Press, 1987.

———. "Pluralism, Democracy, and Catholicism in the Era of World War II." *Review of Politics* 49 (1997) 208–30.

Grant, Philip A., Jr. "Bishop Bernard J. Sheil's Condemnation of Senator Joseph R. McCarthy." *Records of the American Catholic Historical Society of Philadelphia* 97 (1986) 43–50.

Greeley, Andrew M. *The Church and the Suburbs.* New York: Sheed and Ward, 1959.

———. *Strangers in the House: Catholic Youth in America.* New York: Sheed and Ward, 1961.

Gross, Robert. "The Transnational Turn: Rediscovering American Studies in a Wider World." *Journal of American Studies* 34 (2000) 373–93.

Guilday, Peter. *The National Pastorals of the American Hierarchy (1792–1919).* Washington, DC: National Catholic Welfare Council, 1923.

Hagspiel, Bruno. *Along the Mission Trail.* 5 vols. Techny, IL: Mission Press, 1925–1928.

———. *Father Bruno's Vocation Letters.* 2 vols. Techny, IL: Mission Press, 1936.

———. *Financing a Vicariate in the Foreign Mission Field.* Techny, IL: Mission Press, 1924.

———. "The Young Man and Foreign Missions." *America* 12.17 (1915) 408–9.

Halsey, William M. *The Survival of American Innocence: Catholicism in an Era of Disillusionment, 1920–1940.* Notre Dame Studies in American Catholicism 2. Notre Dame, IN: University of Notre Dame Press, 1980.

Hannigan, Greg. "What Kind of Love?" *Cosmic* 1.3 (1969) 2.

Hasting, Adrian, editor. *A World History of Christianity.* Grand Rapids, MI: Eerdmans, 1999.

Hebblethwaite, Peter. "Why Missions?" *Catholic World* 205 (1967) 335–39.

Hecht, Robert A. *An Unordinary Man: A Life of Father John LaFarge, S.J.* ATLA Monograph Series 39. Lanham, MD: Scarecrow, 1996.

Heitmann, John A. "Doing 'True Science': The Early History of the Institutum Divi Thomae, 1935–1951." *Catholic Historical Review* 88 (2002) 702–22.

Hennesey, James J. *American Catholics: A History of the Roman Catholic Community in the United States.* New York: Oxford University Press, 1981.

Herberg, Will. *Protestant, Catholic, Jew: An Essay in American Religious Sociology.* Garden City, NY: Doubleday, 1955.

Higham, John. *Strangers in the Land: Patterns of American Nativism, 1860–1925.* New Brunswick, NJ: Rutgers University Press, 1955.

Hill, Patricia R. *The World Their Household: The American Woman's Foreign Mission Movement and Cultural Transformation, 1870–1920.* Women and Culture Series. Ann Arbor: University of Michigan Press, 1985.

Hillman, Eugene. "Anonymous Christianity and the Missions." *Downside Review* 84 (1966) 361–79.

Hitchcock, James. "Americanism: The Phantom Heresy Reconsidered." In *Faith and Sources of Faith: Proceedings of the Sixth Convention of the Fellowship of Catholic Scholars*, edited by Paul L. Williams, 105–18. Scranton, PA: Northeast Books, 1983.

Hoare, Frank, S.S.C., "The Influence of the 'Crusade' Symbol and the 'War' Metaphor on Motivation and Attitudes of the Maynooth Mission to China, 1918–1929." *U. S. Catholic Historian* 24.3 (2006) 55–74.

Hoffman, Ronan. "Conversion and the Mission of the Church." *Journal of Ecumenical Studies* 5 (1968) 1–20.

———. *The Council and the Missions*. Scholia Series 1. Cincinnati, OH: CSMC Press, 1963.

———. "The Development of Mission Theology in the Twentieth Century." *Theological Studies* 23 (1962) 419–41.

———. "The Missionary Church and New Realities." *Homiletic and Pastoral Review* 68 (1968) 299–304.

Hoffman, Ronan, and James A. Magner. *Latin America: Pattern for the 'Sixties*. CSMC Five-hour Series. Cincinnati, OH: CSMC Press, 1961.

Hogan, Edmund M. *The Irish Missionary Movement: A Historical Survey, 1830–1980*. Washington, DC: The Catholic University of America Press, 1990.

Hogg, W. Richey. "Edinburgh 1910 – Perspective 1980." *Occasional Bulletin of Missionary Research* 4 (1980) 146–53.

———. "Vatican II's *Ad Gentes*: A Twenty-Year Retrospective." *International Bulletin of Missionary Research* 9 (1985) 146–54.

Holland, R. F. *European Decolonization, 1918–1981: An Introductory Survey*. New York: St. Martin's, 1985.

Holmes, J. Derek. *The Papacy in the Modern World, 1914–1978*. New York: Crossroad, 1981.

Hopkins, C. Howard. "John R. Mott (1865–1955) Architect of World Mission and Unity." In *Mission Legacies: Biographical Studies of Leaders of the Modern Missionary Movement*, edited by Gerald H. Anderson, 79–84. American Society of Missiology Series 19. Maryknoll, NY: Orbis, 1994.

———. *John R. Mott, 1865–1955: A Biography*. Grand Rapids, MI: Eerdmans, 1979.

Howard, David M. *Student Power in World Evangelism*. 2nd ed. Downers Grove, IL: InterVarsity, 1979.

Huizinga, Johan. *The Waning of The Middle Ages: A Study of the Forms of Life, Thought and Art in France and the Netherlands in the XIVth and XVth Centuries*. London: Edward Arnold, 1970.

Hunter, Jane. *The Gospel of Gentility: American Women Missionaries in Turn-of-the-Century China*. New Haven, CT: Yale University Press, 1984.

Husslein, Joseph. "A Catholic Students' Convention." *America* 19.11 (1918) 266–67.

———. "The Coming Crusade." *America* 17.8 (1917) 200–201.

Hutchison, William R. *Errand to the World: American Protestant Thought and Foreign Missions*. Chicago: University of Chicago Press, 1987.

———. "A Moral Equivalent for Imperialism: Americans and the Promotion of 'Christian Civilization,' 1880–1910." In *Mission Ideologies in the Imperialist Era: 1880–1910*, Torben Christiensen and William R. Hutchison, 167–78. Århus, Denmark: Aros, 1982.

"An Impressive Aspect of the Catholic University of America." *American Ecclesiastical Review* 85 (1931) 520–24.

Bibliography

Ireland, John. "Father Hecker and America." *The Missionary* 1 (1896) 5.

Irvin, Dale T., and Scott W. Sunquist. *A History of the World Christian Movement*. Vol. 1, *Earliest Christianity to 1453*. Maryknoll, NY: Orbis, 2001.

Janser, Peter T. "The Seminary and Mission Endeavor." In *Catholic Educational Association Proceedings and Addresses*. Sixteenth Annual Meeting, June 23–26, 1919. Columbus, OH: Catholic Educational Association, 1919.

Jay, Eric G. *The Church: Its Changing Image Through Twenty Centuries*. Vol. 2, *1700 to the Present Day*. London: SPCK, 1978.

Jedin, Hubert, and John Patrick Dolan, editors. *History of the Church*. Vols. 5–9. New York: Crossroad, 1980–1982.

Jonas, Thomas J. *The Divided Mind: American Catholic Evangelists in the 1890s*. The Heritage of American Catholicism 17. New York: Garland, 1988.

Kantowicz, Edward R. *Corporation Sole: Cardinal Mundelein and Chicago Catholicism*. Notre Dame Studies in American Catholicism. Notre Dame, IN: University of Notre Dame Press, 1983.

Kasdorf, Hans. "Missiology as a Discipline in Historical Perspective." In *Reflection and Projection: Missiology at the Threshold of 2001: Festschrift in honor of George W. Peters for his eightieth birthday*, edited by Hans Kasdorf and Klaus W. Müller, 219–38. Bad Liebenzell: Verlag der Liebenzeller Mission, 1988.

Kauffman, Christopher J. "Americanism." In *The Modern Catholic Encyclopedia*, edited by Michael Glazier and Monica Hellwig, 24–26. Collegeville, MN: Liturgical, 1994.

———. "Edward McSweeney, the Knights of Columbus, and the Irish-American Response to Anglo-Saxonism, 1900–1925." *American Catholic Studies* 114.4 (2003) 51–65.

———. *Faith and Fraternalism: The History of the Knights of Columbus, 1882–1992*. New York: Harper and Row, 1982.

———. "Formation of American Identities of Three Congregations of Men Religious." *U.S. Catholic Historian* 22 (2004) 127–46.

———. *Mission to Rural America: The Story of W. Howard Bishop, Founder of Glenmary*. New York: Paulist, 1991.

———. *Patriotism and Fraternalism in the Knights of Columbus A History of the Fourth Degree*. New York: Crossroad, 2001.

Keane, John. "The Apostolic Mission House and the Catholic University." *The Missionary* 9 (1904) 9–11.

Keeler, Floyd. "College Sodalities and the Mission Crusade." *America* 23.5 (1920) 103–4.

———. "Mission Study in Our Schools." *The Catholic Educational Review* 21 (1923) 283–86.

———. "Missionary Organization and the Mission Societies." *American Ecclesiastical Review* 74 (1926) 124–28.

Keene, Jennifer D. *The United States and the First World War*. Seminar Studies in History. New York: Longman, 2000.

Kelley, Francis C., editor. *The First American Catholic Missionary Congress: Held Under the Auspices of the Catholic Church Extension Society of the United States of America*. Chicago: J. S. Hyland, 1909.

———. *The Story of Extension*. Chicago: Extension, 1922.

———. *The Two Great American Catholic Missionary Congresses: Held Under the Auspices of the Catholic Church Extension Society of the United States of America*. Chicago: J. S. Hyland, 1914.

Kelly, Timothy. "Suburbanization and the Decline of Catholic Public Ritual in Pittsburgh." *Journal of Social History* 28 (1994) 311–30.
Kennedy, David M. *Over Here: The First World War and American Society*. New York: Oxford University Press, 1980.
Kennedy, Ruby Jo Reeves. "Single or Triple Melting Pot?: Intermarriage in New Haven, 1870–1940." *American Journal of Sociology* 49 (1944) 331–39.
Kennedy, Thomas. "Missions, Catholic." In *The Catholic Encyclopedia* 10:375–78. New York: Encyclopedia Press, 1913.
Kennelly, Karen M. *American Catholic Women: A Historical Exploration*. Makers of the Catholic Community. New York: Macmillan, 1989.
———. "Foreign Missions and the Renewal Movement." *Review for Religious* 49 (1990) 445–63.
Kilby, Karen. *Karl Rahner: Theology and Philosophy*. New York: Routledge, 2004.
King, Clifford J. *I Remember: Memoirs of Clifford J. King, S.V.D.* Techny, IL: Divine Word, 1968.
Knitter, Paul F. *No Other Name? A Critical Survey of Christian Attitudes Toward the World Religions*. American Society of Missiology Series 7. Maryknoll, NY: Orbis, 1985.
Komonchak, Joseph A. "The Local Church and the Church Catholic: The Contemporary Theological Problematic," *Jurist* 52 (1992) 416–47.
Komonchak, Joseph A., and Giuseppe Alberigo. *History of Vatican II*. 5 vols. Translated by Matthew J. O'Connell. Maryknoll, NY: Orbis, 1995–2006.
Koren, Henry. *The Serpent and the Dove: A History of the Congregation of the Holy Ghost in the United States, 1745–1984*. Pittsburgh, PA: Spiritus, 1985.
Kselman, Thomas A., and Steven Avella. "Marian Piety and the Cold War in the United States." *Catholic Historical Review* 72 (1986) 403–24.
Latourelle, René, editor. *Vatican II: Assessment and Perspectives Twenty-Five Years After (1962–1987)*. 3 vols. New York: Paulist, 1988–1989.
Latourette, Kenneth Scott. *A History of the Expansion of Christianity*. 7 vols. New York: Harper & Brothers, 1937–45. Reprint, Grand Rapids, MI: Zondervan, 1970.
———. "The Missionary Awakening Among Roman Catholics in the United States." *International Review of Missions* 11 (1922) 439–44.
Lears, T. J. Jackson. *No Place of Grace: Antimodernism and the Transformation of American Culture, 1880–1920*. New York: Pantheon, 1981.
Lebhar, Neil. "Why Did the Yankees Go Home? A Study of Episcopal Missions, 1953–1977." *Historical Magazine of the Protestant Episcopal Church* 48 (1979) 27–43.
LeBrun, Jacques. "Politics and Spirituality: The Devotion to the Sacred Heart." *Concilium* 69 (1971) 29–43.
Lederer, William J., and Eugene Burdick. *The Ugly American*. New York: Norton, 1958.
Le Guillou, Marie-Joseph. "Mission as an Ecclesiological Theme." In *Re-thinking the Church's Mission*. Concilium 13. New York: Paulist, 1966.
Lord, Daniel A. *Forward, America!* Mission Series 1. New York: Jesuit Mission Press, 1929.
———. *Played by Ear: The Autobiography of Daniel A. Lord, S.J.* Chicago: Loyola University Press, 1956.
Madden, Thomas F. *A Concise History of the Crusades*. Critical Issues in History. Lanham, MD: Rowman and Littlefield, 1999.
———, editor. *The Crusades: The Essential Readings*. Blackwell Essential Readings in History. Malden, MA: Blackwell, 2002.

Bibliography

Massa, Mark. *Catholicism and American Culture: Fulton Sheen, Dorothy Day, and the Notre Dame Football Team.* New York: Crossroad, 1999.

McAvoy, Thomas T. *The Great Crisis in American Catholic History, 1895–1900.* Chicago: Regnery, 1957.

McDonough, Peter. *Men Astutely Trained: A History of the Jesuits in the American Century.* New York: Macmillan, 1992.

McGavran, Donald. *The Conciliar-Evangelical Debate: The Crucial Documents, 1964–1976.* 2nd enl. ed. South Pasadena, CA: William Carey Library, 1977.

McGloin, Joseph T. *Backstage Missionary: Father Dan Lord, S.J.* New York: Pageant, 1958.

McGreevy, John T. *Catholicism and American Freedom.* New York: Norton, 2003.

———. *Parish Boundaries: The Catholic Encounter with Race in the Twentieth-Century Urban North.* Historical Studies of Urban America. Chicago: University of Chicago Press, 1996.

McGuiness, Margaret M. "The Call of the East: The Early Years of the Catholic Near East Welfare Association," *Records of the American Catholic Historical Society of Philadelphia* 103.3–4 (1992) 33–42.

McKeown, Elizabeth. "The National Bishops' Conference: An Analysis of its Origins." *Catholic Historical Review* 66 (1980) 565–83.

———. "The 'National Idea' in the History of the American Episcopal Conference." In *Episcopal Conferences: Historical, Canonical, and Theological Studies,* edited by Thomas J. Reese, 59–84. Washington, DC: Georgetown University Press, 1989.

———. *War and Welfare: American Catholics and World War I.* The Heritage of American Catholicism 21. New York: Garland, 1988.

McManners, John. "The Expansion of Christianity (1500–1800)." In *The Oxford Illustrated History of Christianity,* edited by John McManners, 301–37. New York: Oxford University Press, 1990.

McNamara, Patrick. *A Catholic Cold War: Edmund A. Walsh, S.J., and the Politics of American Anticommunism.* New York: Fordham University Press, 2005.

McNeal, Patricia. "Catholic Conscientious Objection During World War II." *Catholic Historical Review* 61 (1975) 222–42.

McNicholas, John T. *Mosaic of a Bishop: An Autobiographical Appreciation of His Grace, The Most Reverend John T. McNicholas . . . Gained from His Addresses, Sermons and Correspondence.* Paterson, NJ: St. Anthony Guild, 1957.

———. *Our Youth of Tomorrow: Sermon Preached at the Tenth National Convention of the Catholic Students' Mission Crusade, Cleveland, August 18, 1937.* Paterson, NJ: St. Anthony Guild, 1937.

Meigs, Mark. *Optimism at Armageddon: Voices of American Participants in the First World War.* Washington Square, NY: New York University Press, 1997.

Metzler, Josef. "Pius XI (1857–1939) The Missionary Pope." In *Mission Legacies: Biographical Studies of Leaders of the Modern Missionary Movement,* edited by Gerald H. Anderson, 55–61. American Society of Missiology Series 19. Maryknoll, NY: Orbis, 1994.

———, editor. *Sacrae Congregationis de Propaganda Fide memoria rerum, 1622–1972.* Rome: Herder, 1971–1976.

"Millions Let Us Pour Into the Missions." *Catholic Missions* 11.3 (1917) 70.

Minus, Paul M., Jr. *The Catholic Rediscovery of Protestantism: A History of Roman Catholic Ecumenical Pioneering.* An Exploration Book. New York: Paulist, 1976.

"Missioners down 20% in 4 years." *National Catholic Reporter* (November 24, 1972) 5.

Bibliography

"A Modern Conception of the Salvation of the Infidels which Hampers Apostolic Zeal according to Father Karl Rahner." *Christ to the World* 8 (1963) 421–28.

"Monsignor Edward A. Freking." *Centric* 1.4 (1970) 2.

Mosse, George L. *Fallen Soldiers: Reshaping the Memory of the World Wars*. New York: Oxford University Press, 1990.

Mott, John R. *Five Decades and a Forward View*. New York: Harper, 1939.

Müller, Karl. *Josef Schmidlin (1876–1944) Papsthistoriker und Begründer der Katholischen Missionswissenschaft*. Studia Insituti Missiological Societatis Verbi Divini 47. Nettetal: Steyler, 1989.

———. "Joseph Schmidlin (1876–1944) Pioneer of Catholic Missiology." In *Mission Legacies: Biographical Studies of Leaders of the Modern Missionary Movement*, edited by Gerald H. Anderson, 402–9. American Society of Missiology Series 19. Maryknoll, NY: Orbis, 1994.

———. "The Legacy of Joseph Schmidlin." *Occasional Bulletin of Missionary Research* 4.3 (1980) 109–13.

Murphy, Elly, et al., editors. *Hope for the Decade: A Look at the Issues Facing Catholic Youth Ministry*. Washington, DC: National Catholic Youth Organization Federation, 1980.

Nason, Mary Francine. "Educational Activities of Archbishop John T. McNicholas, O.P., 1925–1950." MA thesis, The Catholic University of America, 1955.

National Catholic Reporter. "Missiologist Marks End of Missions." September 20, 1967.

National Catholic Reporter. "Missioners Down 20% in 4 years." November 24, 1972.

National Headquarters of the Holy Name Society. *Jesus, His Name: An Informal Sketch Concerning the Holy Name and the Holy Name Society*. Somerset, OH: Rosary, 1947.

Neill, Stephen. *A History of Christian Missions*. New York: Penguin, 1990.

Nevins, Albert. "End of an Era: The Missions Reappraised." *The Critic* 23.4 (1965) 32–37.

Nuesse, C. Joseph. *The Catholic University of America: A Centennial History*. Washington, DC: Catholic University of America Press, 1990.

Nutt, Rick. "G. Sherwood Eddy and the Attitudes of Protestants in the United States toward Global Mission." *Church History* 66 (1997) 502–21.

O'Brien, David J. *Public Catholicism*. Makers of the Catholic Community. New York: Macmillan, 1989.

Ochs, Stephen J. *Desegregating the Altar: The Josephites and the Struggle for Black Priests, 1871–1960*. Baton Rouge: Louisiana State University Press, 1990.

O'Connell, Marvin R. *John Ireland and the American Catholic Church*. St. Paul: Minnesota Historical Society Press, 1988.

O'Connor, David L. "Defenders of the Faith: American Catholic Lay Organizations and Anticommunism, 1917–1975." PhD diss., State University of New York at Stony Brook, 2000.

O'Malley, John W. *Tradition and Transition: Historical Perspectives on Vatican II*. Theology and Life Series 26. Wilmington, DE: Michael Glazier, 1989.

O'Toole, James M., editor. *Habits of Devotion: Catholic Religious Practice in Twentieth-Century America*. Cushwa Center Studies of Catholicism in Twentieth-Century America. Ithaca, NY: Cornell University Press, 2004.

"Our Soldiers of the Cross." *Catholic Missions* 12.1 (1918) 22.

Parker, Michael. *The Kingdom of Character: The Student Volunteer Movement for Foreign Missions (1886–1926)*. Lanham, MD: University Press of America, 1998.

Bibliography

Pasquini, John J. *Atheism and Salvation: Atheism from the Perspective of Anonymous Christianity in the Thought of the Revolutionary Mystic and Theologian Karl Rahner.* Lanham, MD: University Press of America, 2000.

Patterson, James A. "The Legacy of Robert P. Wilder." *International Bulletin of Missionary Research* 15 (1991) 26–32.

Phillips, Clifton J. "Changing Attitudes in the Student Volunteer Movement of Great Britain and North America, 1886–1928." In *Mission Ideologies in the Imperialist Era: 1880–1910*, edited by Torben Christiensen and William R. Hutchison, 131–45. Århus, Denmark: Aros, 1982.

———. "The Student Volunteer Movement and Its Role in China Missions, 1886–1920." In *The Missionary Enterprise in China and America*, edited by John K. Fairbank, 91–109. Harvard Studies in American-East Asian Relations 6. Cambridge, MA: Harvard University Press, 1974.

Pierson, Paul. "Roman Catholic Missions since Vatican II: An Evangelical Assessment." *International Bulletin of Missionary Research* 9.4 (1985) 165–67.

Piper, John F., Jr. *The American Churches in World War I.* Athens, OH: Ohio University Press, 1985.

———. "The Development of the Missionary Ideas of Robert E. Speer." In *North American Foreign Missions, 1810–1914: Theory, Theology, and Policy*, edited by Wilbert R. Shenk, 261–80. Studies in the History of Chirstian Missions. Grand Rapids, MI: Eerdmans, 2004.

———. *Robert E. Speer: Prophet of the American Church.* Louisville, KY: Geneva, 2000.

Portier, William L. "From Historicity to History: One Theologian's Intergenerational American Catholic Narrative," *U. S. Catholic Historian* 23.2 (2005) 65–72.

———. "Two Generations of American Catholic Expansionism in Europe: Issac Hecker and John J. Keane." In *Rising from History: U. S. Catholic Theology Looks to the Future*, edited by Robert J. Daly, 53–69. Annual Publication of the College Theology Society 30. Lanham, MD: University Press of America, 1984.

Powers, Richard Gid. "American Catholics and Catholic Americans: The Rise and Fall of Catholic Anticommunism," *U. S. Catholic Historian* 22.4 (2004) 17–35.

———. *Not Without Honor: The History of American Anticommunism.* New York: Free Press, 1995.

Putney, Clifford. *Muscular Christianity: Manhood and Sports in Protestant America, 1880–1920.* Cambridge, MA: Harvard University Press, 2001.

Rahner, Karl. "Anonymous and Explicit Faith." In *Experience of the Spirit: Source of Theology*, 52–59. Theological Investigations 16. Translated by David Morland. New York: Seabury, 1979.

———. "Anonymous Christianity and the Missionary Task of the Church." In *Confrontations 2*, 161–78. Theological Investigations 12. Translated by David Bourke. New York: Seabury, 1974.

———. "Anonymous Christians." In *Concerning Vatican Council II*, 390–98. Theological Investigations 6. Translated by Karl-H. Kruger and Boniface Kruger. Baltimore: Helicon, 1969.

———. "Atheism and Implicit Christianity." In *Writings of 1965–1967, 1*, 145–64. Theological Investigations 9. Translated by Graham Harrison. New York: Herder and Herder, 1972.

———. "Observations on the Problem of the 'Anonymous Christian.'" *Confrontations* 2, 280–94. *Theological Investigations* 12. Translated by David Bourke. New York: Seabury, 1974.

Reed, James Eldin. "American Foreign Policy, the Politics of Missions and Josiah Strong, 1890–1900." *Church History* 41 (1972) 230–45.

Reese, Thomas J., editor. *Episcopal Conferences: Historical, Canonical, and Theological Studies.* Washington, DC: Georgetown University Press, 1989.

Reeves, Thomas C. *America's Bishop: The Life and Times of Fulton J. Sheen.* San Francisco: Encounter, 2001.

Reher, Margaret. *Catholic Intellectual Life in America: A Historical Study of Persons and Movements.* Makers of the Catholic Community. New York: Macmillan, 1989.

Ricard, Serge. *An American Empire: Expansionist Cultures and Policies, 1881–1917.* Aix-en-Provence: Université de Provence, 1990.

Rice, Gerard T. *The Bold Experiment: JFK's Peace Corps.* Notre Dame, IN: University of Notre Dame Press, 1985.

Richardson, William J., editor. *Reappraisal: Prelude to Change.* Maryknoll, NY: Maryknoll, 1965.

Riley, Kathleen L. *Fulton J. Sheen: An American Catholic Response to the Twentieth Century.* Staten Island, NY: Alba House, 2004.

Riley-Smith, Jonathan Simon Christopher. *The Crusades: A Short History.* New Haven, CT: Yale University Press, 1987.

Rivers, Caryl. *Aphrodite at Mid-Century: Growing up Catholic and Female in Post-War America.* Garden City, NY: Doubleday, 1973.

Robb, Dennis Michael. "Specialized Catholic Action in the United States, 1936–1949: Ideology, Leadership, and Organization." PhD diss., University of Minnesota, 1972.

Robert, Dana L. *Occupy Until I Come: A. T. Pierson and the Evangelization of the World.* Library of Religious Biography. Grand Rapids, MI: Eerdmans, 2003.

———. "The Origin of the Student Volunteer Watchword: 'The Evangelization of the World in This Generation.'" *International Bulletin of Missionary Research* 10.4 (1986) 146–49.

Roukanen, Mikka. "Catholic Teaching on Non-Christian Religions at the Second Vatican Council." *International Bulletin of Missionary Research* 14 (1990) 56–61.

Rouse, Ruth. *The World's Student Christian Federation: A History of the First Thirty Years.* London: SCM, 1948.

Rowe, John Carlos. "Post-Nationalism, Globalism, and the New American Studies." *Cultural Critique* 40 (1998) 11–28.

Royer, Fanchón. *The Power of Little Children: The Story of Charles Conte De Forbin-Janson, Primate of Lorraine, and the Beginning of the Association of the Holy Childhood.* Fresno, CA: Academy Library Guild, 1954.

Rynne, Xavier. *The Fourth Session: The Debates and Decrees of Vatican Council II September 14 to December 8, 1965.* New York: Farrar, Straus, and Giroux, 1966.

———. *The Third Session: The Debates and Decrees of Vatican Council II September 14 to November 21, 1964.* New York: Farrar, Straus, and Giroux, 1965.

"Save the Babies in Heathendom." *The Missionary* 29.1 (1916) 55.

Schreiter, Robert J. "Changes in Roman Catholic Attitudes toward Proselytism and Mission." In *New Directions in Mission and Evangelization*, vol. 2: *Theological Foundations*, edited by James A. Scherer, 113–25. Maryknoll, NY: Orbis, 1994.

Bibliography

———. "Contextualization from a World Perspective." In *Ministry and Theology in Global Perspective: Contemporary Challenges for the Church*, edited by Don A. Pittman, Ruben L. F. Habito, and Terry C. Muck, 315–27. Grand Rapids, MI: Eerdmans, 1996.

———. *The New Catholicity: Theology Between the Global and the Local*. Faith and Cultural Series. Maryknoll, NY: Orbis, 1997.

Schwager, Frederick. "Mission Movement Among Catholic Students." *America* 12.12 (1915) 290–91.

———. "Mission Movement Among Protestant Students." *America* 12.8 (1914) 192–93.

Shenk, Wilbert R. *Enlarging The Story: Perspectives on Writing World Christian History*. Maryknoll, NY: Orbis, 2002.

Shiflett, Dave. "Uncertain Crusaders: Christians no longer worry much about converting 'heathens.'" *Wall Street Journal*, November 14, 2003.

Showalter, Nathan. "Crusade or Catastrophe? The Student Missions Movement and the First World War." *International Bulletin of Missionary Research* 17 (1993) 13–14, 16–17.

———. *End of a Crusade: The Student Volunteer Movement for Foreign Missions and the Great War*. ATLA Monograph Series 44. Lanham, MD: Scarecrow, 1997.

Slawson, Douglas J. *The Foundation and First Decade of the National Catholic Welfare Council*. Washington, DC: Catholic University of America Press, 1992.

Society for the Propagation of the Faith. *The Mission Apostolate: A Study of the Mission Activity of the Roman Catholic Church*. New York: National Office of the Society for the Propagation of the Faith, 1942.

Society of the Holy Name. *Jesus, His Name: An Informal Sketch Concerning the Holy Name and the Holy Name Society*. Somerset, OH: Rosary, 1947.

Sontag, P. J. *America's Answer or The Great Opportunity for the Boys of America*. Chicago: Loyola University Press, 1919.

Southern, David W. *John LaFarge and the Limits of Catholic Interracialism, 1911–1963*. Baton Rouge: Louisiana State University Press, 1996.

Spaeth, J. Paul. "Books for the World." *Catholic Library World* 29.2 (1957) 82–85.

———, editor. *Perspectives in Religion and Culture*. Cincinnati, OH: Paladin, 1957.

"Spaeth, Joseph Paul." In *Who's Who in the Midwest*, 13th ed., 693. Chicago: A.N. Marquis, 1973.

Sparr, Arnold. *To Promote, Defend, and Redeem: The Catholic Literary Revival and the Cultural Transformation of American Catholicism, 1920–1960*. Contributions to the Study of Religion 25. New York: Greenwood, 1990.

Spickard, Paul R., and Kevin M. Cragg. *A Global History of Christians: How Everyday Believers Experienced Their World*. Grand Rapids, MI: Baker, 1994.

Springhall, John. *Decolonization Since 1945: The Collapse of European Overseas Empires*. Studies in Contemporary History. New York: Palgrave, 2001.

Stackhouse, Max. *Apologia: Contextualization, Globalization, and Mission in Theological Education*. Grand Rapids, MI: Eerdmans, 1988.

Stanley, Brian, editor. *Missions, Nationalism, and the End of Empire*. Studies in the History of Christian Missions. Grand Rapids, MI: Eerdmans, 2003.

Stransky, Thomas F. "Evangelization, Missions, and Social Action: A Roman Catholic Perspective." *Review and Expositor* 79 (1982) 343–51.

Strauss, William, and Neil Howe. *Generations: The History of America's Future, 1584 to 2069*. New York: Morrow, 1991.

Bibliography

Sullivan, Francis A. *Salvation Outside the Church? Tracing the History of the Catholic Response.* New York: Paulist, 1992.

Sykes, Richard J. "A Call to Arms." *Catholic Missions* 12.1 (1918) 15–16.

Synod of Bishops. *The Evangelization of the Modern World.* Washington, DC: United States Catholic Conference, 1973.

Tavard, George H. *Two Centuries of Ecumenism: The Search for Unity.* Notre Dame, IN: Fides, 1960.

Tifft, Thomas W. "McNicholas, John T." In *The Encyclopedia of American Catholic History*, edited by Michael Glazier and Thomas Shelley, 894–95. Collegeville, MN: Liturgical, 1997.

Valera, Edmundo Barreiro. "The Social Gospel and Imperialism." *Listening* 30.3 (1995) 162–77.

Vaughn, Stephen. "Morality and Entertainment: The Origins of the Motion Picture Production Code." *Journal of American History* 77 (1990) 39–65.

Verstraelen, F. J., editor. *Missiology: An Ecumenical Introduction: Texts and Contexts of Global Christianity.* Grand Rapids, MI: Eerdmans, 1995.

Veverka, Fayette Breaux. *For God and Country: Catholic Schooling in the 1920s.* The Heritage of American Catholicism. New York: Garland, 1988.

Wacker, Grant. "The Waning of the Missionary Impulse: The Case of Pearl S. Buck." In *The Foreign Missionary Enterprise at Home: Explorations in North American Cultural History*, edited by Daniel H. Bays and Grant Wacker, 191–205. Religion and American Culture. Tuscaloosa: The University of Alabama Press, 2003.

Wallstrom, Timothy C. *The Creation of a Student Movement to Evangelize the World: A History and Analysis of the Early Stages of the Student Volunteer Movement for Foreign Missions.* Pasadena, CA: William Carey International University, 1980.

Walsh, Frank. *Sin and Censorship: The Catholic Church and the Motion Picture Industry.* New Haven, CT: Yale University Press, 1996.

Walsh, William Thomas. *Our Lady of Fátima.* New York: Macmillan, 1947.

Wangler, Thomas E. "Myth, Worldviews, and Late Nineteenth Century American Catholic Expansionism." In *Rising from History: U. S. Catholic Theology Looks to the Future*, edited Robert J. Daly, 71–82. Annual Publication of the College Theology Society 30. Lanham, MD: University Press of America, 1984.

"We Cannot Escape It." *The Missionary* 6 (1901) 3.

"We Come Not to Conquer but to Win." *The Missionary* 2.8 (1898) 50.

Weaver, Mary Jo, and R. Scott Appleby, editors. *Being Right: Conservative Catholics in America.* Bloomington: Indiana University Press, 1995.

Weldgen, Francis. "A Brief Look at the Growth of Catholic Youth Work in the United States." In *Hope for the Decade: A Look at the Issues Facing Catholic Youth Ministry*, edited by Marisa Guerin, 1–9. Washington, DC: USCC National Catholic Youth Federation, 1980.

Werner, Stephen A. *Prophet of the Christian Social Manifesto: Joseph Husslein, S.J., His Life, Work, and Social Thought.* Marquette Studies in Theology 24. Milwaukee, WI: Marquette University Press, 2001.

White, Joseph M. *The Diocesan Seminary in the United States: A History from the 1780s to the Present.* Notre Dame Studies in American Catholicism. Notre Dame, IN: University of Notre Dame Press, 1989.

Wiebe, Robert H. *The Search for Order, 1877–1920.* Making of America. New York: Hill and Wang, 1967.

Bibliography

Wiest, Jean-Paul. "The Legacy of Vincent Lebbe." *International Bulletin of Missionary Research* 23 (1999) 33–37.

———. *Maryknoll in China: A History, 1918–1955*. Armonk, NY: Sharpe, 1988.

Willging, Eugene P. "The Mission Book Apostolate." *Catholic Library World* 29.2 (1957) 77, 89.

Wilson, Raymond J., Jr. *Communism: A Catholic Survey*. Problems of the Living Church Series. Cincinnati, OH: Catholic Students' Mission Crusade, 1949.

Wiltgen, Ralph M. *The Rhine Flows into the Tiber: A History of Vatican II*. Devon, UK: Augustine, 1978.

Wolff, Bernice. *The Sodality Movement in the United States, 1926–1936*. St. Louis: The Queen's Work, 1939.

"World Missionary Conference." In *Encyclopedia of Protestantism*, edited by Hans J. Hillerbrand, 2049–52. New York: Routhledge, 2004

Wuthnow, Robert. *The Restructuring of American Religion: Society and Faith Since World War II*. Studies in Church and State. Princeton, NJ: Princeton University Press, 1988.

Yates, Timothy. *Christian Mission in the Twentieth Century*. Cambridge: Cambridge University Press, 1994.

Zieger, Robert H. *America's Great War: World War I and the American Experience*. Critical Issues in History. Lanham, MD: Rowan and Littlefield, 2000.

Index

Ad Gentes (Decree on Mission), 131–32, 136, 140
Africa, x, 1, 79, 113, 122; attitudes of American students toward, 114n78; bishops at Vatican II, 129, 131; colonialism in, 3, 124; communism in, 114, 116; Islam in, 41; mission studies of, 24; missionary presence in, 1, 3–5, 24, 66, 119–20, 127; mission studies of, 72; religious vocations, 79
African Americans, 87–89, 97, 148
Akademischer Missionsverein, 33
Albania, 109
Albigensianism, 101
Alter, Karl J., 143, 156–57, 165
America First movement, xi, 103
American Academy of Christian Democracy, 70
American Board of Catholic Missions (ABCM), 35–36, 49, 55, 80, 81
American Catholic Missionary Congresses, 12, 17, 20
American Catholic Students' Foreign Mission League, 37
American Federation of Catholic Societies, 34
Americanism, xi, 5–7, 34, 61 n.18
Anderson, Gerald H., 144
Angelicum, Rome, 134
Anglican Church, *see* Episcopal Church

Anonymous Christianity, 145–46, 148
anti-Catholicism, 23, 59
anticommunism, 98–101, 110–11, 117–18
Apostolic Mission House, Washington, DC, 7–8, 13, 48–49
Appalachia, 151
Aquinas, St. Thomas, 6n12, 60, 68, 95, 115, 117
Arnold, Nancy, 51
Asia: American aid to, 126; bishops at Vatican II, 129, 131; colonialism in, 124; communism in, 107–9, 112–15; missionary presence in, 1–3, 5, 45–46, 85, 119; students from, 21, 113
Asia minor, 41
Association for International Development (AID), 121
atheism, 60, 101, 104–5, 116
Australia, 50
Austria, 33, 50, 109

Baltimore, Maryland, ix, 12, 17, 34, 88, 96
Baltimore Catechism, 66
Bea, Augustin, 142–43
Beckman, Francis J. L., 40, 56–57, 66, 72, 82, 84, 93–94, 102–4
Benedict XV, Pope, 29, 31
birth control, 92
Bishop, William Howard, 97

Index

Blue Army of Fatima, 111
Bolshevik Revolution, 97–99, 112
  See also communism
Bosch, David, 144, 147, 152
Boston, Massachusetts, ix, 12, 37, 49, 55
Brandewie, Ernest, xi
Braun, Matthias, SVD, 33
Brors, Francis X., SJ, 42
Buddhism, 65, 107
Bulgaria, 109
Burdick, Eugene, 126
Burke, B. Ellen, 18

Calvin, John, 143
Campaign for Human Development, 151
Canada, 11, 17, 33–34, 50
Canevin, Regis, 36
Carbonneau, Robert, CP, xi, 55
Carden, John, 126
Carey, Patrick, 110
Catholic Action, xiii, 73, 75, 161, 164; and the mission movement, 78, 84–86, 89–90, 93
Catholic Church Extension Society, 12
Catholic Daughters of America, 111
Catholic Evidence Guild, 86
Catholic Foreign Mission Society of America. *See* Maryknoll
Catholic Hospital Association, 35
Catholic Interracial Council, 88, 165
  See also racism
Catholic Missionary Union, 48
Catholic Near East Welfare Association, 49–50
Catholic Relief Services, 151
Catholic Students' Mission Crusade (CSMC): and anticommunism, 92, 97–120, 122, 140, 166; conventions, 51–52, 58, 72–79, 81–82, 87, 94, 97, 101–3, 112–14, 121, 136, 140, 143, 147, 151, 156, 159–60, 162–64; dissolution of, 157–65; early leadership, 37–41, 44–46, 48–51, 55–58; and ecumenism, 141–44, 148–50, 152; founding, 37–44, 46–53; membership, ix–x, 41, 44, 46–55, 91, 122, 158–59; mission education, x, 58, 66, 70–72, 82, 88, 137, 140, 143; Ritual of Initiation, 62, 65–68, 79, 82–83; and Vatican II, 132, 134–41, 152, 166
Catholic Telegraph, Cincinnati, 55, 57
Catholic Truth Society (Hong Kong), 115
Catholic University of America, Washington, DC, 5, 49, 87, 116, 137; Apostolic Mission House at, 13, 48–49; CSMC meetings/conventions at, 51, 75, 78, 103; Crusade Conference of Clerics and Religious, 118–19; Thomas Shahan, rector, 40, 55
Catholic Worker, The, 102
  See also Day, Dorothy
Catholic Youth Organization (CYO), 35, 84
Cavanaugh, John, CSC, 36–37
Chicago, Illinois: American Catholic Mission Congress at, 12, 17; International Eucharistic Congress (1926) at, 74
Child Knights of the Cross, 18–19
China: American depictions of, 64–65, 70; attitudes of American students toward, 114n78; communism in, x, 107–9, 112, 114–15; Honan Province, 46; mission studies of, 24, 72; missionary presence/aid to, 16–17, 31, 38, 45–46, 66, 71, 91, 108, 125; religious

Index

vocations in, 79, 83; Shatung Province, 45
China Missionary Bulletin, 115
Chinese Catholic Students' Society, 113
Chinnici, Joseph P., 75, 154
chivalry, 29, 42–44, 156
Christian Family Movement, 161
Cicognani, Amleto, 104
Cincinnati, Ohio, 94; American Board of Catholic Missions meeting in, 55; headquarters for the CSMC in, 49–50, 55–56, 61, 70 (*see also* Crusade Castle); mission promotion in, 63, 75–78; Society for the Propagation of the Faith meeting in, 81
Cincinnati, Ohio, Archdiocese of, 56–57, 71–72n59, 96, 97, 105, 134n33
civil rights movement, 123, 151, 161
Clark, Robert B., SVD, ix, 39, 45–46
Clarke College, Dubuque, Iowa, 78
clergy, indigenous, 4, 32, 83, 129
Cleveland, Ohio, 79, 101
Cold War, xi, xiii, 92, 98, 109–10, 125, 164–166. *See also* communism and anticommunism
colleges. *See* education, Catholic
Collegio San Tommaso, Rome, 95
colonialism, 31, 123–24, 150
Columbans (Society of St. Columban), 38, 50n83, 107
Comboni, Daniel, 4
Comboni Missionaries (Verona Fathers), 55, 97, 166
communism, 92, 97–120, 122, 140, 166. *See also* anticommunism
computers, 116–117, 147
Confraternity of Christian Doctrine (CCD), 47
Congar, Yves, OP, 115

Congregational Home Missionary Society, 9
Congregation for the Propagation of the Faith. *See Propaganda Fide*
Congregation of the Missions. *See* Lazarists
Congregation of the Sacred Hearts of Jesus and Mary (Picpus Fathers), 3
Connare, William G., 157, 160, 162
Considine, John J., MM, 52, 120–21, 149
Cornell University, 22
Coveyou, Walter, C. P., 76
Crusade Castle, Cincinnati, 61, 70–72, 81–82
crusades, 41–43
Cuba, 14, 126
Curley, Michael, 34
Cushing, Richard, 49, 120
Czechoslovakia, 109

Day, Dorothy, 161
Dayton, Ohio, University of, 78
De Hueck, Catherine, 161
Denmark, 115
de' Nobili, Robert, 2
Des Moines, Iowa, 25
Dewey, John, 116
Diem, Ngo Dinh, 113
Dietz, Frederick C., MM, 71
Dietz, Peter E., 70–71
disease, 136, 148, 150
Divine Word Missionaries (Society of the Divine Word), ix, 4, 19, 36–40, 45–47, 54
Divini Redemptoris (1937), 99, 104
Dodge, Ralph, 126
Dominicans, 3, 96
Dooley, Thomas, 113
Dorr, Donal, 133
Doyle, Alexander, CSP, 7–9, 12
Dreamer Awakes, The, 63–65, 69–70
Dries, Angelyn, OSF, ix, xi, 6

Index

Dubuque, Iowa, 78, 94
Duff, Edward J., SJ, 142
Dulles, Avery, 138–39
Duluth, Minnesota, 97

ecumenism, xiii, 123, 133–34, 141–44, 148–50, 152
Eddy, G. Sherwood, 23
Edinburgh, Scotland: world missionary conference in, 24, 141
education, Catholic: character of educational system, 47–48, 52; higher education, 35–37, 39, 47, 117; Jesuit schools, 62; McNicholas, John T., and, 95–96; racial integration, 88; recruiting CSMC members, 39–41, 46–47, 50–53, 158–59; scholasticism, 60, 99, 117; seminaries, 36–37, 39, 46–47
education, mission, x, xiii, 24, 58, 66, 70–72, 80, 82, 88, 99, 120, 137, 140, 143
education, public, 86, 101, 159
Egypt, 125
Einstein, Albert, 116
Elliot, Walter, CSP, 12
England, 4, 50
Episcopal Church, 48, 143
Estonia, 109
Ethnological Missionary Museum, Rome, 83
Eucharistic Congress, International (1926), 74
Eucharistic Crusade, 43
Europe: Catholicism in, 9, 23; colonization by, 3, 124–25; Eastern Europe, 109–10, 114; immigrants from, 5; missionaries and missionary aid from, 4, 11, 16, 27–29, 31, 50–51, 120; missionary presence in, 1–3; totalitarianism in, 25
Ezekiel, the prophet, 131

Family Rosary Crusade, 43
Far East, 38
Fatima, Portugal, Our Lady of, 111–12
Federation of Catholic College Clubs, 35
Field Afar, The, 13, 18–19, see also Maryknoll
Forbin-Janson, Charles de, 3, 15–16
France: missionaries and missionary aid from, 3–4
Franciscan Friars of the Atonement, 48
Franciscans, 2–3, 11, 166
Franco, Francisco, 100
Freking, Edward A., 57, 93–94, 103, 134–35, 156–57, 165
Freri, Joseph, 20
Freud, Sigmund, 116
Friendship House, 161

Gaudium et Spes (Constitution on the Church in the Modern World), 133
German Americans, 27, 45, 70
Germany: immigrants from, 5; missionaries and missionary aid from, 4, 27–28, 33, 38, 42, 45, 50
Giantkiller, The, 62, 69, 70
Gibbons, James, 31
Gillard, John T., SSJ, 87–89
Gilson, Etienne, 115
Gleason, Philip, 158
Glenmary Home Missioners, 97, 166
God Wills It!, 42–43, 63, see also *Dreamer Awakes*
Goodman, Benny, 94
Grail Movement, 121, 161
Great Commission (Matthew 28:19), 1, 133
Great Depression, 25, 85
Greek Orthodox, 143
Greeley, Andrew, 165

Gregory XV, Pope, 2–4
Gregory XVI, Pope, 3–4
Gremillion, Joseph A., 151
Gruhn, Frederick, SVD, 45
Guatemala, 125

Hagspiel, Bruno, SVD, 19, 38–39, 43–44, 47
Handly, John M., CSP, 40, 41n52, 48
Harty, Jeremiah, 36
Hayes, Patrick, 36
Hebblethwaite, Peter, SJ, 128
Hecker, Isaac, CSP, 5, 8, 11
Heithaus, Claude, SJ, 88
Hitler, Adolph, 99, see also Nazism
Hoffman, Ronan R., 137–40, 149
Holbein, Godfrey, CP, 76
Holland. See Netherlands
Holy Childhood Association, 3, 15–19, 32, 34, 72, 157, 162
Holy Ghost Fathers. See Spiritans
Holy Land, 41, 60
Holy Name Society, 34, 74, 96, 161
Holy See. See Vatican
home missions, 10, 12, 36, 79, 85, see also rural apostolate
Homer, 115
Hong Kong, 115
Hungary, 109
hunger, 136
Hurley, Joseph P., 103–4
Husslein, Joseph, SJ, 39–40

Illich, Ivan, 127–28, 149
illiteracy, 136, 148, 150
imperialism, religious, 9–10, 14, 23, 32, 125–26, 148, 150
India, 36, 66, 72, 79, 112, 115
Institutum Divi Thomae, Cincinnati, Ohio, 96
Inter-Seminary Missionary Alliance, 22
International Catholic Auxiliaries, 121

International Missionary Conference. See Edinburgh, Scotland
interracial justice, xi, 86–89, 165
Iran, 125
Ireland, 33–34, 50
Ireland, John, 5–6, 8, 13–14
Irish Americans, 5, 27
Italian Americans, 27

Janser, Peter, SVD, 45, 47
Janssen, Arnold, SVD, 4
Japan, 24, 45–46, 64, 66, 102–3, 112–13, 115
Japanese Catholic Students in America, 113
Jaricot, Pauline, 3, 16
Jehovah's Witnesses, 143
Jesuits (Society of Jesus), 43; American mission promotion by, 30, 39, 62–63, 85, 140; and the Holy Childhood Association, 17; educational institutions, 62, 73, 88; missionary efforts of, 2–4, 11, 166
Jewish people, 103n33, 142–43
Joan of Arc, St., 68
Johnson, Lyndon B., 151
John XXIII, Pope, 119, 129–30, 135, 141
Justice and Peace, Pontifical Commission on, 136

Keane, John J., 5, 13, 35
Keefe, Anselm M., O.Praem., 79
Keeler, Floyd G., 48–49, 50n81, 51, 55
Keller, James, MM, 115
Kelley, Francis Clement, 12
Kennedy, John F., 121
Kennedy School of Mission, 33n21
Kenrick Seminary, St. Louis, Missouri, 46

Index

King, Clifford J., SVD, ix, 37–41, 44–46, 50–51, 59, 108, 112, 125, 157, 166
Klocker, Henry J., 80, 134–135, 157–58, 164
Knights of Columbus, 34, 43, 100
Knights of Labor, 43
Knights of the Cross, 18–19
Knights of the Labarum, 23
Korea, 72, 112–13
Küng, Hans, 143

Labodie, William O., 105–6, 109
LaFarge, John, SJ, 85, 87
laity, 74–75, 151; and anticommunism, 98; and John T. McNicholas, 95–96; as missionaries, 118–19, 121–22; in the CSMC, 48, 54, 56–58, 89, 105, 113, 136, 140; criticism of missions, 128–29; mission support organizations, 3, 18, 36–37, 162
Lamont, Donal, 131
Laos, 125
Latin America, 23; communism in, 114; missionary presence in, 49, 119–22, 127, 149; students from, 113; study of, 137, *see also* Papal Volunteers for Latin America (PAVLA)
Latourette, Kenneth Scott, 19n53, 22–23
Latvia, 109
Lazarists, 3
Lebbe, Vincent, 31
Legion of Decency, 93
Leibold, Paul F., 157
Lenin, Vladimir, 116
Leopoldine Society (*Leopoldinische Stiftung*), 4, 11
Leo XIII, Pope, 6
liberalism, 60, 97
Life and Work Movement, 141

Lincoln, Nebraska, 56
Lipa, Phillipines, 111
literature, Catholic, 18–20, 30, 58, 100, 111, 115–16, 142
Lithuania, 109
Little Missionary, The, 19, 38n42, 44n65
Loras Colege, Dubuque, Iowa, 78
Lord, Daniel A., SJ, xiii, 61–71, 73–74, 78n81, 79, 93
Louis, St., 68
Lourdes, France, Our Lady of, 79, 111
Ludwig Society (*Ludwig Missionsverein*), 4
Lumen Gentium (Dogmatic Constitution on the Church), 133, 160
Luther, Martin, 143

MacKaye, Percy, 63
Mallon, Vincent, MM, 128
manifest destiny, 7, 10, 14, 26
Marian apparitions, 110–12, *see also* Mary, devotion to
Marists, 3
Marx, 106, 112
Mary, devotion to, 16, 43, 70, 110–12
Maryknoll, 11, 36–37, 50, 52, 124, 128, 166; in China, 71, 107; in Latin America, 120; preparatory seminary in Clarks Green, Pennsylvania, 49; seminary in Glen Ellyn, Illinois, 158; seminary/house of studies in Ossining, New York, 44, 47, 120; *see also* Field Afar
Maryknoll Magazine, 149
materialism, xi, xiii, 60, 92, 99, 164
Maximum Illud (1919), 31–32
Maynooth Seminary, Ireland, 33–34, 50
McCarthy, Joseph, 117–18

Index

McCarthyism, 117–18, *see also* anticommunism
McGreevy, John, 148, 153
McGuire, Frederick, CM, 143, 149
McNicholas, John T., 73, 86, 93–97, 101–4, 134
medievalism, xii–xiii, 43–44, 59–66, 69–71, 74–75, 77–78, 82, 89–90, 166
Merton, Thomas, 115
Mexican Revolution, 98
Mexico, 17, 100, 109, 127
militarism, 30, 44, 59, 78, 156
Mill Hill Fathers, 4
Mindszenty, Josef, 110
Minh, Ho Chi, 113
missiology, 32–33, 131, 137, 140, 144, 147, 149
missionaries, critique of, 124–29, 146, 149; financing of, 41, 80–81; from America, 10, 14–15, 20, 166; lay, 118–22; need for and recruitment of, 44, 66, 79, 118–20; number of, 120, 124; origin of, 1–4; Protestant, 10, 20–21, 23–24; training of, 8, 127; and World War I, 27–32
Missionaries of Our Lady of Africa (White Fathers), 3
Missionary, The, 49
Missionary Index of Catholic Americans, 119
Missionary Oblates of Mary Immaculate, 3
Missionary Society of St. James the Apostle, 49, 120
Missionary Society of St. Paul the Apostle. *See* Paulists
Missionary Union of the Clergy, 32, 34
Moeller, Henry, 36, 55–57, 95
Moody, Dwight L., 21
Mormons, 143

Moscow, Russia, 103
Mott, John R., 22–24
Mount Hermon, Massachusetts, 21
Mount St. Joseph High School, Baltimore, Maryland, 88
Mount St. Mary's Seminary of the West, Cincinnati, Ohio, 37, 40, 47, 49, 55–57, 134
movies, 92–94
Mundelein, George, 36, 45, 74
Münster School of Mission Science, University of Münster, 32–33
music, 92–94
Mussolini, 99
Mystical Body of Christ, 87, 150

National Catholic Educational Association (NCEA), 96, 120
National Catholic Rural Life Conference, 47, 86, 97
National Catholic War Council (NCWC), 28, 35–36
National Catholic Welfare Conference (NCWC), 34, 49, 96, 121, 149
National Conference of Catholic Charities, 35
National Council of Catholic Women, 94
National Federation of Catholic College Students, 144
nationalism, xi, 14–15, 30–32, 44, 59–60, 75, 99
National Student Christian Federation (NSCF), 25
Native Americans, 65
Nazism, 92, 100, 102–4
Necedah, Wisconsin, 111
negro apostolate. *See* African American apostolate
Netherlands, 4, 33, 38, 50, 109
Nevins, Albert J., MM, 149–50
Newman Student Federation, 25, 144
New Orleans, Louisiana, ix, 17, 54

193

Index

newspapers, Catholic, 55, 118, 154, 169, *see also Catholic Telegraph*
New York, New York, 17–18, 36–37, 39, 49, 55, 96, 110, 113, 127
Niagara University, 78
Norris, James J., 151
North Korea. *See* Korea
Nostra Aetate (Declaration on the Relation of the Church to Non-Christian Religions), 133
Notre Dame, University of, 36–37, 78–79, 114, 116, 140, 147, 162
Notre Dame College, Maryland, 51

Oblates of Mary Immaculate, 3, 38
O'Callaghan, Peter J., CSP, 48
O'Connell, Denis J., 5
Oklahoma City, Oklahoma, 12
O'Meara, Edward T., 157
O'Reilly, James P., 111
Our Sunday Visitor, 119

"pagan babies," 16–19, 150
paganism: and communism, 105; critique of 64–67, 69–70, 79, 99
pageants, ix, xiii, 61–65, 69–70
Papal Volunteers for Latin America (PAVLA), 121–22, 136
Passionists (Congregation of the Passion), 55, 76
Paulists, 5, 7–8, 12, 18, 36, 40–41, 48–49
Paul VI, Pope, 131, 151
Peace Corps, 121, 136, 151
peace movement, Catholic, 112–13, 150–51, 156, 161
Pearl Harbor, 102–3
Peter the Hermit, 67
Peyton, Patrick, CSC, 43
Philippines, 14, 24, 115
philosophy, 5, 60, 97, 100–101, 114–16, 118, *see also* scholasticism

Pierson, Arthur T., 21–22
Pittsburgh, Pennsylvania, 17, 36, 55, 63, 141
Pius IX, Pope, 4, 17
Pius X, Pope, 11
Pius XI, Pope, 18, 82–84
Pius XII, Pope, 119, 141
Poland, 109–10
pontifical mission societies, 18, 34, 83, 157, 163
Pontifical Missionary Union, 83
Populorum Progressio (1967), 151
poverty, material, xiv, 8, 17, 67, 136, 148, 150–52, 156; voluntary, xi, 106
Presbyterian Board of Foreign Missions, 23
Princeton, 22
Propaganda Fide, 2–3, 11, 29, 36, 82–83, 120, 129
Propagation of the Faith, Society for the (U.S.), xiii, 3, 12, 20, 32, 34, 80–83, 127, 134, 147, 157
Protestantism: ecumenical impulse, 141–44; missionary impulse of, ix, 2–3, 9–11, 19–26, 29, 32, 39, 126; relationship to the Catholic Church, x, xii, 2, 6–11, 77, 79, 93, 99
Protestant missions. *See* missionaries, Protestant *and* Student Volunteer Movement for Foreign Missions
Protestant Reformation, 2, 19, 102
publications, mission, 18–21, 49–50, 81, 118–19, 124
Puerto Rico, 14

Quadragesimo Anno (1931), 86
Queen's Work, The, 62

racism, xiii, 87, 123; and interracial justice, 87–89, 145, 165
Rahner, Karl, SJ, 145–147

Ramparts, 127
Reitan, Augustus O., 157
Rhodesia. *See* Zimbabwe
Ricci, Matteo, 2
Rivers, Caryl, 147
Romania, 109
Rome. *See* Vatican
Roosevelt, Franklin D., 103–4
rosary. *See* Mary, devotion to
Rossum, Willem van, 82
rural apostolate, xiii, 12, 35, 47, 55, 86, 90, 97, 136, 148, 165; *see also* home missions
Russia, xi, 100, 103–6, 111–12

St. Augustine, Florida, 103
St. Augustine's Seminary, Bay St. Louis, Mississippi, 88
St. Columban Seminary, Galway, Ireland, 50
St. Francis de Sales Seminary, Milwaukee, Wisconsin, 36, 46
St. Gregory Seminary, Cincinnati, Ohio, 57, 134
St. John's Seminary, Boston, Massachusetts, 37
St. John's University, Collegeville, Minnesota, 46–47
St. Joseph Society for Foreign Missions. *See* Mill Hill Fathers
St. Louis, Missouri, 46, 55, 62–63, 69
St. Louis University, St. Louis, Missouri, 88
St. Mary's College, Notre Dame, Indiana, 140
St. Mary's Mission House, Techny, Illinois, 37–39, 44
St. Meinrad Seminary, Indiana, 46
Salesians, 4
Salina, Kansas, 57
salvation, 16; of non-Christians, 144–48
Salvation Army, 43
Sartre, Jean Paul, 116

Scalabrini Fathers, 55
Scherer, James A., 126
Schillebeeckx, Edward, OP, 145
Schmidlin, Josef/Joseph, 32–33, 71
scholasticism, 5, 60, 96, 99, 106, 117, *see also* education, Catholic
schools. *See* education, Catholic
Schumacher, Alphonse L., 40
Secretariat for Promoting Christian Unity, 142
secularism, xiv, 4, 60, 92, 95, 97, 99, 101, 114–16, 118, 123, 139, 147, 164
seminaries. *See* education, Catholic
Seton Hall University, 113
Seybold, Clement, CP, 76
Shahan, Thomas J., 40, 55
Shakespeare, 115
Sheen, Fulton J., 100, 115, 127
Shield, The, x, 57–58, 61, 100, 102, 104–12, 114–17, 119–22, 126–27, 132, 135, 137, 142–43, 148, 152–55
sisters, ix, 11, 16, 56, 66, 91, 108, 119, 136, *see also* vocations, religious
Smith, Vincent E., 116–17
Social Gospel movement, 7, 9–11, 24, 26
socialism, xiii, 106
Society of Jesus. *See* Jesuits
Society of Mary. *See* Marists
Society of St. Columban. *See* Columbans.
Society of St. Francis de Sales. *See* Salesians
Society of St. Peter the Apostle, 83
Society of the Divine Word. *See* Divine Word Missionaries
Society of the Foreign Missions of Paris, 3
Society of the Sons of the Sacred Heart (Verona Fathers). *See* Comboni Missionaries

Index

sodality movement, 62, 73–74, 84, 100, 166
Sontag, P. J., SJ, 30, 44
South Korea. *See* Korea
Soviet Union. *See* Russia
Spaeth, J. Paul, 57–58, 105, 115, 143
Spaeth, Louise (Scheuerman), 58
Spain, 2, 14, 33–34, 41, 50, 102
Spanish-American War, 7
Spanish Civil War, 98, 100, 109
Speer, Robert E., 23
Spellman, Francis, 100, 110, 113
Spiritans, 3, 17
Stalin, 99, 109
Stepinac, Alojzije, 110
Stevens, Thomas Wood, 63
Stransky, Thomas, CSP, 130n18, 144, 149
Strong, Josiah, 9–10
student mission societies, 22, 36–37, 51; *see also* Catholic Students' Mission Crusade *and* Student Volunteer Movement for Foreign Missions (SVM), ix, 21–25, 39, 158
Stuhlmueller, Carroll, C.P., 141
Summa Theologica, 95
Switzerland, 33–34, 50
Sykes, Richard J., SJ, 30

Testem Benevolentiae (1899), 6, *see also* Americanism
Thill, Francis A., 40, 56–57, 73, 76–77, 81–82, 93, 105–6
Thiry, Theodore, SJ, 17
Thomism. *See* scholasticism
Tordesillas, Treaty of (1493), 2
totalitarianism, 25, 92, 97–102, 106, 110
Trappists, 108
Trinity College, Washington, DC, 37, 51

U.S. Catholic Conference. *See* National Catholic Welfare Conference
Union of Soviet Socialist Republics. *See* Russia
Unitatis Redintegratio (Decree on Ecumenism), 133
United Nations, 105, 119
United States Catholic Mission Council, 140–41, 162
United Student Christian Council, 25
University Christian Movement, 25, 144, 158
Urban College (*Collegio Urbano di Propaganda*), 32–33, 83

Vatican (Holy See/Rome), 83, 104; approach to the United States, 5–6; approval of the CSMC, 79–84, 92, 162; direction of missionary efforts, 2, 32, 36
Vatican Council II, xi, xiii, 123, 129–42, 151–52, 158, 160–61, 164, 166; *Ad Gentes* (Decree on Missions), 131–32, 136, 140; *Gaudium et Spes* (Constitution on the Church in the Modern World), 133; *Lumen Gentium* (Dogmatic Constitution on the Church), 133, 160; *Nostra Aetate* (Declaration on the Relation of the Church to Non-Christian Religions), 133; *Unitatis Redintegratio* (Decree on Ecumenism), 133
Verona Fathers. *See* Comboni Missionaries
Versailles Treaty, 28
Vietnam, 112–13
Vietnam Conflict, xiii, 113, 123, 156, 166

Index

Vietnamese Catholic Students in America, 113
Virgil, 115
vocations, religious and missionary, 29, 45–46, 53, 79, 118–19, 122, 129, 149, 166

Walsh, Edmund A., SJ, 100
Walsh, James A., 37
Walsh, William Thomas, 111–12
Washington, DC, 8, 37, 40, 49, 51, 54–55, 63, 73, 75, 78, 103, 137, 141
Weigel, Gustave, SJ, 143
West Baden College, West Baden Springs, Indiana, 140
Wiest, Jean-Paul, xi
Wilder, Robert P., 22
Willging, Eugene, 116
Willms, John, C.S.Sp., 17–18
Wilson, Raymond J., Jr., 105
women, 38, 134; in the CSMC, 51–54, 68; missionary and mission support roles for, 3, 23, 37, 42, 119, 121; pagan, 67, 69
women's suffrage, 27
World Council of Churches, 141–42
World Mission Sunday, 83
World War I, xi–xii, 18, 27–34, 43, 59, 76, 103, 107, 166
World War II, xi, xiii, 91–92, 102–7, 166; and isolationism, *see* America First movement
World's Student Christian Federation, 24
Wright, John J., 141

Xavier, St. Francis, 2, 45, 62
Xavier Society of the Rhineland, 4
Xavier University, Cincinnati, Ohio, 57, 105n41

Yale University, 22

Yalta Conference, 109
Yang, Thaddeus, OSB, 107
Young Men's Christian Association (YMCA), 22
Young Women's Christian Association (YWCA), 22
youth and missions, 15–19, *see also* Catholic Students' Mission Crusade *and* Student Volunteer Movement for Foreign Missions
Yugoslavia, 109–10

Zimbabwe, 131

www.ingramcontent.com/pod-product-compliance
Lightning Source LLC
Chambersburg PA
CBHW060609230426
43670CB00011B/2042